The Melted Pot
Antisemitism, Diversity, and the Limits of Tolerance

Harry Saul Markham

The Melted Pot
Antisemitism, Diversity, and the Limits of Tolerance

Harry Saul Markham

Academica Press
Washington

Library of Congress Cataloging-in-Publication Data

Names: Markham, Harry Saul (author)

Title: The melted pot : diversity, antisemitism, and the limits of tolerance | Markham, Harry Saul.

Description: Washington : Academica Press, 2025. | Includes references.

Identifiers: LCCN 2025937172 | ISBN 9781680534061 (hardcover) | 9781680534078 (paperback) | 9781680534085 (e-book)

Copyright 2025 Harry Saul Markham

Dedication

This book is dedicated to the memory of my grandparents, Eva and Jack Sherman, and Ida and Norman Markham. Without their influence and inspiration, as proud and loyal British Jews, I would not have written this book. Their kindness, love, and warmth touched all who were fortunate enough to know them. This is a small token of my appreciation for everything they did for me and my siblings. May their memory be a blessing.

Praise for *The Melted Pot*

"This is a magnificent contribution to a subject that needs exactly this kind of sane, balanced and forward thinking. A wonderful cooperation between people of different communities and faiths this important book might even be said to give … *hope*."
– Sir Stephen Fry, comedian, actor, writer, and presenter

"Are you shocked by the rise of authoritarian populism in Europe? Stunned by the rise of antisemitism in the continent that seemed to have learned the lessons of the Holocaust? Flabbergasted that the apparently irresistible idea of a liberal, cosmopolitan world order is plunging in popularity? If so, there must be something about the present you're not understanding. With style, humanity, and good sense, Harry Markham diagnoses the problems that Europe has blundered into and points the way toward restoring the vision that once inspired it."
– Steven Pinker, Johnstone Professor of Psychology, Harvard University, and the author of *Enlightenment Now*

"Multiculturalism is the collectivist philosophy that was enthusiastically applied in the West in the last few decades. It has hollowed out European and American institutions and rendered nationhood meaningless. It has become among other things a vehicle that enables Anti-Semitism. Everyone needs to read Harry Saul Markham's book, *The Melted Pot*, not only to understand how this happened, but crucially what to do about it."
– Ayaan Hirsi Ali, Human Rights Activist & Bestselling Author, Research Fellow, The Hoover Institution

"*The Melted Pot* is a rare and necessary book, which calls for honest conversation about the challenges and promises of multiculturalism. This

urgent and brave book offers not just critique, but a roadmap for renewal—a path toward a multiculturalism that does not compromise on democratic principles. Read this book!"
– Natan Sharansky, human rights activist, former political prisoner, and author of *The Case for Democracy*, a *New York Times* Bestseller

"We need more books like this exposing not only the evils but also the dangers of tolerating antisemitism."
– Professor Alan Dershowitz, Harvard University, best-selling author, leading lawyer

"The key point of agreement between the far left and the far right appears to be persistent antisemitism. Harry Saul Markham's *The Melted Pot* is a much-needed contribution to our understanding of how this most ancient and repugnant of prejudices has lately regained its momentum. At a time when self-proclaimed "anti-fascists" are enabling fascism to flourish, Markham's passionate and enlightening book could not be more timely.
– Andrew Doyle, bestselling author and broadcaster

"Harry Markham takes an honest look at the urgent problems facing the European continent, and the paradoxical clash between a desire to promote multiculturalism and a desire for government to respect and support productive discussion and debate. Unless we take an honest look in the mirror, it is unlikely that current dangerous trends will reverse. And this is exactly what The Melted Pot does. Important reading for anyone concerned about these issues today."
– Lawrence M. Krauss, President, The Origins Project foundation and bestselling author of A Universe from Nothing, the Edge of Knowledge, and the forthcoming War on Science

"As a Muslim and Arab who is deeply committed to fostering Jewish-Muslim understanding and promoting peace in the Middle East, I recognize the urgent need for honest conversations about rising antisemitism and its impact on our societies. *The Melted Pot* is a courageous and timely work

that challenges us to confront uncomfortable truths about the unintended consequences of some policies and the dangers of extremism."
– Fatema Al Harbi, First Bahrani Peace Activist to EU, Gulf Affairs Director at Sharika, Leading Peace Advocate

"Harry Saul Markham makes a powerful, personal case for a renewal of centrist national integrationism in western European societies like Britain. The political mainstream, wedded to a left-liberalism born – ironically – out of antisemitism, is laying the groundwork for a new epoch of Jewish persecution. Tolerating the dangerous level of antisemitism present in many sections of Muslim Europe in the name of political correctness can only hasten Europe's sad journey towards illiberalism and division. For the sake of the Jews, liberalism and western civilization, Markham urges us to get control of our borders and foster commonality rather than difference if we hope to make a multicultural society work in our culturally and demographically turbulent century."
– Eric Kaufmann, Professor of Politics, University of Buckingham, and author of *Taboo: How Making Race Sacred Led to a Cultural Revolution*

"As Harry Markham points out, the insidious nature of antisemitism threatens both Jewish people and the nature of our entire democracy. Too many people seem blind to antisemitism or appear to tolerate it, almost as if it is not as serious as other forms of racism. Harry isn't afraid to go where others fear to tread and this book is a welcome contribution to the debate on how best to counter antisemitism."
– Iain Dale, leading national broadcaster and author

"Far from any reactionary or nostalgic manifestos, [Markham's] book offers both a virulent denunciation of the consequences of ideological multiculturalism, and a plea for 'the dignity of difference:' the conditions that will allow the emergence of a truly multicultural society to emerge. This is what makes his book so original, urgent, and necessary."
– Marc Weitzmann, leading French journalist and novelist

"*The Melted Pot* is a compelling attempt to illuminate how the progressive

and humanitarian principles of Europe are being gradually and steadily undermined due to unbridled political correctness and an unholy alliance between radical Islam and European anti-Semitism. In such turbulent times, Harry Markham graciously offers a viewpoint that encourages efforts to foster cohesion and shared values instead of polarizing identity politics. The book is worth a read for those who believe that introspection might help us strengthen the forgotten vow "Never again" and resuscitate liberalism in its glory."
– Khadija Khan, Journalist and broadcaster

"*The Melted Pot* is a timely and essential read for anyone concerned about the future of social cohesion in the UK. Harry Saul Markham confronts hard questions surrounding multiculturalism, extremism, and the rising tide of intolerance with clarity and courage. In a world where extremist ideologies threaten the fabric of our society, this book provides a much-needed call for honest dialogue and principled action. A vital contribution to an urgent conversation, it is a must-read for policymakers, community leaders, and anyone invested in fostering a truly inclusive and united Britain at ease with itself."
– Mohammed Abbasi, Deputy Chair, The Association of British Muslims

"This is a vital and timely book. It is deeply troubling that, less than a century after the most horrific crimes in human history, too many self-proclaimed anti-racists and advocates of multiculturalism are either unwilling or unable to confront the uncomfortable truth behind its resurgence, let alone take action against it. Harry Markham offers a courageous and refreshingly balanced path forward, showing how we confront this civilizational threat and reclaim liberal values - the very principles that safeguard all people, including ethnic and religious minorities."
– Inaya Folarin Iman, journalist and founder of The Equiano Project, an anti-racism charity

"*The Melted Pot* offers a sobering account of the fragility and limits of Western Europe's tolerance. Markham delves deep into the roots of European antisemitism and its newfound alliance with radical Islam. *The*

Melted Pot calls for an urgent reckoning of the individual and collective responsibility behind antisemitism. It sheds an unforgiving light on the failures of divisive diversity policies."
– Marie Daouda, University of Oxford

"*The Melted Pot* takes a bold step in confronting one of the most critical issues of our time: the rise of antisemitism in the West and beyond. In a world where radical ideologies are gaining ground and even Muslims who speak out for peace are silenced by labels like "Islamophobe," Harry Saul Markham has written a difficult but essential book that bravely confronts the truth of what is really happening. This book is for anyone seeking to understand the lived experiences of Jewish people in the West, rather than relying on trendy, ignorant narratives."
– Faezeh Alavi, policy researcher, artist, and Iranian Muslim advocate for peace in the Middle East

"With profound courage and incisive acumen, Harry Markham has undertaken a desperately needed investigation into the rising antisemitism that plagues the Western world and beyond. This book is a must read for anyone who wishes to have a deeper understanding of this growing threat to society. It is deeply insightful, informative, and transformative."
– Professor David Patterson, University of Texas at Dallas

"With precision, conviction, and courage, Harry Saul Markham dissects the paradox of tolerance: how, in our attempt to build a pluralistic utopia, we have cultivated new dogmas, new blindness, and new dangers. He challenges us to act before the foundations of liberal democracy crumble under the weight of its own illusions. This book is essential reading for anyone who still believes in the promise of Europe—not as a museum of past glories, nor as a battlefield of competing victimhoods, but as a living experiment in freedom, dignity, and the difficult art of coexistence."
– Pascal Bruckner, author of *The Tyranny of Western Guilt: An Essay on Western Masochism*

"Much has been written on contemporary European antisemitism, yet few authors are as uniquely positioned to address the academic avalanche as Harry Markham. Like countless students, he has witnessed pedagogical authoritarianism in the making from the classroom to the courtyards, yet he departs from many on campus in his willingness to confront it. Markham thus offers fresh insights that render this read on antisemitism novel."
– Professor R. Amy Elman, author of *The European Union, Antisemitism, and the Politics of Denial*

"Since the horrific events of October 7, 2023, this book, perhaps more than ever before, is a must read for all those concerned at trajectory of our societies. As a concerned Muslim, Brit, and someone who has for the last 20 years been involved in trying to combat extremism and racism, I am delighted to commend this important and timely contribution."
– Haras Rafiq, Trustee of Secure Canada and former trustee of the UK Charity Muslims Against Antisemitism and former CEO of the counter-extremist organization, Quilliam International

"*The Melted Pot* is a passionate call to confront antisemitism within Muslim communities without demonizing all Muslims. Markham explores why this conversation has been avoided for so long and why addressing it is crucial. This book is essential reading for anyone deeply concerned about rising antisemitism and seeking to understand the lived experience of a young British Jew in today's climate."
– Dr. Gunther Jikeli, Erna B. Rosenfeld Associate Professor, Institute for the Study of Contemporary Antisemitism, author of *European Muslim Antisemitism*

"At a time when antisemitism has gained widespread influence and when tolerance is in serious trouble it is important that we understand the issues at stake. Harry Saul Markham's *The Melted Pot: Diversity, Antisemitism, and the Limits of Tolerance* offers an important counterpoint to the outlook of the intolerant elites who dominate our culture. Read this book!"
– Professor Frank Furedi, University of Kent

Acknowledgements

This book was written over the course of a few years. There are many deserving of thanks, and it is not possible to mention all those involved throughout this arduous process, especially to all those who were kind enough to endorse this work. You know who you are!

However, there are some people I feel compelled to name. Firstly, none of this would have been possible without the unwavering love and support of my dear parents, Deborah and David Markham, and siblings, Candy and Ross. I also thank my dear friend, Golda, who first encouraged me to write this book in the summer of 2021, even when I had major doubts. Thank you for always believing in me! Along with these people, I offer my sincere gratitude to my inspirational friend, Professor David Patterson, who was kind enough to give up his precious time to read each chapter with a close and critical eye. With him, I pay homage to my entire ISGAP family, including Professors Katherine Aron-Beller, Günther Jikeli, Katherine Harbord, Amy Elman, Christine Maxwell, Haras Rafiq, and others, for their faith in me, and this project. And I would be remiss not to thank Sheikh Paul, of the Association of British Muslims, not only for his kindness and generosity, but for inspiring me, every day, in his important mission to promote peace between the spiritual descendants of Abraham.

This book was meant to be published in the October of 2024, to mark the first anniversary of the horrors of October 7th. However, the publisher I was due to publish with, decided, at the last minute, to withdraw its offer of publication. As such, I was left despondent, and without a prospect of this project seeing the light of day. However, with immense thanks to my good friend, Robert McLiam Wilson, and several others, I was encouraged not to give up. Indeed, from the day this book was cancelled, my agent, Matthew Hamilton of The Hamilton Agency, has been on my side. Despite all the setbacks, he worked tirelessly to get this over the line. I wouldn't have done this without him, so thank you, Matthew! And, of course, you would not be reading this without my publisher, Academica Press, and its champion of free-speech President and CEO Dr. Paul du Quenoy, who has supported me, and this work, from day one.

All those I have thanked, and those I haven't, have made valued contributions to the final product. However, every shortcoming of this book is mine. On a final note, these past few months have been challenging for me, and I would not have got through it without the love and affection of my dear partner, Arielle Zilkha, and for that, my Ella, I am forever grateful.

Foreword

As the Managing Director of the Association of British Muslims, it is with a profound sense of responsibility and urgency that I pen this foreword for Harry Saul Markham's *The Melted Pot: Antisemitism, Diversity and The Limits of Tolerance*. This book arrives at a critical juncture in our nation's journey, offering a compelling exploration of the challenges and paradoxes inherent in our multicultural landscape.

As an unwaveringly devout Muslim and proud Englishman and Briton, my life stands testament to the harmonious coexistence of diverse identities. This unique interweaving of faith and nationality underpins my deep commitment to classical liberal and democratic ideals. These values form the bedrock of our society, fostering an environment where diversity is not just tolerated but celebrated. Yet, it is with a heavy heart that I observe the growing shadow of extremism, both Islamist and other forms, casting a long, ominous pall over the United Kingdom.

The growth of extremism is a tide against which we must all swim. Islamist extremism poses a grave threat – not just to the societal fabric of our beloved country but also to the very essence of Islam, a religion of peace and compassion. Markham's book is a crucial narrative that echoes my sentiments, warning of the perils of extremism and the distortion of Islamic teachings for nefarious ends.

Yet, the concern does not end with Islamism. The proliferation of extremist ideologies has a ripple effect, impacting minorities of all faiths – Jews, Hindus, Sikhs, and indeed, fellow Muslims who find themselves increasingly alienated. Many Muslims feel trapped between the rising tide of radical ideologies within their communities, often steeped in conspiracy theories, and the reactionary swell towards far-right ideologies in broader society. This dichotomy is not just disheartening; it is a clarion call for introspection and action.

The presence of Islamist organizations in the UK, and incidents involving grooming gangs where the perpetrators were predominantly

Muslim, have fueled a narrative that threatens to overshadow the contributions and the inherent goodness of the vast majority of British Muslims. This narrative, left unchecked, not only distorts the reality of our diverse communities but also feeds into a cycle of mistrust and fear.

As British Muslims, we stand at a critical juncture. We must confront these challenges head on, fostering dialogue and understanding, not just within our communities but across all

sections of British society. Our faith teaches us the values of peace, empathy, and respect – principles that align seamlessly with the ethos of a modern, democratic Britain.

The Melted Pot is more than a book; it is a mirror reflecting our society's current struggles. It calls upon us to look beyond superficial narratives, to address the underlying issues that fuel extremism, and to recommit to the ideals of unity and understanding. This book is a valuable contribution to a conversation that is as necessary as it is urgent, reminding us of the power of shared humanity to overcome the challenges of our times.

In closing, I extend my gratitude to Harry Saul Markham for this enlightening work. It is a pivotal addition to the discourse on multiculturalism and societal cohesion, urging us all to strive for a future where diversity is not just an aspiration but a reality, where every individual, irrespective of faith or background, can thrive in a society anchored in respect, understanding, and shared values.

Sheikh (Kyai) Paul Salahudin Armstrong
Managing Director, The Association of British Muslims

Preface

When I completed this manuscript on October 5, 2023, I sought to convey a message of hope. After all, as my dear mother would emphasize, most people are not antisemites, nor are they tolerant of extremism, and if things turned sour, they would stand by their Jewish neighbors, and do what is right. In that positive spirit, the final pages of this book attempted to vindicate my mother's optimism. It may take a long time, and will involve many difficult conversations, but the route out of this mess is not closed off. At least, not yet.

My sanguinity, however, was to be short-lived. When all seemed calm, a couple of days later, on October 7, we awoke to unspeakable devastation. In what has since been described as Israel's 9/11 (although, proportionately speaking, far more deadly), the place where Jews are ostensibly most safe, witnessed the deadliest and most barbaric assault on Jewish life since the Holocaust; resulting in the brutalization and butchering of over 1200 children, women, and men, in cold-blood. Reminiscent of fascist atrocities only eighty years ago, in which extreme violence and sexual brutality were intrinsic to the modus operandi of totalitarian armies, trained Hamas operatives and their allies, at the crack of dawn, broke into the southern part of the country from Gaza, where their murderous barbarity raged to an unprecedented degree, and inflicted unbridled terror on families, on attendees at a music festival, and on any target they could find. With a nightmarish horror unthinkable in this century, these squads of genocidal and infanticidal terror, sadistically, remorselessly, and callously tortured their 'prey,' that being, babies, children, the elderly, young women, and other defenseless innocents. Their resolve was not only to slaughter, but as Professor David Paterson put it, it was to "assault and torture, butcher, rape, mutilate, behead, and burn alive… to the point where it was impossible to visually identify the dead." This went beyond killing. This was about destroying the very essence, the very holiness, the very dignity, of each human life, unfortunate enough to suffer at the hands of this machine of indescribable evil.

Yet this bloody rampage did not end with death. Their incursion resulted in the kidnapping of 242 people, including babies, children, and the most vulnerable, and at the time of writing, many are still being held hostage. But this is no ordinary hostage situation. They are immured in dungeons of torture. Their bestial and merciless guards delight in the physical and mental anguish which they exact. And since October 7, Hamas have made no attempt to cover up their crimes. They live-streamed their iniquities for all to see, and continue to post footage, as a means of psychological warfare, of a cruelty which plunges into the deepest pits of human depravity. Unlike the Nazis, who went to extreme measures to conceal and deny their wickedness, their ideological descendants in Hamas have made no such effort. Quite the opposite. They took pride - and continue to relish - in broadcasting their atrocities. They want the world to see every last lurid detail of their continued affront to human life. Despite this, there are an astounding number of people who minimize or flagrantly deny, without apology or hesitation, what took place, and what is still taking place in the labyrinth of underground tunnels in Gaza. Unsurprising, of course, if you know anything about the history of either antisemitism or misogyny. This is a deadly fusion which excels in denialism. Nevertheless, examining the philosophical origins of Hamas' savagery, French philosopher, Pascal Bruckner, observes:

> *This is the era of the happy massacre. Corpses are dragged behind a 4x4 while its occupants shriek with joy; a decapitated head is kicked about like a football or a woman's severed breast is tossed around like a toy; the enemies of God are beheaded to the sound of laughter and a musical score—this is something like genocidal euphoria. Just as Levi Strauss distinguished the cooked from the raw, so we must distinguish the Nazis' cold and bureaucratic death machine from the murderous fervor of jihadism. The Nazis sometimes showed frenzied sadism towards their victims, but their genocidal program was meticulously planned and methodically implemented. Allah's fanatics, on the other hand, are eager to get their hands dirty, and their orgies of cruelty are messy and personal. They resemble the Hutu extremists who cleaved their enemies*

open with machetes and then rested in the evening; they pounce on the bodies of their victims, crushing, burning, and mutilating them with insatiable passion.[1]

However, what occurred ought to be understood not only by the instruments of terror employed, or the monstrous celebration of such wicked acts, but by Hamas' calculated timing. Bad enough this happening on shabbat, or the sabbath, a time when families come together to mark the end of the week, Saturday, October 7, was also Simchat Torah, the day when Jews rejoice at the conclusion and restart of the annual Torah reading. The timing of Hamas' butchery has gone largely unnoticed and unmentioned. And that's understandable; it seems so insignificant in the grand scheme of things. But according to Professor Patterson, this is no mere detail, and it is no coincidence. "In this timing," he avers, "we see what the murderous Hamas anti-Zionists are anti-: their radical assault on the existence of the "Zionist Entity" is an assault on the Torah that goes forth from Zion" (Micah 4:2). He adds that, "It is an assault on the Torah that attests to the infinite dearness of the other human being and to the infinite responsibility of each of us for the other." And he concludes, "It is an assault on the commandments to love God and neighbor and stranger."[2] This observation matters as it illuminates what that day marked: not only Hamas' most murderous incursion, but the beginning of a global insurgency, or "intifada" against Jews, and everything Jews represent.

Those of us outside Israel cannot begin to comprehend, much less articulate, the impact of such a bloodcurdling atrocity on this small nation. The villainy of October 7 shattered and demoralized the Israeli people; and it marked a departure from perceived security to a widespread sense of vulnerability. And these sentiments have reverberated across the Jewish world. Events of this kind are not new, of course. History repeats itself, and any student of Jewish history will confirm that this was yet another tragedy in a long history of tragedies in what is a primordial, protean, indestructible, almost divine, hatred.

---

[1] Bruckner, Pascal. "The Genocidal Imagination." Quillette, December 12, 2023. https://quillette.com/2023/12/12/the-genocidal-imagination/
[2] In private correspondence with me.

Yet this book is not written in order to examine the geopolitical foundations of what occurred. Rather, through exploring events in the years preceding October 7, this work details the political, cultural, and social origins of what has since unfolded, and taken hold in Western-Europe. Contrary to the view of many policymakers and much of the commentariat, this insurgency against Jews, as well as against liberal democracy, is not because of a resumption of violence in the Middle East. While some of the data and information in this book may seem outdated, since I began this project almost four years ago, as each chapter details, events since October 7 have accentuated, not invented, the issues which have since become portentous and mainstream. What is positively a crisis facing both Jews and civilization has been decades in the making. And unless there is dramatic and seismic change, through their own blind spots and negligence, Western European leaders will pave the way for the end of the liberal-democracies which they proclaim to champion and defend.

This is a book that a publisher cancelled because it tackles issues of a "sensitive nature." But now, as the following pages detail, it is time for a bold, honest, and significant challenge to an issue which will determine the future of the societies which we call home. This is a book for all people who wish to see our civilization remain free, democratic, and above all, secure.

Contents

Acknowledgements xv

Foreword xvii

Preface xix

Introduction 1

Chapter One:
What is going on? 21

The Brutality: 23

The Data and Victims: 32

The Perpetrators: 37

The Warning Signs: 43

Final Remarks: 54

Chapter Two:
Where is this hatred coming from? 55

Some Data 60

Section One: Historical developments 69

Section Two: Communal Antisemitism 80

1. Social 80

2. Institutionalised Jew-hatred 89

3. Media 93

Section Three: Anti-Israelism and its Extreme Alliances 96

The Troubling Future 106

Chapter Three:
Why are we here? **109**

Section One: The Politics of Fear... 112

Section Two: Politics of Numbers.. 134

Section Three: The Politics of Identity... 153

Concluding Thoughts 173

Chapter Four:
How do we get out of this? **179**

Section One: To Confront Reality and Reclaim 185

Section Two: Prevent & Enforce the Law.. 189

Section Three: Non-Jewish ally-building... 198

Section Four: Amplification, not Reformation 204

Section Five: Restructuring Society:
A New Vision for Western Europe... 211

Final reflections 216

Afterword: The Road to October 7th 219

Introduction

"You're all in serious danger," declared the policeman to my terrified mother. Although it wasn't just my mother who was terrified. We all were. But recounting the events of that fateful, warm spring afternoon is no easy task. And for someone who is an outrageous schmoozer, being lost for words is not something to which I am accustomed. Yet, as best I can, I must try to convey the enormity of what we experienced. Since this ordeal not only led me to reassess my place as a young Jew living in Britain, but to ask, how on the streets of our country, our progressive and tolerant country, one minority might feel so threatened by another minority.

So, with that, I must do something out of character, and begin on a rather somber note. We thus turn to London, on the 11th of May, 2021, during Israel's war with Hamas. Much like previous periods of intense fighting, a pro-Palestinian demonstration was arranged to take place in Westminster, just outside the Prime Minister's residence in Downing Street. And this city was not alone. Similar events took place throughout Western Europe and across the globe. All of which drew substantial crowds. As a group of roughly fifteen activists against antisemitism, many of whom were grandparents, including my mother, we made the decision to head into Central London, and not allow what we knew would be an anti-Israel hate fest, to go unchallenged. The least we could do was show our friends and family in Israel that they were not alone, and that we were not going to be quiet in the face of those calling for the destruction of the relatively young Jewish state. With the words of John Stuart Mill, often misattributed to Edmund Burke, ringing in my ears, "the only thing necessary for the triumph of evil is for good men to do nothing," I could not possibly stand by, and do nothing. But while we have attended many protests of this kind, nothing prepared us for what we faced on that day.

Arriving in our designated area, meters away from the main crowd, guarded by a row of police and a small metal barrier, we were stunned by the sheer number of activists who had gathered. In a matter of minutes, their numbers had swelled from a few hundred to a couple of thousand. Although they were mostly young or middle-aged Muslim men, what was particularly disturbing was the number of children who had accompanied their parents. As if this was an agreeable day out for the whole family, they had brought their children, many of whom were draped in Palestinian colors and scarfs, to an event which wound up being far from a protest for peace and justice for Palestinians. This was to be something much more sinister.

One might think, of course, given our comparably infinitesimal numbers, our presence would go unnoticed, or ignored. Those in front of us, however, did not agree. As their numbers grew in this febrile atmosphere, a large mob splintered off from the main demonstration, and encircled us: this small group of Israel flag waving, hava nagila singing, albeit tone deaf, counter-protestors. They decided to ignore their various speakers, which included a hero of theirs, Jeremy Corbyn, the disgraced former leader of the Labor Party, and we became the focus, indeed the target, of what was to be a baying and forbidding mob.

With more joining their ranks, scores of charged men, with a murderous fury beaming from their piercing stares, as if we had become their prey, began chanting in Arabic. Making as much bone-chilling noise as possible, their aim was to intimidate us. And, by Jove, this was box office intimidation. Only a few minutes after this predatory behavior, one of their men broke out, jumped over a fence, and wrestled an Israel flag off one of our activists, injuring her in the process. Witnessing this, in support of their comrade, his mates began to chant "Allahu Akbar," and more frighteningly, began to push at the barrier, with the intention of taking it down. Had they succeeded, and had the police not held their line, it is reasonable to suggest you might not be reading this. Thankfully, though seriously outnumbered, somehow, the police did hold the line.

Of course, naturally, at this point, the anxiety began to kick in. But then, who wouldn't be anxious in such a situation? Behind a protected cage, we were confronted by a sea of seething, hate-ridden, almost foaming at the mouth men, for whom it was an ineffable pleasure to see this small group terrified. In the midst of this raging chaos, aside from hearing one or more individuals chant, "put away your Jewish flags," there were bangs; terrifying, close to vomit-inducing, thunderous bangs. As you do at any protest, especially one which is explicitly peaceful, they were setting off these blinding and garish flares, which ordinarily one might find only on a sinking ship. Although these demonstrations, I suppose, are full of fantastic surprises. If this wasn't enough, a few moments later, a very large rock was hurled towards us, which very nearly landed on my friend's head. Had it succeeded in reaching its intended target, any one of us, they would have been seriously injured, or worse. One can only surmise that you do not find a large rock outside the street in which the Prime Minister resides. Someone brought this rock from home with the sole purpose of bombarding any pro-Israel gathering.

At this point, trembling with trepidation, I turned to my mother, and said, "we need to get out. Now!" With dread in her eyes, like everyone else, she agreed. This was no typical demonstration which went a bit fruity. We were surrounded by a marauding sea of men, who, at boiling point, were ready, indeed eager, to unleash their bloodthirsty wrath on a small group of Jewish activists. In that moment, it seemed we all became theists, and prayed that the outmanned police line stayed in place. In the end, it did, and our worst fears were not realized. But we were lucky.

Thankfully, coming to our rescue, were police reinforcements trained to deal with hostile crowds. They formed a large cordon around us, and speedily pushed us to safety. As we were weaving through this venomous crowd, I remember saying to myself 'be prepared for a punch or a knife,' all while trying to reassure my mother that everything was going to be okay. That didn't help much. One of their more dedicated foot soldiers jumped on my friend, also a student, causing another activist, a grandfather, to fall to the ground. Fearing there would be a stampede, he was able to get back on his feet. How he did this, I have no idea. All I know was that despite this police exit lasting only a few minutes, this incident, reminiscent of historic anti-Jewish riots, felt like one long, inescapable terror.

While this frightful experience was unimaginable, to say the very least, the police plan worked. Although shaken, and perhaps emotionally scarred, we all got to safety. The warning to my mother from the police officer was no exaggeration. Had the police not been there, or removed us to safety, I have no idea if I'd be here to tell the tale. That night, however, I returned home, overcome with despair and anxiety, and I thought to myself, how could it be that in the 21st century, a large group of Muslim men, many with their children, almost lynched a small group of Jews in the center of London, a city which is widely celebrated for its multiculturalism and diversity? It was this question which marked the beginning of this book, an investigation into what has gone so desperately wrong in Britain, and Western Europe, in recent years.

This riot was blockbuster levels of distressing; and it certainly was an award winner for antisemitism in the May of 2021. Yet, sadly, it was one amongst a plethora of antisemitic and anti-democratic intimidation in that month. Unfortunately, that period was a very busy time for antisemites all over the globe. Jew-hating was big business. It was just like the good old days.

In a report on UK-based antisemitic incidents in the period between the 8th of May and the 7th of June 2021, the Community Security Trust, the main body for recording antisemitism in the UK, found that antisemitic incidents in the UK were up by 365%. In other words, there were 628 instances of criminal antisemitism, compared to 135 incidents in the preceding 31 days. This 628 figure, they say, is the highest number they have ever recorded in a month-long period. No wonder they named their report 'The Month of Hate.'[3] Given the fact that there were just so many instances, it is impossible to detail each one. And I won't even try. However, in addition to what we experienced, some of the most distressing instances included a convoy of pro-Palestinian cars in Finchley, an area in which many Jews live, blaring "fuck the Jews. Rape their daughters," which did not lead to any convictions.[4] In fact, the Crown Prosecution Service decided to drop all charges against the men in the car, who were seemingly so eager to intimidate the local Jewish community that they

---

[3] The month of hate, CST. Available at: https://cst.org.uk/data/file/4/a/The_Month_of_Hate.1626263072.pdf

[4] 4 held over antisemitic 'F*** their mothers, rape their daughters' *London convoy* | The Times of Israel

travelled a staggering 216 miles, coming all the way from Blackburn.[5] But threatening Jews with rape, and getting away with it, is something to which we are regrettably familiar. Nonetheless, other incidents included the vandalization of a Messianic Synagogue with the words, "Kike Free Palestine," along with a Nazi swastika drawn on its front door.[6] In at least one demonstration, the words of the Islamic battle cry, ""Khaybar Khaybar, ya yahud, Jaish Muhammad, sa yahud" (Jews, remember Khaybar the army of Muhammad is returning"), which references a massacre of Jews by Muslim forces, was chanted on the streets of London. After attempting, albeit unsuccessfully, to counter a large pro-Israel solidarity demonstration in the same city, a group of Muslim men, walking next to a lot of police, were shouting, "We'll find some Jews there. We want the Zionists; we want their blood."[7] And the police, witnessing this, did nothing. Last, but certainly not least, in this month alone, there were 93 recorded incidents of antisemitism involving school children, 61 of which took place in school grounds. In fact, throughout that period, schools became intimidating environments for Jewish students and staff.[8]

This, however, went well beyond the shores of Blighty. That year, 2021, was the worst year for antisemitic attacks in a decade, according to a report from the Jewish Agency and the World Zionist Organization. The report notes that, on average in that year, there were more than ten reports of antisemitic incidents each day, with almost 50 per cent of these cases taking place in Europe.[9] Although not all incidents were connected to events in the Middle East, the report makes it clear that anti-Jewish hostility reached its cruel apotheosis during this time. Like in the UK,

---

[5] Ferrer, Richard. "Disgust over CPS Decision to Drop Charges Against All Palestine Convoy Suspects." *Jewish News*, 18 Nov. 2022, https://www.jewishnews.co.uk/disgust-over-cps-decision-to-drop-charges-against-remaining-palestine-convoy-suspects/.
[6] Norwich rabbi praises local support after synagogue graffiti (2021) BBC News. Available at: https://www.bbc.co.uk/news/uk-england-norfolk-57244844
[7] "Police Officer Is Filmed Ignoring 'We'll Find Jews, We Want Blood' Death Threats." *Jewish News*, 21 May 2021, https://www.jewishnews.co.uk/police-officer-is-filmed-ignoring-well-find-jews-we-want-blood-death-threats/.
[8] CST, 'Month of Hate,' p.5
[9] "World Zionist Organization and Jewish Agency for Israel." *The State of Antisemitism in 2021*. p.10. Gov.il, Jan. 2022, https://www.gov.il/BlobFolder/news/wzo2 4012022/en/file_2021%20report-final.pdf.

incidents include vandalism of Jewish property, murderous chants at demonstrations, and verbal and physical attacks on individuals. In fact, so concerned was the French government that they decided to ban pro-Palestinian street protests.[10]

Across the world, it became apparent that it was bloody hard to be a Jew. However, few commentators readily acknowledged that a great many, perhaps the bulk of the perpetrators of these hostilities in the May of 2021, were Muslim. No doubt others were also involved, too. At our May 11th event, the crowd included a fascinating assemblage of white leftists, and— to the best of my recollection— a neo-Nazi who approached me, and while performing a Sieg Heil, whispered, "You're not going home tonight." Although unmistakably an unholy alliance of extreme, anti-democratic fanatics, in that month, those of a Muslim background were disproportionately represented in antisemitic offences. There are those, of course, who downplay any mention of this.

Worse, there are strenuous and tawdry attempts made to justify this strain of Jew-bashing. Most obvious, the actions of Israel and her government. The Palestinian issue is of supreme importance to Muslims around the world, and so, when tensions are high in the region, inevitably, there is going to be more pro-Palestinian activity, and some of this can disintegrate into antisemitism. But this does not mean, so the argument goes, that such people are motivated by an anti-Jewish animus. If only those conniving Israelis did not have the temerity to defend themselves from terror, and do what any other country on earth would do, there would be no need for Jew-hate. It's the victims' own darn fault. Others, while also indulging in the trend of victim blaming, may also suggest that this anti- Jewish hostility and violence is a reaction to oppressive social and economic factors which afflict large parts of Western Europe's Muslim communities. Unwittingly speaking in antisemitic terms, they say that Muslims in Western Europe are oppressed in multiple ways, and so the way some Muslims express their frustration is through attacking members of what they regard as an oppressive white, European hegemony, in which

---

[10] Nadi, Selim. "Emmanuel Macron's Government Has Banned Palestine Solidarity Demonstrations." *Jacobin*, 14 May 2021, https://jacobin.com/2021/05/macron-france-palestine-israel-protests-banned.

Jews form a central and foundational part. Therefore, antisemitism again becomes a predictable development, since Jews are at the center of this imagined hegemon, which is regarded to be the source of their oppression, And so, in both cases, the argument is that if these things were to be dealt with, that is, if Israel were to cease its actions (as well as, for many, cease to exist), and the various social and economic grievances were to be resolved, there would not be a problem of antisemitism amongst Muslims. These fallacious arguments not only exonerate Muslim perpetrators of antisemitism of any real responsibility, bad enough though that is, but they provide a cover, a defense, a justification, for activities which, had they been committed by a heterosexual man with blonde hair and blue eyes, would be rightly and unreservedly condemned.

Unfortunately for those who subscribe to this 'get out of jail card,' their arguments stand neither the test of history nor that of reality. Now, while it could be said that the factors above may well exacerbate hostilities, it is not the cause of the anti-Jewish hostility and violence we are seeing on the streets of Western Europe. Rather, these factors, credible though they sound, serve as a convenient distraction. There is a reason why Günther Jikeli, a first-rate scholar in this field, notes, "the review of surveys from different European countries demonstrates that the level of antisemitic attitudes is significantly higher among Muslims than among non-Muslims, although many European Muslims do not share antisemitic beliefs."[11] There is a reason why parts of France and Sweden have become arguably uninhabitable for Jews. There is a reason why Jews say that antisemitism is the biggest problem in their home nation, and identify Muslims as one of, if not the most significant, perpetrators of antisemitic hostility and violence.

There is, indeed, a particular problem of antisemitism within Western Europe's Muslim communities. In fact, Medhi Hassan, a practicing British-Muslim, in an article some years ago for The New Statesman, stated, "It pains me to have to admit this, but anti-Semitism isn't just tolerated in some sections of the British Muslim community; it's routine

---

[11] Jikeli, Günther. *Antisemitic Attitudes among Muslims in Europe: A Survey Review.* ISGAP, May 2015, https://isgap.org/wp-content/uploads/2015/05/Jikeli_Antisemitic_Attitudes_among_Muslims_in_Europe1.pdf. p.19

and commonplace. Any Muslims reading this article – if they are honest with themselves – will know instantly what I am referring to. It's our dirty little secret. You could call it the banality of Muslim anti-Semitism."[12] It's not often I say this, but Medhi is right. I would argue, however, that this is not only the case in Britain. This virus infects Muslim communities across the continent, and around the world.

In the case of Western Europe, this form of intolerance, because of multiculturalism, is tolerated and has regrettably flourished. With its emphasis on the imperatives of diversity and acceptance of all, and thus a subsequent reluctance and even refusal on the part of our leaders to promote shared values and identity, antisemitism in our Muslim communities becomes not only acceptable, but most disturbingly, it becomes inevitable. This anti-Jewish thinking, as well as a lack of social cohesion which have emerged from multiculturalism are not, as thought in some circles, the symptoms of a failure. Rather, they are the symptoms of a profound delusion, which has gripped our liberal leaders for decades. Despite the best intentions of these politicians, the melting pot, which should hold us all together, has liquified, and has allowed for what is decidedly a major threat not only to Jews, but to the very future of our liberal democracies, to flourish with little resistance And this, I argue, is the answer to the question I posed after May 11th.

It is, no doubt, the strangest of ironies that Jews, of all people, are the ones to pay the price for this delusion. The very values which became foundational in our civilization, in large part because of Jewish suffering in the Second World War, are precisely the values that have enabled these new threats to Jewish life in the region. This book explores the nature of this new menace, and details what must be done to protect minority rights, and make the most of living in diverse societies. Before turning to this, however, it is important to be clear on *terms and critical distinctions.*

Firstly, defining what constitutes Western Europe is not as straightforward as it seems. This has always been more of a political region

---

[12] Hasan, Mehdi. "The Sorry Truth Is That the Virus of Anti-Semitism Has Infected the British Muslim Community." *New Statesman*, 21 Mar. 2013, https://www.newstatesman.com/politics/2013/03/sorry-truth-virus-anti-semitism-has-infected-british-muslim-community

than a clear, geographical one. During the Second World War, Western Europe meant the allied powers and their neutral neighbors. Of course, Germany and Italy, which today are regarded as Western European, were certainly not in the 1930s and 1940s. During the Cold War, this region came to mean the states which were not under Soviet rule in Eastern Europe. And today, in a post-Cold War world, like in the past, Western Europe refers to a set of shared political and social values between states. As such, for this work, I am referring to the UK, Belgium, France, Germany, Sweden, Denmark and the Netherlands. These countries are not located within one part of Europe, yet, despite the many differences they have with one another, these countries are (largely) stable, diverse, liberal democracies.

This region, more than any other, is at the epicenter of debates and issues surrounding multiculturalism, Islamism, and integration. To be clear, while the concentration of Muslims in Western Europe has significantly increased over the years, with the majority residing in the UK, France, and Germany, there is no one way to be a Muslim. It is often said - 'two Jews, three opinions.' This is no less of a truism for Muslims. Like Jews, our cousins, are a diverse people, with multiple identities and various cultures. Thus, this work is certainly not to suggest all Muslims adhere to the views and ideas I am describing. Many actively rebuke such dangerous attitudes. And do so precisely because they are devout and proud of their faith. However, here in Western Europe, within our Muslim communities, there is a distinct issue of what I describe as 'Islamist thinking,' a term to which I shall return in a moment. But, for now, to put this into perspective, in the August of 2022, on a summer fellowship with the Institute for the Study of Global Antisemitism and Policy at the University of Oxford, I had the pleasure of meeting Fatema Al Harbi, the first Bahraini citizen to have visited Israel. She now works as an activist in her home country, educating Muslims in her country about the Holocaust and the history of antisemitism, as well as promoting peace between Jews and Arabs. She is a remarkable, inspiring and courageous individual. But she is safer doing this work in Manama or Dubai than in Paris, Malmo, or London. Something has gone terribly awry in our neck of the woods.

Before we unpack this, when talking about Islam and Islamism, important distinctions and qualifications are required. Far too often these terms are conflated. This work is not arguing that Islam, a religion, which consists of a set of diverse ideas and values, is inherently responsible for this anti-Jewish hostility. For there are the Fatemas of the Muslim world, and there are many like her, who reject this kind of bigotry, again, because they are true to their Islam. Rather, what is responsible is Islamism, and the normalization of what I describe as 'Islamist-thinking' within our Muslim communities. Defining Islamism, Peter Mandeville, a leading scholar of Islam, says that this describes, "forms of political theory and practice that have as their goal the establishment of an Islamic political order in the sense of a state whose governmental principles, institutions, and legal systems derive directly from the Sharia [Islamic law]."[13] In other words, the rejection of liberal democracy, and the belief that it is necessary to impose a particular value system and interpretation of Islamic law over the rest of society. Central to this is antisemitism, and associated homophobia, sexism, and of course, totalitarianism. Unfortunately, such dangerous ideas have become alarmingly common in these communities. They are not, as thought by many, marginal or fringe.

For this reason, the term 'extremists,' to a great degree, is no longer useful. We face ordinary people who subscribe, often without thought, to ideas in conflict with the ideals which underpin Western democratic civilization. As such, this book, though acknowledging the fact many do not give credence to these ideas, encourages an approach which views Muslim perpetrators of abuse, harassment and violence against Jews to be the products of communities in which such attitudes have become, in many quarters, mainstream. The fertile ground laid by non-violent, hate-filled rhetoric, or Islamist thinking, often paves the way for violence and criminal activity.

At this stage, it should also be said that while Islam and Islamism are certainly not synonymous, one should not make the mistake of entirely divorcing the former from the latter. After all, there is no Islamism without the first five letters of that word and thus, we do need to recognize that

---

[13] Cited here Maher, Shiraz. "Understanding Islamism. Policy Exchange," 2021, https://policyexchange.org.uk/wp-content/uploads/Understanding-Islamism.pdf.

Islamism is, at its core, a plausible interpretation of Islamic doctrine. But because of the sheer variety of theological interpretations which exists within Islam, as with any religion, I use the term 'Islamist-thinking' given that it is much more of a qualified and accurate description of the various factors I am writing about.

When it comes to multiculturalism, this term is equally ambiguous. There is no universal definition, and the way it manifests differs from country to country. The French, for instance, view multiculturalism as anathema, and regard it as an expression of separatism, or *communautarisme*. Nevertheless, to varying extents, all countries in the region experience it. A useful definition is given by the European Union (EU), which states that multiculturalism is a 'policy that endorses the principle of cultural diversity and supports the right of different cultural and ethnic groups to retain distinctive cultural identities ensuring their equitable access to society, encompassing constitutional principles and commonly shared values prevailing in the society.'[14] Generally speaking, in the case of Western Europe, I am unconvinced by the latter part of this definition. We are deprived of 'commonly shared values prevailing in the society,' which all, regardless of faith or background, can identify with. As such, my definition is much simpler. Notwithstanding differences between countries, in practice, multiculturalism is both a policy and a philosophy, which allows for, and often celebrates, a plurality of cultures living side by side (although increasingly less so), with each retaining their distinct customs and traditions, but with little or no emphasis being placed upon that which binds different communities together. Regardless of state policies, this is a state of affairs which Western European states are now having to contend with, and not only is this dividing communities, but it is also allowing for the toleration of ideals and values which are undeserving, and even exploitative, of our tolerance.

At the outset, however, it needs to be said that while this work is written in opposition to multiculturalism, it is very much in favor of societies which are multicultural, and those which embrace what the late

---

[14] "Multiculturalism." *European Commission - Migration and Home Affairs*, https://home-affairs.ec.europa.eu/networks/european-migration-network-emn/emn-asylum-and-migration-glossary/glossary/multiculturalism_en.

Chief-Rabbi Jonathan Sacks described as 'the dignity of difference.' This work, in no way, is written in opposition to diversity. After all, yours truly is a Jew with East European origins, and would not be here, in Britain, if it were not for diversity. But to ensure the preservation of our diverse societies, our leaders must be prepared to confront that which runs the risk of undermining Western Europe's meritorious progress over the years, and which would return us to a dark place. As the great philosopher, Karl Popper, put it in his work, The *Open Society and Its Enemies*, which he wrote during the Nazi reign, "If we extend unlimited tolerance even to those who are intolerant, if we are not prepared to defend a tolerant society against the onslaught of the intolerant, then the tolerant will be destroyed, and tolerance with them."[15] What we are confronting is indeed a threat to the very essence and foundations of our liberal-democratic civilization.

Now, I bet your bottom shekel, many of you, with hot-blooded exasperation, will point to the ubiquity of antisemitism. And you would be right to do so. From Britain to South Africa, and from Afghanistan to China, no one community or culture has ownership of Jew-bashing. A 2014 poll from the Anti-Defamation League, found that 24 per cent of the population in Western Europe agreed to at least six out of eleven antisemitic stereotypes.[16] In a post-Holocaust, post-colonial, postmodern world, that statistic is disturbing, to say the least. But the point is, this poison transcends all religious and political boundaries. And, of course, it is not only a consequence of the Islamist threat for why Synagogues and Jewish schools (including my alma mater) have airport-like security and prison-like gates upon entry. Remember, it was white-supremacists, not Islamists, who were responsible for the attacks in Pittsburgh, Texas, Poway, Kansas City, Halle, and more. This threat remains strong, and not one to be perfunctorily shrugged off with weasel words.

And, of course, none of this is new. In a piece for Liberation, Robert McLiam Wilson, who now writes for Charlie Hebdo, rightly pointed out,

---

[15] Popper, Karl (1945). "Chapter 7, The Principle of Leadership." The Open Society and Its Enemies (Volume 1). Routledge. pp. 265–266.
[16] Anti-Defamation League. "ADL Poll of Over 100 Countries Finds More Than One-Quarter of Those Surveyed Infected with Anti-Semitic Attitudes." Press Release, May 13, 2014. https://www.adl.org/resources/press-release/adl-poll-over-100-countries-finds-more-one-quarter-those-surveyed-infected.

"In the churning washing machine of human race hatred, anti-Semitism is the fabric that never loses its color. We've been at this stuff for millennia. All of us."[17] He isn't wrong. I recall my grandparents discussing with me their struggles as young Jews in 1930s London. It wasn't easy. My grandmother would lament about her experiences on Easter, when she was chased around the school by students and staff for being an effing 'Christ Killer.' And later, during the war, in the public air raid shelters of her street, she was told, "this is your fault. Go back to Palestine." The irony, of course, is that today, a number of Jews are told, often by those proclaiming to represent all-things progressive, to 'get out of Palestine.' Nevertheless, though what my family faced back in the day was comparably minor to what their counterparts were facing just across the channel, the virulent hatred which they would encounter led my paternal grandfather to change the family name from 'Marks' to 'Markham' to make us sound more English and less 'Jewy,' so we'd able to "fit in." Well, all I can say to that is my family trying to sound less "Jewy" and more English, is like me trying to go a day without complaining about my acid reflux – the truth is, neither has happened, or will ever happen.

However, the point here is that while antisemitism has a long-standing history within the West, and even though it remains widespread in society, there is a fundamental question of scale. The unpalatable truth for many, as we shall see, is that many Jews in Western Europe are concerned by the Islamist threat more than they are any other. And for good reason. Although there have been other social, political, and economic grievances resulting from the failure to manage cultural diversity, this work concentrates on anti-Jewish thinking for two reasons. Firstly, on a personal note, as a young British Jew, what this book explores has profound consequences for my future, and that of my counterparts in Western Europe. Secondly, I use contemporary antisemitism, particularly its Islamist incarnation, the most concerning of all its varied expressions, as a means of gauging the wider problems of multiculturalism. Since what happens to Jews almost always has implications for the welfare of us all.

This is understood by exploring the nature of this plague. Never has antisemitism been a mere xenophobia or racism. It has never just been a

---

[17] Translated into English by Mcliam Wilson in private correspondence.

plain loathing of Jews or an odious contempt for Judaism. If only! Although it can be expressed in these terms, what gives Jew-hate its distinct "color" is that it is more like a paranoid psychosis in which the thoughts and ideas of antisemites are not only divorced from reality, but are its very negation. Their *weltanschauung, or worldview, is polluted with conspiratorial and demonic delusion.* We Jews are not attacked for what we are: a small and diverse religious civilization. We are attacked *for what we are not: an imaginary or mythical collective, responsible for all that is corrosive in a society.* The antisemite, unable to succumb to reason and logic, invents myths, and in his or her charade, dresses such falsehoods as indisputable facts. As rightly observed by David Patterson, an eminent scholar of Jewish Studies, "For the antisemite, the premise is not that all Jews are evil but that all evil is Jewish."[18] It follows, therefore, that if society is freed from its Jews, better known in German as Judenfrei, it is freed from those evils.

This 'diabolical causality,' as described by the late French historian, Leon Poliakov, has distinguished antisemitism from every other prejudice under the sun. For Christian antisemites, past and present, it is thought for the world to be saved from its godlessness, at first, those Christ-killers, those Jews guilty of killing the son of God, had to be converted, expelled, or worse. Otherwise, mankind would be deprived of its impending redemption. Taking some inspiration from this, for European fascists, society could only be freed from communism, "race mixing," feminism, gay-rights, and all the other ideals fascists reject, when the cause of these 'degenerate' developments, the Jews, are eliminated. Similarly, communists thought that to be freed from the evils of capitalism, society must first be freed of its proponents. Yes, those "huckstering" Jews. Today, in the name of human rights and progressivism, for there to be an end to all things Western, a civilization which cannot shake off its eternal sins, the world must first be freed from the nation which is perceived to be the West's most sacrilegious invention, the State of Israel, which just happens to be the world's only Jewish-majority state. Indeed, in all these and other examples, Jean-Paul Sartre in his thought-provoking 1946 work,

---

[18] David Patterson. *Judaism, Antisemitism, and Holocaust: Making the Connections.* Cambridge: Cambridge University Press, 2022. p.100

Anti-Semite and Jew, reasoned, "anti-Semitism is a conception of the Manichean and primitive world in which hatred for the Jew arises as a great explanatory myth."[19] To those whose worldview is understood through this psychosis, or as Leon Pinsker put it in 1882, an incurable 'demonopathy,' to eliminate the perfidious Jews is to eliminate the cause of all that is evil. This is not written to absolve the antisemite, but to shed light on why, inevitably, we all become targets.

Back in the day, my old, East-End Jewish grandfather, like many Jews back then (because they could be their own bosses), was a black taxi driver in London. It was said, in those days, you could tell how well the economy was doing by how well the black cabbies were doing. If the taxi trade was doing well, so was the economy. Similarly, we can measure a society's commitment to liberal democracy and a society's commitment to the 'dignity of difference' by the way a society treats its Jews, historically Europe's oldest and ultimate other. As Jonathan Sacks rightly pointed out, "antisemitism is not really about Jews. It is about how societies treat the Other, the one-not-like-us." And therefore, he declared, "A nation that has no room for difference has no room for humanity."[20] It is no coincidence that most, if not every, anti-democratic and totalitarian movement in European history has had a particular problem with Jews. It's the disdain for Jews, and everything perceived to be of Jewish origin, which brings together capitalists and socialists, nationalists and internationalists, racists and liberals, intellectuals and hoodlums, theists and atheists. This psychosis has been and continues to be the common denominator, perhaps even First Cause, in all movements and ideologies, which reject the fundamentals of liberal democracy.

Visiting the Weiner Holocaust Library in London, I discovered that in France, the Dreyfus Affair, in which a highly prominent French-Jewish officer was falsely accused and convicted of treason, this "became a symbol and rallying point for antisemites and the opponents of liberalism and republicanism on the one side, and defenders of French democracy on

---

[19] Sartre, Jean-Paul. *Anti-Semite and Jew.* Translated by George J. Becker, Schocken Books, 1948. P.107
[20] Sacks, Jonathan. "The Hate that Starts with Jews Never Ends There." *The Rabbi Sacks Legacy*, 16 Aug. 2014, https://rabbisacks.org/archive/hate-starts-jews-never-ends-there/

the other."[21] In other words, the perception of this Jew, and by extension, the Jews, was fundamental to the way French society perceived democracy. Those who were opposed to it, were largely of the view that Dreyfus was guilty, and those in favor of democracy, largely believed Dreyfus was innocent. In his analysis of this affair, the late Christopher Hitchens described how the term "intellectual," as a term of insult, owes its origins to what occurred during this period. He noted that it was a charge thrown by the anti-Dreyfusards towards the Jews and those in support of Dreyfus. In Hitch's interpretation, then, the assault on Dreyfus was one upon the very foundations of modernity, freedom, and enlightenment. In that spirit, just like then, where our societies stand on its Jews today, is where it stands on all the values integral to our liberal-democracies. Accordingly, though this book pays much attention to what Jews are experiencing, I explore broader themes of democracy, populism, extremism, and identity. The crux of my argument is that Western Europe is sleepwalking into a crisis of and for civilization. What is at stake here is more than the future of Jews. It is about the very future of our shared humanity.[22]

With that, in Chapter One, I explore why it is that despite Western Europe's progress over the years, large numbers of Jews are concerned for their futures. Through using surveys, data and anecdotal evidence, I analyze what is going on within this region, and what many of its Jews are experiencing. What we experienced on May 11th was not that dissimilar from anti-Jewish pogroms of the past. This Russian word, meaning, "to wreak havoc, or to demolish violently," were local affairs across Eastern and Central Europe. Although sometimes prompted by the elite and the state, these were groups of local people who, on their own volition, violently rose up against their Jewish neighbors. While those involved in that May 11th mob were incensed by a vast amount of misinformation and distorted imagery from both the media and academia, they were very much a group of wrathful, but ordinary Muslim men. Many of whom came from

---

[21] Cited at "Fighting Antisemitism from Dreyfus to Today," Wiener Holocaust Library, London.
[22] "Christopher Hitchens on Antisemitism." https://www.youtube.com/watch?v=eMGwcZPbLHw

places in which anti-Jewish thinking is the norm. They were not necessarily affiliated with any particular organization. They came on their own volition. What we experienced will become a regular fixture in more cities and towns across the region if we do not confront the extent to which Jew-hate has found an accommodating environment within our Muslim communities. The result of which would make life for Jews, and everyone else for that matter, intolerable.

Accordingly, leading on from this, Chapter Two explores what is motivating Muslim antisemitism, why it exists, and what the future could look like if no action is taken. The fact is, we cannot begin to understand what is causing this unless we look beyond the odious criminality of the individuals who carry out these anti-Jewish crimes. As such, this chapter dwells on three factors, namely historical developments, communal antisemitism, and anti-Israelism. By addressing the sources of where this is coming from, we can establish what must be done to stop it.

Before we turn to this, however, in Chapter Three, the question to which we must investigate is why this intolerance has been able to thrive in a civilization which boasts universalism and tolerance for all. By evaluating three factors, the politics of fear, the politics of numbers, and the politics of identity, this chapter not only attempts to answer why multiculturalism has, unwittingly, become the means to a terrible end, but why our leaders have been, as I argue, negligent, and even, in some cases, complicit, in this threat to Jewish-life and our liberal democracies. Again, by understanding the political, social, and cultural roots of this crisis, we are in a much better place to possibly put up some resistance to this worsening situation.

And lastly, in Chapter Four, I offer, or try to at least, a message of hope. Although things are bleak, it is not too late for there to be lasting and credible change. To that end, this chapter wrestles with five areas: 1. To Confront Reality and Reclaim, 2. To Prevent & Enforce the Law, 3. The importance of non-Jewish ally-building, 4. Amplification, not Reformation, and 5. Restructuring Society: A New Vision for Western Europe. The purpose of this chapter is to put the case forward for a new model for managing diversity here in Western Europe; one which makes the most of the enriching benefits of diversity, one which confronts extremism, and also one which rebuilds trust in mainstream politics, or parties which ideologically exist both in and around the orbit of centrism, and critically, believe in sustaining liberal-democratic societies and processes.

This work is written, in part, because of the growth of parties, rightly or wrongly, dubbed as populist and/or even extreme. However, I take the view that their appeal and success at the ballot box is more of a reflection of the failure of mainstream politics than of their success, which, in the context of this book, describes parties that have tendencies to veer towards both the hard left and hard right. At present, it seems the only political movements willing to discuss some of these uncomfortable truths about multiculturalism are precisely the parties casually derided as anti-democratic. If anything, those parties are offering vehicles through which people can feel some degree of democratic representation. However, those who believe in sustaining liberal-democratic politics cannot afford to leave people's legitimate concerns with multiculturalism in what has been described as the 'taboo zone.' The alternative is what we see all over the region. At the last French election, if we combine the first-round votes for Marine Le Pen and Eric Zemmour, both populist right leaders, Emmanuel Macron, the so-called centrist, would have lost the popular vote. It is also worth noting, if we were to add the votes for Jean-Luc Mélenchon, a populist left leader, France's Jeremy Corbyn, French society voted overwhelmingly against the liberal status quo. Of course, we are seeing similar patterns throughout Western Europe and beyond, need I mention Brexit, Trump or Meloni? There is a demonstrable and widespread disillusionment with mainstream politics, and the growth of populist movements is not the cause, but the natural reaction. Mainstream centrists and social democrats must be willing to reclaim the debate on these issues, or else, we leave it to the populist, and sometimes, anti-democratic, forces. And, if left unchecked, in the long run, this could prove to undermine the very democracies these movements are proclaiming to defend.

What we experienced on May 11th serves as a warning to us all. If we do not stand up to violent antisemitic and anti-democratic forces, we shall pay the price in the years to come. What is being addressed is not a parochial issue. It is one of the most burning cultural crises of our age. We ignore it at our own peril.

Now, what's going on in Western Europe? To this, we now turn.

Chapter One:
What is going on?

In case it wasn't clear already: my family and I have a shared proclivity for discussing the existential questions facing Jews and civilization. In fact, in recent months, perhaps because of this book, it seems all we speak about is why people dislike us, and what this means for us and our deliciously complex identities. Sometimes, I just want to discuss my weekend plans (not that I ever have any), or the best series currently on Netflix, and yet there we are, in the kitchen, cacophonously debating the reasons for why people want us in the sea. I feel for our poor neighbors, of course. But we are by no means alone. This debate rages in many Jewish homes throughout the world.

Speaking of the Jews today in Europe, Hans Christian Krüger, the former Deputy-Secretary General of the Council of Europe, the continent's leading body for human rights and democracy, remarked, "Your presence reminds us about our raison d'être, about our roots and hopes. Indeed, the very concept of the Council of Europe would not have arisen without a cataclysm, what was World War II, without Shoah and racist lessons of the totalitarian wave that swept across Europe…"[23] The haunting legacies of unparalleled suffering and barbarity which engulfed swathes of Europe throughout the Nazi Holocaust, has inspired, as Levy and Sznaizer put it, an 'epochal break,' from all the things which allowed such unspeakable evil to flourish.[24] Indeed, Mr Kruger was right to point

---

[23] "The Universalist Nature of the Jewish Peoples Message," Hans Christian Kruger in *Ben-Itto,* Hadassa, et al., editors. *Justice*, no. 23, Spring 2000, International Association of Jewish Lawyers and Jurists, https://www.ijl.org/justicem/Mag%20No.23%20Spring%202000.pdf

[24] Cited in Seymour, David M. ""New Europe," Holocaust Memory, and Antisemitism." *Global Antisemitism: A Crisis of Modernity*, edited by Charles Asher Small, vol. 1, Brill, 2013, pp. 19–26.

out that the immensity of human wickedness in this period paved the way for the intellectual, social, and political construction of a new postwar Europe. Whereas this civilization was once characterized by nationalism, racism and anti-democratic politics, this 'New Europe,' is defined by its commitment to democracy, tolerance, universalism, and human-rights.

Thank goodness for that. The very systems and structures which allowed this Shoah, this catastrophe, to take place, have now, for the most part, been marginalized for the sake of this post-nation state, pan-European community – which, as the motto of the European Union makes clear, celebrates 'unity in diversity.' The former President of the European Commission, when accepting a Nobel Peace Prize on behalf of the EU stated, "The genius of the founding fathers was precisely in understanding that to guarantee peace in the 20th century, nations needed to think beyond the nation-state."[25] Given the transformation from fascism and war to democracy and peace, how could this progress be anything but good, especially for the continent's Jews, the very people whose martyrdom has spawned this new epoch in European history?

Yet, despite Europe's progress, however, its response to the historic suffering of Jews is a fantasy. For many, the harrowing images of piled up, Jewish corpses have become emblematic of the continent's nationalist, exclusionary, and racist past. The brutality Jews endured has been subsumed into a wider, universal message of all that is wrong with Europe's foundations, and thus the moral imperative of the postwar core maxim, namely, to 'think beyond the nation state.' Liberals may have thought, and continue to think, that this is the only way to ensure such horrors can never happen again. But they are wrong. The pursuit of liberal never-againism has not emancipated Europe from the shackles of antisemitism, but in fact, has become the partner-in-crime of this primordial beast. The tyrant facing Jews, indeed civilization, is not a dictator with a peculiar moustache, but the delusions of the well-intentioned.

---

[25] Van Rompuy, Herman, and José Manuel Durão Barroso. "From War to Peace: A European Tale." *European Commission*, 10 Dec. 2012, https://ec.europa.eu/commission/presscorner/detail/en/SPEECH_12_930

In 1920, the great Yiddish author and playwright, Sholem Aleichem, wrote a play describing the tribulations of Jewish life in the Russian Empire. It follows a Russian-gentile, Ivanov, who initially dismisses the idea that being a Jew is hard. Upon the suggestion of an acquaintance, he takes on the challenge of being one for a year, and the play details his day-to-day struggles of this decision, be that state sanctioned antisemitism, socioeconomic discrimination, threats of a pogrom, accusations of ritual murder, and more. At the end, Ivanov realized the immensity of this struggle, and rightly concluded, as the play is entitled, *Shver Tsu Zayn a Yid*, It's Hard to be a Jew.

A hundred and four years later, a lot has changed. Neither Russia nor any European nation has state sanctioned antisemitism, where pogroms and discrimination are a part of daily life. However, the denial over the realities of contemporary antisemitism remains, as does, in some places, the threat to Jewish lives. And if only the scholars, politicians, and journalists who minimize this issue were to be like Ivanov, and become a Jew for a year, they would realize, for many of us, it ain't easy.

The Brutality

To understand why, we begin in Bagneux, a rundown, poverty-stricken Parisian suburb, or Banlieue. On the 20th of January, 2006, life for the Halimis, a small and poor Jewish family, was to change forever. The oldest child, Illan, an unassuming, but outgoing 23-year-old, lived with his observant mother and two sisters. Life was hard for this family, and Illan had to take on the role of father figure, as well as working as a salesman in a Parisian phone store. Despite the tribulations, they were a close and loving family. Yet, on that day, thinking he was going to the home of a beguiling young woman, whom he had met in his store, he was led to what she and her friends had been planning for months: the abduction of an innocent Jew by a gang made up of around fifty people, calling themselves the "Gang des barbares," the Gang of Barbarians, led by Youssouf Fofana, who was born and bred in these suburbs as a second-generation Ivorian. They had tried these villainous operations for months, as they thought 'all Jews were rich,' and that by abducting a Jew, they would make their fortune. Until now they had no success. But young Illan, through this sickening episode of entrapment and extortion, was to pay the ultimate price.

Demanding a staggering 450,000 Euros for his release over a course of 600 agonizing phone calls, Foufana sent pictures to the Halimis via email of their Illan brutalized. His head was shaved, his cheek was sliced with a knife, with blood streaming down his face, and a few days later, cigarette burns appeared on his forehead, with open wounds everywhere which, again, were gushing out blood. With each passing day, in addition to the beatings and torture, Illan was also left on a on a freezing boiler room floor, wrapped up from head to toe, dressed like a 'mummy,' fed through just a straw, only able to urinate into a bottle, and defecate into a plastic bag. The Halimis were powerless to save their boy. Not only was the exorbitant ransom money out of reach, but they had no idea where he was. Lasting for twenty-four days, also the title of a spine-chilling film of this affair, the exquisite agony this family suffered was not to end with his release. After some time of not hearing anything further from his captors, Illan Halimi was found, struggling to walk on the tracks of a Paris suburb trainline, where the gang dumped him. As well as being naked and handcuffed, he was bleeding from multiple stab wounds, burns covered 80 per cent of his body, an ear and a toe had been forcibly cut off, and his genitals were mutilated. An ambulance was called, but he died en route to the hospital.[26]

When Fofana was tried, he declared "Allah will be victorious," and was sentenced to life imprisonment, while more than twenty others received lesser sentences. This, however, was by no means the last instance of brutal Islamist violence against Jews. This was the beginning.

Six years later, on the 19th of March 2012, a Jewish high school, in Toulouse was the target of 23-year-old, Mohammed Merah, born in France to Algerian parents. He murdered four people at this school, three of whom were young children. This Islamist began his killing spree eight days

---

[26] From a range of sources: Freund, Deborah. "The Shocking Murder of Ilan Halimi." *Aish.com*, https://aish.com/the-shocking-murder-of-ilan-halimi/. "Remembering Ilan Halimi." *American Jewish Committee*, 12 Feb. 2020, https://www.ajc.org/news/remembering-ilan-halimi. "The First Victim: Remembering Ilan Halimi." *American Jewish Committee*, 12 Feb. 2016, https://www.ajc.org/news/the-first-victim-remembering-ilan-halimi.

earlier. On the 11th, he shot dead an off-duty paratrooper, Master Sergeant Imad Ibn-Ziaten, right in the head, outside the Chateau de l'Hers school in Toulouse. Merah was able to flee the scene the quickly on his motorcycle. Four days later, on the 15th March, Merah shot dead, while they were withdrawing money from an ATM near their barracks, a 25- year-old Corporal, Abel Chennouf, and a 23-year-old Private, Mohamed Legouad. He also seriously wounded another. As on the 11th, he was able to escape the scene on his motorcycle.

But he was not finished. A few days later, he would go to the Ozar Hatorah school, since renamed Ohr Torah, and savagely murder his last victims. It was to be the first time Jewish children had been killed in Europe since the Holocaust. The Ozar Hatorah schools, of which there are several, were established for young Jews from Middle Eastern and North African backgrounds. The school, in fact, was known chiefly for being a place of academic excellence. Even to this day, this school remains a high achieving school. Yet the butchery of March 19th was to leave Ohr Hatorah irredeemably scarred.

At 8:00 AM, Merah arrived on his motorbike, and immediately fired several bullets towards the front of the school. According to the local prosecutor, Michel Valet, Merah "shot at everything he could see, children and adults, and some children were chased into the school." His first victim at the school, and fourth over this eight-day period, was Jonathan Sandle, a 30-year-old rabbi, father and teacher, who was trying to protect his two young boys from this bloodthirsty Jihadist. However, after killing their father, Merah then savagely killed those defenseless boys – Arié aged just 5, and his brother, Gabriel, aged just 3. He then pursued an 8-year-old girl, who would become his seventh and final victim. This girl, Myriam Monsonego, fled for her life into the courtyard, where he caught her by the hair, and attempted to shoot her. He discovered that his gun was jammed, and so in these few moments of inexpressible wickedness, he took out a separate gun in his possession, and shot this poor little girl in the head. Upon hearing the shootings, the head teacher and father of Myriam, Yaacov Monsonego came outside to the school yard only to see his daughter, his child, murdered. Merah also left several people wounded, leaving one seventeen-year-old boy gravely injured . Like in his previous senseless and callous attacks, he fled the scene.

This time, though, he did not get far. At this point, the French authorities embarked on one of, if not the biggest, manhunts in French history. Eventually, Mohammed Merah was shot dead by police in a siege on the 22nd of March 2012. In the words of Nicole Yardeni, who led the regional branch of CRIF, the leading body for Jewish affairs in France, "It is unbearable that someone be able to dehumanize children to this point." And this is not only true in the case of Merah. This trend of employing the most heinous and unspeakable modes of murder is a major common denominator we see throughout these savage crimes.[27]

Despite the tragedy which unfolded at this place of learning, the school continued to thrive, but sadly, it was to face other, albeit less serious, incidents of antisemitism. As if it had become a prison, with a new high wall and barbed wire put in place, Ohr Torah received innumerable threats and insults. In 2014, two years after the attack, a man would post a picture of himself doing the quenelle, an inverted Nazi salute first performed by the notorious antisemite and comedian, Dieudonné M'bala M'bala. In July of that year, a man would throw a Molotov cocktail at the school building. In comparison to what happened in 2012, these incidents are minor, but they represent how one anti-Jewish attack is a source of inspiration for others.[28]

On a personal note, I will never forget the day the Ozar Hatorah shootings happened. I had just turned 12, and heard the tragic news on my way to my Jewish high school. And like other people in my class and Jews throughout the world, I immediately thought to myself, could this happen here? Indeed, like others, I thought, is it even safe to attend my Jewish school, knowing that this kind of thing could happen here? This reaction, which doubtless was shared by my peers, illustrates the way in which these barbaric murders send shockwaves throughout the Jewish world. They serve as a reminder that life for Jews, even in this post-Holocaust age, is not impervious to the murderous wrath of the unrelenting beast that is Jew-hate.

---

[27] Mohamed Merah | Counter Extremism Project.
[28] Nazi-style quenelle salute performed at Toulouse Jewish school | The Times of Israel.

Yet, the shooting of innocent Jewish children was not enough for Islamists. A couple of years later, on the 24th May 2014, the Jewish Museum in Brussels, was the target of Mehdi Nemmouche, a repeat offender, born in France to Algerian parents. Here, in the Belgian capital, Mr. Nemmouche, with the support of Nacer Bendrer, the man who supplied him with a Kalashnikov assault rifle and a handgun, murdered four innocent people. Like Mohammed Merah, Mehdi Nemmouche loathed Jews. In fact, while serving his fifth sentence, a report notes that Nemmouche "asked for a television set to follow – 'with jubilation' the saga of the killer [Mohammed Merah] on a scooter." A few days later, he was recorded by the prison warden saying, "I feel great this morning. I could well picture myself shooting up a little Jewish girl today." As expected, upon his release, this soon-to-be murderer was no gefilte-fish-loving, committed liberal, philosemite. Rather, he moved to Molenbeek-Saint-Jean, a municipality within Brussels which has earned a reputation for being an Islamist hotspot, and from there, much like his hero Merah, on New Years Eve 2012, travelled to the Middle East, arriving in Syria. While there, he worked as a prison guard for Islamic State, largely working with captured French journalists. Later, when brought to trial in the January of 2019, some of those journalists who were held captive by Nemmouche, claimed that his schadenfreude was in witnessing his prisoners suffer, and that he was "filled with hate especially towards the Jews and Shia Muslims." But, again, just like with Merah, Western-Europe allowed this committed Jihadist back into its shores. And he was determined to find some Jewish targets.

Courtesy of his friend, he got hold of a Kalashnikov and a pistol. He arrived at the Jewish Museum, and murdered two Israeli tourists, a French volunteer, and a Belgian receptionist, in the heart of the country's capital. This was, in fact, the first terror attack committed by a Jihadist returning from the war in Syria. At his trial, like many killers before him, he was remorseless. In fact, before the jurors left the courtroom to deliberate, Nemmouche folded his arms, offered the court a perfunctory and unperturbed smirk, and said with ease, "life goes on." However, even after his defense lawyer blamed Mossad for this atrocity (even when Jews are killed, it's still, somehow, their fault), he was found guilty and received a life sentence, and his accomplice, Nacer Bendrer, was imprisoned for 15 years.[29]

After 2015, violent and deadly anti-Jewish violence would reach a new high across Western Europe. On the 9th of January 2015, at the Hypercacher Kosher supermarket, Amedy Coulibaly, a French-Malian Jihadist, in sync with Islamist shootings by Saïd and Chérif Kouachi (his Jihadist-trained-friends) at the office of Charlie Hebdo two days earlier, in which 12 people were murdered, raided this supermarket in Paris, immediately killing four people, all of whom Jews, before taking hostages. Just a month later, on the night of the 14th of February, in Copenhagen's Great Synagogue was the target of Omar Abdel Hamid El-Hussein, who murdered a young Jewish man, who was on security duty during a bat-mitzvah celebration, as well as wounding two police officers. That afternoon, he shot dead one person at an exhibition in the Danish capital entitled "Art, Blasphemy and Freedom of Expression," and later that night, he attacked the synagogue. Most recently, in the August of 2022, Eliahou Haddad, a Jewish man living in Longperrier, France, aged 34, was axed to death by his Muslim neighbor, who confessed his guilt to local police.[30]

Before looking at the situation in numbers, there are two final examples worth highlighting as they are particularly depraved. And like most of these murderous assaults, we return to Paris and its banlieues. The first is the 2017 murder of Lucie Attal Halimi, posthumously named Sara Halimi, a 65-year-old retired doctor and schoolteacher, the second, which occurred a year later, is the murder of Mireille Knoll, an 85-year-old Holocaust survivor.

We begin with Sarah Halimi. It's probably best to start with her name. Her Hebrew name was Sarah, and Halimi came from her former husband, Yaacov Hallimi, with whom she divorced decades earlier. No one is quite sure why she was posthumously given that name. One suspects, however, she was known by Sarah Halimi to draw a symbolic parallel between her

---

[29] Silber, Mitchell D. "Terrorist Attacks Against Jewish Targets in the West (2012-2019): The Atlantic Divide Between European and American Attackers." *CTC Sentinel*, vol. 12, no. 5, Combating Terrorism Center at West Point, May/June 2019, p.33.

[30] ibid pp 31-35; Klein, Zvika. "Jewish French Man Murdered with Ax, Face Burned by Roommate – Report." *The Jerusalem Post*, 29 Aug. 2022, https://www.jpost.com/diaspora/antisemitism/article-715842

murder and that of Ilan Halimi eleven years earlier. That is, Sarah Halimi was perceived to be the next Illan Hallimi, the latest Jew to be a victim of this savagery.

Like with Illan Halimi, Sarah lived in an apartment located within a city, in a social housing project in the Parisian suburbs. In the early hours of the 4th April 2017, Sarah Halimi was violently beaten, and subsequently murdered, by being thrown out of her third-floor balcony. She was asleep when the man and neighbor who would soon murder her, Kobili Traoré, a 27-year-old Franco-Malian Muslim, entered her apartment, and woke her up. In his gruesome assault, her skull was crushed, and the nightgown she was wearing - colored white with some blue - was soaked with her blood. This barbaric crime lasted a staggering fifty minutes. Just imagine. Fifty minutes of a 27-year-old man brutally attacking a 65-year-old grandmother, before ultimately defenestrating her. While beating her, neighbors heard him call her a "dirty Jew," while reciting verses from the Quran and chanting "Allahu Akbar." He then, after these 50 minutes, finally threw her from her balcony. Once he saw on the floor, in a river of her own blood, Traoré chanted from the balcony, "I killed the sheitan!" This is the Arabic word for "devil." According to neighbors, at this point, he again repeatedly shouted, "Allahu Akbar." Like in previous incidents, what is shocking is not only her murder, but the way in which she was so cruelly murdered. For Traoré not only killed, but he callously tortured his elderly Jewish victim.[31]

Although we have seen similar incidents, what was particularly disturbing, indeed outrageous, about this affair was how the courts subsequently dealt with Kobili Traoré. The country's highest court, the Court of Cassation, ruled in the April of 2021 that Traoré could not be tried because, on the night of the murder, he took marijuana, and this, therefore, absolves him of all culpability. It should be noted, however, that in 2017, a man who had been drinking and threw his dog out of the

---

[31] Liphshiz, Cnaan. "French Parliamentary Report on Sarah Halimi Murder Reopens Wounds It Sought to Heal." *The Times of Israel*, 22 Jan. 2022, https://www.timesofisrael.com/french-parliamentary-report-on-sarah-halimi-murder-reopens-wounds-it-sought-to-heal/

window, was sentenced to prison. A fine example of 'Jews Don't Count.'[32]

In any case, this was not the first time the French courts decided not to prosecute an Islamist killer. In 2003, Sebastien Selam, a 23-year-old French-Moroccan Jew, also in the Parisian suburbs, was murdered from multiple stabbings, by his childhood friend Adel Amastaibou, a man who previously violently assaulted a random rabbi in the street. In the parking lot where this Islamist thug murdered Salem, he proudly declared, "I killed my Jew! I'll go to heaven! Allah made me do it!" It was decided, contrary to the advice of the psychiatrist who interviewed him, that Adel Amastaibou's mind was "altered at the time of the act," and was unable to stand trial, and therefore, was absolved of all responsibility.[33]

What a similar picture we see in the case of Kobili Traoré. This man did not become a murderous antisemite after smoking marijuana. He had long terrified Sara Halimi. According to an interview with Sarah's brother and the Guardian's James McAuley, Sarah would tell her brother that she would only feel safe if this man were locked up, after he had verbally abused her in the building's elevator.[34] And it should be said, he later confessed to authorities that he knew she was an Orthodox-Jewish woman. Traoré's alibi, therefore, simply does not hold.

Some years later, Sarah Halimi's family and Jews around the world are still in pursuit of justice. What they rightly point out is that this decision from France's highest court set a precedent that if you kill a Jew, and at the time you were high or intoxicated, the case against you could well be dismissed. As the front cover of Charlie Hebdo, the French satirical magazine, put it on the 28th of April 2021, with a Muslim man holding a

---

[32] "We Demand Justice for Sarah Halimi: A Grandmother Stabbed to Death Because She Was Jewish." *Action Network*, https://actionnetwork.org/petitions/we-demand-justice-for-sarah-halimi-a-grandmother-stabbed-to-death-because-she-was-jewish

[33] Klein, Zvika. "Jewish French Man Murdered with Ax, Face Burned by Roommate – Report." *The Jerusalem Post*, 29 Aug. 2022, https://www.jpost.com/diaspora/antisemitism/article-715842. Weitzmann, Marc. "How 'The Deranged Ones' Are Reshaping France." *Tablet Magazine*, 29 Jan. 2015, https://www.tabletmag.com/sections/news/articles/terror-anti-semitism-france

[34] McAuley, James. "How the Murders of Two Elderly Jewish Women Shook France." *The Guardian*, 27 Nov. 2018, https://www.theguardian.com/world/2018/nov/27/how-the-murders-of-two-elderly-jewish-women-shook-france-antisemitism-mireille-knoll-sarah-halimi

knife, lighting his joints from a Menorah, "Faut-il dépénaliser l'antisémitisme?" (Should we decriminalize antisemitism?) The magazine was right. The decision not to take a strong stand against this kind of unspeakable violence serves only to embolden the Traorés of tomorrow.

No doubt the lack of justice Traoré faced enabled Yacine Mihoub and Alex Carrimbacus in their murder of Mirelle Knoll, our second and last victim, a year later, on the 23rd of March, 2018. An 85-year-old Holocaust survivor and an escapee of the Vil D'hiv roundup in 1942, Knoll, who was also suffering from Parkinsons in her old age, was savagely murdered in her home (also located in a suburb). Both men, aged 31 and 25 respectively, had their problems. They met in prison while serving sentences for sexual assault, robbery, and violence. Like with Traoré, Mihoub had psychiatric and alcohol related issues. In a similar fashion to the murder of Sarah Halimi, Mihoub and Carrimbacus broke into her home, it is claimed, on the basis that "She's a Jew. She must have money." Upon forcing themselves into her home, Mihoub repeatedly stabbed the woman who lived next to his own mother, and who acted as a "surrogate grandmother," before setting her apartment on fire, and leaving her blood-soaked to burn, at least partly. It is claimed that Mihoub, who was the one found guilty of murder, repeatedly chanted "Allahu Akbar" while slashing her to death.

When it came to this three-week trial, in this case, the French courts got it right and confirmed that this was fueled by a blaze of Judenhass. Yacine Mihoub was sent to prison for life, while Alex Carrimbacus received a sentence of 15 years for burglary with antisemitic motivations. A harrowing episode, but thankfully, the French courts, this time, got it right.[35]

The examples I have considered are not exhaustive. The list could have been longer. Nevertheless, what matters here, aside from the common denominators here being the geographical proximity they have with one another, the jail time each spent (where some of whom were radicalized), as well as the authorities failing to keep Jihadists out of Western Europe, all points to which we shall return, is that these instances of murderous

---

[35] "Mireille Knoll: Killer of French Holocaust Survivor Jailed for Life." *BBC News*, 3 Feb. 2022, https://www.bbc.co.uk/news/world-europe-59239981.

antisemitism have traumatizing repercussions on the way Jews view both their own identity and their place in Western Europe.

The Data and Victims

However, though leaving many desperately fearful, since such events seldom occur, it would be wrong to suggest that these events are the principal source of Jewish concerns in the region. Much more frequent are the almost daily instances of anti-Jewish harassment, abuse, and violence. Such acts are wider ranging, but as the data demonstrates, things are far from good. Altogether, recent years have left Jews feeling deeply unnerved about what lies ahead. These fears were expressed in two major surveys of European Jews in both 2018 and 2019. Both conducted by the European Union's Agency for Fundamental Rights (FRA), an independent body in the EU for the promotion of human rights and anti-racism, these surveys made for an agonizing read. The former, and its second such survey, published in 2018, was the largest ever poll on the Jews of Europe; it reached 16,500 Jews across 12 EU member states. The latter, published in 2019, reached 2,700 young Jews on the continent. Although this data is an average, most respondents came from France, UK, and Germany, where most of Europe's Jews live.

Both painted a sorry picture for those who embrace this `New Europe.` The 2018 report identified that nine in ten of the respondents believed that antisemitism had increased in their country five years before the survey.[36] In fact, more than eight in ten considered it to be a serious problem, and many of whom see it as the most serious social or political problem where they live.[37] Young Jews share the concerns of their elders. The 2019 survey points out that well over 80 per cent of young Jews say that antisemitism is a problem in their country and believe it has grown in

---

[36] European Union Agency for Fundamental Rights (FRA). *Experiences and Perceptions of Antisemitism: Second Survey on Discrimination and Hate Crime Against Jews in the EU.* Dec. 2018, https://fra.europa.eu/sites/default/files/fra_uploads/fra-2018-experiences-and-perceptions-of-antisemitism-survey_en.pdf. p.11
[37] Ibid.

the past five years.[38] These fears have not emerged in a vacuum. A notable revelation came in 2019, when the governments of both France and Germany, the former home to the largest and the latter home to the third largest Jewish communities in Europe, recorded rates of antisemitism they had not seen in years. In France, the number of offences against Jews surged by 74 per cent from the previous year, while, in Germany, the number of violent attacks had increased by a staggering 60 per cent.[39] In the Netherlands, The Center for Information and Documentation Israel (CIDI), the main body for recording antisemitism in the country, said that 2019 had the highest number for antisemitic incidents since the organization began publishing its reports in 1982.[40] There isn't the space to consider all the data, however, in the past few years, we have seen similar statistics throughout the region. And let's not forget the surge of anti-Jewish activity around the world in 2021, where in many places, post-Holocaust antisemitism reached record highs.

If we return to the FRA data, we can see that a startling number of Jews have been the victims of such incidents. The 2018 survey found that hundreds of Jews had experienced a physical antisemitic attack, and one in four experienced antisemitic harassment in the 12 months prior to the survey.[41] It added that one in five claimed that they were aware of a relative or people close to them that had been abused, harassed, or even physically attacked.[42] For young Jews, again, we see a similar picture. It found that young Jews are more likely to experience antisemitism than their elder counterparts.[43] In fact, almost 50 per cent of the young Jews surveyed say they had been the victim of one antisemitic incident in the

---

[38] "European Union Agency for Fundamental Rights (FRA)." *Young Jewish Europeans: Perceptions and Experiences of Antisemitism.* 2019, https://fra.europa.eu/sites/default/files/fra_uploads/fra-2019-young-jewish-europeans_en.pdf. p.3
[39] Henley, Jon. "Antisemitism Rising Sharply Across Europe, Latest Figures Show." *The Guardian*, 15 Feb. 2019, https://www.theguardian.com/news/2019/feb/15/antisemitism-rising-sharply-across-europe-latest-figures-show.
[40] "Centrum Informatie en Documentatie Israël (CIDI)." *CIDI Monitor: Antisemitic Incidents 2019 – English Summary.* 2020, https://www.cidi.nl/wp-content/uploads/2020/02/English-Summary-CIDI-Monitor-Antisemitic-Incidents-2019.pdf.
[41] FRA, 2018, p.12.
[42] Ibid.
[43] FRA, 2019, p.21.

12 months prior to the survey.[44] And this resurgence of anti-Jewish activity contributes to many of Europe's Jews hiding their Jewish identity in public. In fact, the 2018 report notes that 49 per cent of Jews at least sometimes wear, carry or display items that could identify them as Jewish. Of those respondents, over two thirds (71 per cent) at least occasionally avoid doing so.[45] Broken down, on a national level, this translates into 82 per cent in France, 80 per cent in Denmark, 78 per cent in Sweden, and 75 per cent in Germany, occasionally avoid looking conspicuously Jewish.[46] Indeed, a number of Jews, one in three, often avoid attending Jewish events or places because they do not feel safe.[47] When asking young Jews for their experiences on this matter, among those surveyed, 73 per cent of the young Jewish Europeans who wear, carry or display things that might help people recognize that they are Jewish, do not do so, at least on occasion, because they are concerned for their safety.[48] Indeed, of those who never wear, carry or display such items, 45 per cent do not do so due to similar concerns.[49]

A few years ago, when in Paris, I visited the Jewish quarter, located in Le Marais, an elegant part of the French capital, a small gem for the city's Jewish and gay communities. I remember walking into a bakery, wearing a big Star of David necklace, and the lady behind the counter, with some vehemence, insisted that I remove or hide it. She said words to the effect of, "it's not safe to show that you're Jewish in Paris." While I was aware of antisemitism in the country, I found it to be chutzpah on steroids that I was being told to conceal my identity on the streets of a city that was under Nazi occupation less than eighty years ago. Yet many Jews, across Western Europe, identify with this disenchantment, and have heeded the call from the 19th century poet, Yehuda Leib Gordon, "Be a man in the streets and a Jew at home." A good Jew, it seems, is a hiding Jew.

To hide one's identity is borne out of a sense that the risks are not worth it. Respondents to the FRA surveys speak to this sentiment. A

---

[44] ibid, p.26.
[45] FRA, 2018, p.31.
[46] FRA, 2018, p.37.
[47] ibid, p.12.
[48] FRA, 2019, p.31.
[49] ibid.

woman aged 20-24, living in Denmark stated, "The way things are now, I experience, for example, that 'Jew' is a widespread cuss word in Copenhagen. As a Jew who has grown up in Denmark, I have always avoided showing/telling people I am a Jew."[50] A 30–34-year-old man, living in Britain, said, "I walk down a main street every Shabbos, {and] I don't think a week goes by that I don't get a hoot or middle fingers. It's very intimidating."[51] A woman aged 55-59, living in the Netherlands, pointed out, "When going to a Jewish event, no matter how small, you always need to register and only then do you get to know the location. That you don't feel safe at all any more to go somewhere where many Jews come together."[52] In France, a woman aged 40-44 said, "Due to antisemitism at our children's school, and in the [REGION] where we live, we have had to move to a different town where the costs are much higher. Financially, life is more difficult, and we can't leave France because of our jobs."[53] In Sweden, a woman aged 40-44, asserted, "None of my friends where I live or who I work with know that I'm a Jew. Our children don't know about my Jewish background, because I am terrified that they would get comments on that in school. I no longer visit the synagogue, because it's not worth it if we'd be targeted for something. The best thing was when I got married, because now my last name is "Svensson.""[54] Indeed, when considering what has occurred in recent years, these concerns are perfectly understandable.

Such realities, however, do not just affect individual Jews, often with very bruising consequences: they also serve to undermine a Jewish way of life. I came to appreciate this in the December of 2021. A group of Jews, largely teenagers, were out on Oxford Street, London, celebrating Channukah on a big open-roof bus. This festival isn't just an opportunity to scoff doughnuts and latkes, and suffer from gastric discomfort as a result, it is also the time when Jews celebrate their triumph over anti-Jewish persecution, and more importantly, celebrate the restoration of Jewish control in Israel from colonial Greek forces. What began as an

---

[50] FRA, 2018, p.48.
[51] ibid.
[52] ibid, p.37.
[53] ibid, p.39.
[54] ibid, p.37.

occasion of frivolity in the bustle of London's busiest street, ended in a mob of young Asian men (few, if any, mainstream news source mentioned their ethnicity) being abusive and intimidating, resulting in this group being forced back onto their bus. By no means was this mob dissimilar from the thugs we faced on May the 11th. They were hurling insults, chanting about Palestine, doing Nazi salutes, spitting on the bus windows, and slapping the bus, some with their shoes. Like all such incidents, it was a dismaying assault upon not only their religious freedoms, but their human rights and human dignity.

In its reporting of this criminal activity, the BBC, the national broadcaster of the UK, disgraced itself (once again) by making repeated references to the allegation that there was an anti-Muslim slur uttered by one of the Jewish victims. Even when this was challenged, and when confronted with overwhelming evidence which found this to be an incontrovertible falsehood, the BBC refused to change their minds. Almost a year later, on the 7th November, 2022, Ofcom, the country's agency for media standards, found Britain's largest media source had failed "to observe its Editorial Guidelines on due impartiality and due accuracy."[55] This reflects a much deeper issue, namely, a fear of confronting the harsh truths to do with Islamist antisemitism. We shall return to this in Chapter 3.

However, to no small extent, events of this kind, which have become far too common, have left many Jews feeling that they want to leave this region. Both FRA surveys reveal that a large proportion of Jews have considered leaving for Israel and elsewhere. The 2018 report notes that in the five years before the survey, more than a third of Jews thought about leaving because they did not feel safe as a Jew in the country where they live. For young Jews, that number is around 4 out of 10. Clearly, the stark realities of antisemitism have left an indelible mark on Jewish life, leaving many to believe there is no future for Jews in countries which have been home for generations.

---

[55] *Ofcom*. "Ofcom Concludes Investigation into the BBC's Coverage of Antisemitic Attack." Published December 15, 2022. Accessed March 31, 2025. https://www.ofcom.org.uk/tv-radio-and-on-demand/broadcast-standards/ofcom-concludes-investigation-into-the-bbcs-coverage-of-antisemitic-attack/

I am writing this a few nights after having dinner in Jerusalem with several young French Jews. They have all left their country of birth for Israel. When I asked each one why, all of them said, as well as leaving to build a Jewish life in Israel, they just don't feel safe as Jews in France. Simply put, they see no future in their country of birth. For a number of Jews in France, particularly those of an Algerian background, they are thinking along the lines of their ancestors back in the Algerian war- "le cercueil ou la valise"—"the coffin or the suitcase." This is a sentiment one can find not only in France, but across the region.

The perpetrators

So why, then, are Jews feeling like this? Back in the day, when my parents were growing up, and I was a mere twinkle in my father's eye, antisemites, the dangerous ones at least, tended to be neo-Nazis, most of whom with disastrous haircuts. These days, such charged hate-merchants are few and far between, and for those that still operate, they largely operate in the arena of cyberspace. For many, the recent rise in right-wing populism, and in some places, far-right activities, is a source of consternation. But hardcore fascism with rising political clout? This does not exist, at least not in any meaningful sense. For the most part, perpetrators of antisemitic incidents are not those on the edges of the right. This is not the reason why large numbers of Jews in the region are expressing grave concerns about their futures. Rather, as recent reports have shown, including the FRA surveys, the perpetrators of these incidents within Western Europe disproportionately involve those of a Muslim background. And in some places, Muslims are the most notable perpetrators of antisemitic violence, abuse and harassment.

Before we look at the data and reports on this issue, in brief, let's compare the situation of antisemitism in Hungary and Poland from that of Western Europe. A report initiated by the Action and Protection League, a European organization for combatting antisemitism, found that although there are widespread antisemitic beliefs in Hungary and Poland (and Greece), there are fewer antisemitic incidents compared to Western-

Europe.[56] These societies in Eastern Europe suffer with a Jew-hate problem, and it is a historic one. Conversely, if we look at the same data when it comes to Western Europe, the overwhelming majority of people in the region repudiate these conspiratorial and baseless theories. And yet, antisemitic violence in the latter is higher. There are, it would seem, two plausible explanations for this. One, most Europe's Jews live within Western Europe, and so, just on a probability front, there is a greater likelihood of a Jew being the victim of antisemitism in this region than in Central or Eastern Europe. Secondly, and perhaps more importantly, there is the role of antisemitism amongst Muslims.

Returning to those FRA surveys, both gave respondents several options to describe the perpetrator(s) of the most serious incident of antisemitic harassment in the five years prior to the survey, and one of those was the description: "someone with an extreme Muslim view." This approach to understanding who Jews identify as perpetrators is flawed twofold. Firstly, not every instance of antisemitism is a serious form of harassment. Needless to say, there are multiple expressions of antisemitism– and "serious harassment" is just one, albeit frequently more common, example. Besides, any form of racist harassment is surely serious by its very nature. Secondly, the perpetrators may be Muslim and not necessarily express views which would be regarded as "extreme Muslim views." After all, what even is an "extreme Muslim view?" This point is particularly important, and we shall return to it in a moment.

Despite these criticisms, this specific part of the report, at the very least, gives us a critical insight into where much of the antisemitism is coming from. Thus in 2018, of the respondents in the 12 countries who say they have been the victim of a serious antisemitic harassment in the five years before the survey, 30 per cent stated that their perpetrator was "someone with extreme Muslim views," and the report notes that many of these respondents selected this in combination with another category.[57] Likewise, in the 2019 survey of young Jews, asking a similar question,

---

[56] Kovács, András, Fischer, Gyorgy "Antisemitic Prejudices in Europe: Survey in 16 European Countries." Action and Protection League. 2021: https://archive.jpr.org.uk/object-2408
[57] FRA, 2018, p.53.

reported that in the past year, a third of victims of antisemitic harassment, and over half of the cases of violence, were said to be committed by 'someone with a Muslim extremist view.'[58] Across the region, Jews are increasingly identifying their assailant as not some incensed skinhead, but members of a different cultural and ethnic minority.

At this stage, however, two further things need to be said about this data. The first, and we return to the point made some moments ago, the report limits its utility in restricting the option to 'extreme Muslim view.' Primarily with the 2018 report, the largest category victims of 'serious harassment' selected was, on average, 'someone I cannot describe' (31 per cent of victims said this).[59] As such, it is plausible that many of the perpetrators in this category were Muslim, but not necessarily - as far as those surveyed were concerned- with extreme Muslim views. What, after all, constitutes an 'extreme' Muslim view? How, indeed, is this even measured? Notwithstanding these important questions, one can assume that because respondents were unable to determine if their attacker had an extreme Muslim view, they went with the unsure option. This would mean those of a Muslim background are more involved in antisemitic incidents than these surveys reveal. Lastly, given that this report included countries with relatively small Muslim communities, this data is an average. To have a comprehensive understanding of Muslim antisemitism within Western Europe, we will need to look at the data where the bulk of Europe's Muslims live. And when we do, we can see that rates of this Jew-hate within Western Europe is much higher than the European average. For instance, in France 33 per cent of respondents, in Sweden 40 per cent of the respondents, in Germany 41 per cent of the respondents, and in the Netherlands 35 per cent of respondents described their assailant as "someone with Muslim extremist views."[60] Clearly, although this data has its limitations, it serves to illustrate why Jews in Western Europe are largely not so concerned by antisemitism from its old school sources. Western Europe is witnessing something new.

---

[58] FRA, 2019, p.8.
[59] FRA, 2018, p.10.
[60] FRA, 2018, p.54.

The FRA surveys are not alone in making these revelations. And by no means are these studies novel. In 2003, an important finding was made by the Center for Research on Antisemitism (CRA) in Berlin. On behalf of the European Monitoring Center for Racism and Xenophobia (EUMC), the predecessor to the FRA, the CRA gathered the data on antisemitism collected by agencies from all European countries, and they found that, "the anti-Semitic incidents in the monitoring period were committed above all either by right-wing extremists or radical Islamists or young Muslims mostly of Arab descent, who are often themselves potential victims of exclusion and racism."[61] Moreover, it added that "physical attacks on Jews and the desecration and destruction of synagogues were acts mainly committed by young Muslim perpetrators..." most of which were committed during or after pro-Palestinian demonstrations. When such revelations were made discovery was made, this report was shelved. As R. Amy Elman points out in her ground-breaking study, *The European Union, Antisemitism, and the Politics of Denial*, it "unsettled the EUMC," adding that in a letter to the authors of this report, the powers that be at the EUMC reaffirmed that they "must be seen as bringing groups together, not as acting divisively."[62] In that spirit, concerns were hushed up. It is better, in this view, to keep quiet than to rock the boat, and do what is necessary to push back against a troubling trend.

However, although this denial over the issue of Muslim antisemitism continues (as we shall see), the data which analyses the nature of antisemitic incidents within the region reveals why it can no longer be ignored, downplayed, distorted, or denied. Since the early 2000s, there have been notable studies on this issue which need to be, at the very least, mentioned. In the Netherlands, CIDI found that between 2002-2006, it was estimated that 33 to 40 per cent of antisemitic incidents reported to them were committed by North Africans, most of whom were Moroccan. Yet

---

[61] Cited in Bergmann, Werner, and Juliane Wetzel. "Manifestations of Anti-Semitism in the European Union: First Semester 2002 Synthesis Report." *Vienna: European Monitoring Center on Racism and Xenophobia*, 2003. https://www.erinnern.at/themen/e_bibliothek/antisemitismus-1/431_anti-semitism_in_the_european_union.pdf. p.7.
[62] Elman, R. Amy. *The European Union, Antisemitism, and the Politics of Denial*. Lincoln: University of Nebraska Press, 2015. p.66.

Moroccans represented just 2 per cent of the population.[63] Similarly, in their annual report in 2012, the British-based CST found that of the 169 antisemitic incidents where the perpetrator could be identified, 31 per cent were South or East Asians, and 11 per cent were Arab or North African. According to Gerstenfeld, the majority, perhaps the entirety of that 42 per cent, were Muslim. Yet, again, in that year, Muslims only made up 5 per cent of the British population. In France, antisemitic incidents have sharply increased in the years between 1994 and 2012. Gunther Jikeli elucidates that although Jews make up less than 1 per cent of the total population, they have been a target of about a third or more of all registered hate incidents. In fact, since 2000, "the number of identified Arab Muslim perpetrators has exceeded the number of identified perpetrators of extreme right." He also points out that, as well as there being a sharp rise of antisemitic violence since the beginning of this century, the majority of perpetrators of violent antisemitic acts are now Arab-Muslims.[64] In France, given the way the French do things, particularly with regard to keeping religion well out of the public sphere, it is difficult to know what percentage of the population is Muslim. However, conservative estimates predict that around 10 per cent of the population in France is Muslim, meaning, like the aforementioned places, we can say that those of a Muslim are increasingly, significantly, and most of all, disproportionately, the perpetrators of Jew-hate. We are seeing a similar picture in Germany, Denmark and Sweden.

However, like with other studies, there are major issues with the data, which leads to what can be described as 'antisemitism-distortion,' meaning a contrived effort to misrepresent the realities Jews are facing. An egregious case of this is within Germany. In a piece for The New York Times Magazine, *The New German Anti-Semitism*, James Angelos, a Berlin based journalist, discusses the multifaceted nature of antisemitism within Germany. He rightly points out that "police statistics attribute 89 percent of all anti-Semitic crimes to right-wing extremists." However, as

---

[63] Cited in Gerstenfeld, Manfred. "Muslim Antisemitism in Europe." *Journal for the Study of Antisemitism 5, no. 1* (2013): 195-229. p.200.
[64] Jikeli, Günther. "Explaining the Discrepancy of Antisemitic Acts and Attitudes in 21st Century France." *Contemporary Jewry* 37, no. 2 (2017): 257–73. http://www.jstor.org/stable/26346553

he notes, the police often do this even when they have no proof that the motivation was far-right. This is a serious failing on the part of those responsible for combatting antisemitism.[65] Speaking of the data recorded by the German Federal Office for the Protection of the Constitution, Germany's domestic intelligence agency, Gunther Jikeli noted that the organization registers only three groups of perpetrators of antisemitism: right-wing, left-wing, and foreign perpetrators.[66] This, for reasons already discussed, is extremely problematic, since it presents those who make decisions with a skewed understanding of the depths of this problem. This, of course, undermines the efficacy of any policies, if any exist to begin with, to arrest this social bug. And by no means is Germany alone. This is conspicuous throughout the region.

In investigating Jewish attitudes to contemporary antisemitism, I undertook a study of my own, asking Jews my age, twenty-one back then, to share with me their experiences of antisemitism. Take, for instance, Jack, a 30- year-old Jewish man from London. He said, "Islamism is everywhere and accounts for a huge portion of antisemitism I have faced." He added that, "I have heard casual conversations [INVOLVING MUSLIMS] calling for the death of Jews, blaming Jews for absurd issues (controlling Hollywood, new world order etc), declarations of a coming judgement day in which all Jews will be killed. I have EVEN seen a video shared online of a guide to slicing the throat of a Jew." He concluded by saying, "Islamism is the principal source of fear I face as a Jew."

Another Brit, Em, a nineteen-year-old girl from up north, also described her experiences of antisemitism in her school. She explained that "Due to there not being a Jewish presence in the city of derby (the last shul closed in 1987) I couldn't attend a Jewish school." As a result, she said, "I went to a local secondary school which was 90% Pakistani Muslim. The lack of diversity served as a breeding ground for extremist Islamist anti-semitism. A boy threatened to set me on fire as "all Jewish women should be burnt to death or beheaded," I was repeatedly told that "if [I] was a man

---

[65] Angelos, James. "The New German Anti-Semitism." *New York Times Magazine,* May 21, 2019. https://www.nytimes.com/2019/05/21/magazine/anti-semitism-germany.html

[66] Jikeli, Günther. "European Muslim Antisemitism: Why Young Urban Males Say They Don't Like Jews." *Bloomington: Indiana University Press*, 2015.

I'd have my head kicked in" etc. during the summer of 2019 during the Hamas bombings, girls from my year who I had known for years were running round the sixth form with Palestinian flags sewn to their hijabs screaming "kill their wives, rape their daughters, make them pay for Palestine." I wouldn't say school was a particularly positive experience."

Respondents from within the continent also shared similar sentiments. For instance, Arthur, a twenty-four-year-old Jew living in Berlin. He, like others in the survey, agrees that while antisemitism does cross borders, there is a particular problem of violent Islamist antisemitism. He argued, "In big cities (especially Berlin), male jews cannot wear a kippah without being offended or even attacked. These attacks are recently caused by young groups of Arabic men out of antisemitic circles."

The warning signs

To state the obvious, the background of the perpetrators of these crimes matter. While it is comforting that governments speak of tackling antisemitism across society, there needs to be explicit attention given to this specific problem. To ignore the elephant in the room, as governments in the region are currently doing, has rendered the nice words from governments as redundant. Currently, in our region, we have at least two areas where this problem is particularly acute and visible, namely, Malmö, Sweden's third largest city, and the banlieues, those rundown suburbs of Paris. It is important to explore the situation in these places, for though different, in both, multiculturalism has put their Jews in great danger, and consequently, their Jewish communities are dwindling. These areas serve as warnings to Western European leaders: if this situation persists, more will head down this path of becoming Judenfrei.

To begin with, Malmö, this city is home to over 350,000 people, and is characterized by its cultural and ethnic diversity. One-third of the population is foreign-born, and the largest groups of such come from Iraq and Syria. The Jews of this city, who number around 500 (in Sweden, there are 15,000-20,000 Jews), arrived in 1871. It is a well-established, albeit tiny and fragile, Jewish community.

In recent years, this city has earned a reputation of being a hotspot of Islamist antisemitism. For the avoidance of doubt, antisemitism in

Sweden, is not new. The country has never been Scandinavia's Goldene Medina. To this day, antisemitic attitudes remain widespread in this country, and to some extent, like other countries, Islamist Jew hate is a product of this. However, it's in Malmö, where, because of Islamism, things have been particularly sour. In fact, in 2010 the Simon Wiesenthal Center, one of the leading institutes for the study of global antisemitism, issued a travel warning for Jews travelling to Malmö, stating that Jews who visit should take "extreme caution when visiting southern Sweden."[67] A 2021 report undertaken by Malmö's municipality stated that schools are unsafe for Jewish students, who are subjected to verbal and physical attacks. In a letter written by one of the city's synagogues, the leaders of the community described the city as "a no-go zone for Jews around the world."[68]

When looking at some incidents of antisemitism against this tiny community, one can understand why many of its residents identify with Sholem Aleichem's agonizing assertion, 'shver tzu zayn a yid,' it is hard to be a Jew. In a superb article, *Can Malmö Solve Its Antisemitism Problem?*, Liam Hore interviewed Rabbi Shneur Kesselman, one of the city's few visible Jews. He says that since moving to the community in 2004 from Detroit, "I've been cursed at in various shapes and forms, many times in Arabic, in Swedish, and 99 percent of the time by people with a Middle Eastern or North African background." Describing one example, the Rabbi said, "The most recent violent incident was in the summer when I had a glass bottle thrown at me in the middle of the city... it came from a group of four or five immigrants while I was walking home from the synagogue just before Shabbat and speaking on my phone to my mom."[69]

---

[67] Simon Wiesenthal Center. "Simon Wiesenthal Center to Issue Travel Advisory for Sweden - Officials Confer With Swedish Justice Minister Beatrice Ask." Last modified December 14, 2010. https://www.wiesenthal.com/about/news/simon-wiesenthal-center-to-3.html

[68] Spencer, Robert. "Sweden: Jewish Congregation in Muslim-Dominated Malmö Says City Is Already a 'No-Go Zone' for Jews." *Jihad Watch,* June 6, 2019. https://jihadwatch.org/2019/06/sweden-jewish-congregation-in-muslim-dominated-malmo-says-city-is-already-a-no-go-zone-for-jews

[69] Liam Hoare. "Can Malmö Solve Its Antisemitism Problem?" *Moment Magazine,* November 22, 2022. https://momentmag.com/can-malmo-solve-its-antisemitism-problem/

Speaking of this Rabbi, the Swedish politician, Ilan Sadé, pointed out, "The police file on the attacks against the Chabad rabbi of Malmö is as thick as a Dostoevsky book…There are about 160 to 180 cases registered: anything from spitting on him to cursing and harassing him."[70] And that's just for one Jew!

Disgracefully, the Rabbi has not been alone. There are many more examples which speak to the troubles in this city. In 2008, a Jewish pro-peace demonstration was interrupted by a large group of Muslim and left-wing activists, who attacked Jewish demonstrators with bottles and fireworks.[71] In 2009, Molotov cocktails were thrown at the local Jewish funeral home.[72] In the same year, when the Israeli tennis delegation came to Malmo, there were 200-300 violent demonstrators with stones, fireworks and paint bombs.[73] This was an anti-Jewish riot. No surprise, therefore, that in 2009, over half of all hate crimes in the city were against Jews.[74] In 2012, an explosion was detonated outside the Jewish community center.[75] In 2015, pro-Palestine demonstrators were chanting, "slaughter the Jews, stab soldiers...," "heroes to carry out attack after attack," as well as "start the third intifada."[76] Two years later, demonstrators in the city chanted, "We have announced the intifada from

---

[70] Stavrou, David. "World Leaders Came and Went, but Nordic City's Fight Against Antisemitism Continues." *Haaretz,* October 21, 2021. https://www.haaretz.com/world-news/europe/2021-10-21/ty-article/.premium/world-leaders-came-and-went-but-nordic-citys-fight-against-antisemitism-continues/0000017f-e648-dc7e-adff-f6ed213b0000

[71] Liam Hoare, Nov 2022.

[72] TOI staff, "Second Jewish Building in Sweden Attacked in Attempted Firebombing." *The Times of Israel,* December 11, 2017. https://www.timesofisrael.com/second-jewish-building-in-sweden-attacked-in-attempted-firebombing/

[73] Liam Hoare, November 2022.

[74] Meo, Nick. "Jews Leave Swedish City after Sharp Rise in Anti-Semitic Hate Crimes." *The Telegraph,* March 7, 2010. https://www.telegraph.co.uk/news/worldnews/europe/sweden/7278532/Jews-leave-Swedish-city-after-sharp-rise-in-anti-Semitic-hate-crimes.html

[75] TOI Staff, "Explosion Rocks Jewish Community Center in Malmö, Sweden." *The Times of Israel,* September 8, 2012. https://www.timesofisrael.com/explosion-rocks-jewish-community-center-in-malmo-sweden/

[76] JTA "Pro-Palestinian Protesters in Sweden Chant 'Slaughter the Jews.'" *The Times of Israel,* October, 2015, https://www.timesofisrael.com/pro-palestinian-protesters-in-sweden-chant-slaughter-the-jews/

Malmö. We want our freedom back, and we will shoot the Jews."[77] In the same year, in the city of Gothenburg, also in the South of Sweden, a synagogue, which at the time had a number Jewish children inside, was firebombed by a gang of a dozen men, following an anti-Israel demonstration. Thankfully, no one was hurt.[78]

There is, unsurprisingly, the regular, and even daily experiences of antisemitic harassment, abuse and violence. Speaking of the situation in the city, Judith Popinski, a Holocaust survivor, stated that "Malmö reminds me of the anti-Semitism I felt as a child in Poland before the war."[79] Many agree with her. Indeed, the city's Jewish population over the past twenty years has halved. The synagogue which wrote the letter had a membership of 842 members in 1999, and as of 2019, it had just 387 members. In the letter written by the community's synagogue, they gave a stark warning that "the Jewish congregation will soon disappear if nothing is done drastically."[80] The question which many Jews in the city (and beyond) are now grappling with is if in twenty years the Jewish population of this city has halved, what will the city look like in the next twenty years? If things do not change, that question begs an answer which few thought possible when envisioning a Europe of tolerance, openness, and diversity.

For the Jews of France, the realities of Malmö are all too familiar. In their 2022 analysis, Fondation pour l'innovation politique, known as Fondapol, along with the AJC, found that 85 per cent of French Jews consider antisemitism to be widespread, with 73 per cent of which arguing that it is getting worse.[81] Although chilling, tis hardly staggering. There is,

---

[77] TOI Staff, "Second Jewish Building in Sweden Attacked in Attempted Firebombing." *The Times of Israel,* December 11, 2017. https://www.timesofisrael.com/second-jewish-building-in-sweden-attacked-in-attempted-firebombing/
[78] "Firebombs Hurled at Synagogue in Sweden After Protest March Over Jerusalem." *The Times of Israel,* December 10, 2017. https://www.timesofisrael.com/firebombs-hurled-at-synagogue-in-sweden-after-protest-march-over-jerusalem/
[79] Cited in Elman, R. Amy. "The European Union, Antisemitism, and the Politics of Denial." Lincoln: University of Nebraska Press, 2015. p.85.
[80] Cited in Robert Spencer, 2019.
[81] Legrand, François, Simone Rodan-Benzaquen, Anne-Sophie Sebban-Bécache, and Dominique Reynié. "An Analysis of Antisemitism in France: 2022 Edition." Paris: *Fondation pour l'innovation politique and American Jewish Committee,* 2022. https://ajcfrance.com/wp-content/uploads/2022/01/fondapol-study-antisemitism-in-

alas, a distinct manifestation of anti-Jewish exclusion within the secular republic. Of course, ça va sans dire, as a Francophone on steroids, and someone who firmly believes in its status as a secular liberal democracy, this isn't to pour scorn on a system which is the vanguard of individual liberty. Indeed, the France of today has moved a long way from the widely read conspiracies of the ratbag Drumont and his sordid Antisemitic League of France, or the anti-Jewish policies enacted by the Vichy Government. And it must never be forgotten the number of those within France, either in the resistance or in the church, who protected Jews from the Nazi evil, and made the ultimate sacrifice in doing so. The fact 75 per cent of French Jews survived the Shoah owes itself, to no small extent, to the bravery of French patriots. But romanticization is never healthy (even if Paris is the city of love). Like other countries, French leaders regularly insist antisemitism is the "enemy of the republic," adding sentiments such as, "it is antithetical to the values of France." Those who do deny or downplay the particularity of French antisemitism would do well to remember the terms upon which Jews were granted de joure citizenship. When discussing Jewish emancipation in 1789, the Count of Clermont-Tonnerre declared in the French National Assembly, "Jews should be denied everything as a nation, but granted everything as individuals," insisting that "[t]he existence of a nation within a nation is unacceptable to our country."[82]

While France was certainly ahead of its counterparts in terms of granting its Jews citizenship as individuals, within this liberal framework, is the necessary othering of Jew; the sense that Jewishness, as a collective hegemon, undermines a nation. Traces of this perception, which was later seen in Napoleon's Grand Sanhedrin of 1805, in which Jewish leaders were posed with questions about the degree to which their Jewish counterparts were loyal to the Republic over Judaism, remain to this day. Perhaps we can describe this as banal antisemitism, that is, casual, unwitting, thoughtless, but deeply entrenched, expressions of Jew-

---

france-edition-2022-legrand-rodan-benzaquen-sebban-becache-reynie-03-2022.pdf. p.5.
[82] Cited in "France." Lapidus Center for the Historical Analysis of Transatlantic Antisemitism. Center for Jewish History. https://www.cjh.org/lapidus/France.html

bashing. For instance, I discovered that when people in France hurt or injure their elbow, they exclaim, "ah, le petit juif" – "ah, my little Jew." Where this comes from, I am not sure, and neither, it would seem, are the people who leap to this kind of unconscious invective. Regardless, such expressions illustrate the permanence and pervasiveness of this societal plague. Like Sweden, none of this is new, nor something which can be attributed to one community.

Nevertheless, in his 2015 book, Une France antijuive? Regards sur la Nouvelle Configuration Judeophobe (An Anti-Jewish France? (Glimpses of the New Judeophobic Configuration), Pierre-André Taguieff, the leading expert in French antisemitism, points out that what exists today is not a continuation of the old hatred, as endorsed and propagated by the likes of Drummont and the Catholic Church. Rather, he describes this as "a reinvention, an entirely new birth, revealing in sociohistorical terms more discontinuities than continuities, more differences than resemblances."[83] While no doubt this banal antisemitism has percolated down to various communities who have made France their home, and has played an important role in cultivating a general perception of Jewishness, this Islamist strain is an aberration from the old ways.

Like in the rest of Western Europe, it isn't far-right extremism that constitutes the bulk of concerns shared by French-Jews. Of those surveyed by Fondapol, 62 per cent and 45 per cent argue that the two driving factors of antisemitism are the rejection of Israel, and Islamist ideas, respectively.[84] These ideas are, as we shall see, closely and inextricably connected. The concerns surrounding Jew-hatred remain widespread, across the country, from Rouen to Marseilles. When I began writing this section, I wasn't sure which place to write about. I was, after all, spoiled for choice. However, after some thought, I felt compelled to write about the banlieues, given my earlier references to them, and the fact that the situation there is distinctly striking and significant.

---

[83] Author's translation from French, Taguieff, Pierre-André. *Une France antijuive ? Regards sur la nouvelle configuration judéophobe: Antisionisme, propalestinisme, islamisme*. Paris: CNRS Éditions, 2015. p.1.
[84] Fondapol, 2022, p.5.

The banlieues, which literally translates as suburbs, have taken on a particular connotation in recent years. The term, which can also be understood as "banlieues défavorisées" (disadvantaged suburbs), has come to mean immigrant-heavy slums, in which there is not only a clear lack of integration, but also an abundance of poverty, crime and overpopulated cités, or large housing projects. While there are also affluent banlieues, I am referring to those with clear economic, social, and class-based issues. Since 2000, and particularly after 2014, they have, like Malmo, earned a reputation of being a 'no go zone' for Jews. And this isn't just the case for Jews. For many, as the title of Emmanuel Brenner's 2002 book on the breakdown of social order within France puts it, these areas are the "Lost territories of the Republic." Adding to this, in a compelling essay for The New Yorker, George Packer makes the point that given the highway which encircles Paris is known as the Périphérique, people describe entering or leaving the banlieues as "crossing the Périphérique," as if it were another country entirely. He points to the fact that within these banlieues, people joke that when going to Paris, one requires a visa and vaccination card.[85]

This impression that between the banlieues and Paris (and the rest of France), there are "two parallel worlds," as described by Mehdi Meklat, is something relatively recent.[86] In the 1950s, because of the post-war housing crisis within France, a large-scale housing program was initiated. These so-called cités, which for many years were home to many middle-class, Français de souche, or native French, were built quickly, with not the best quality materials, to house as many as possible. However, in the early 1970s, things began to change. It was at this stage when the French government encouraged homeownership, and as such, many of these middle-class families moved out. In their stead, the government obliged social housing landlords to home immigrants in these cités. These immigrants had arrived from former French colonies and began to work as low-skilled manual workers. Consequently, as Juliet Carpenter, one of the leading experts of the French banlieues opined, "from the auspicious

---

[85] Packer, George. "The Other France, The New Yorker," August 24, 2015. https://www.newyorker.com/magazine/2015/08/31/the-other-france.
[86] cited in ibid.

beginnings of the cités as places of modernity and optimism, the banlieue housing estates were increasingly characterized by deprivation, a high ethnic minority population, and economic and social exclusion."[87]

Thousands of Jews, arriving to France from the homes they were forced out of in North Africa, also settled in these unattractive, uncared for projects. And, for the most part, Jews and their Muslims lived and worked together in peace. One place in particular, Sarcelles, north-east of Paris, earned the nickname 'La Petite Jérusalem,' or 'The Little Jerusalem.' For years, this city was a kaleidoscope of Jewish life; a hub for those who sought to maintain traditions in their new country.

However, like many of these banlieues, Sarcelles is no longer the haven it once was. In the summer of 2014, life for Jews in this Little Jerusalem was to drastically change. Following Israel's Operation in Gaza, "Protective Edge," the streets of Sarcelles became home to what was an Islamist pogrom against their Jewish neighbors. After pro-Palestinian rioters failed to set fire to the Synagogue, while chanting "death to the Jews," they went on a rampage, looting Jewish stores, and setting fire to cars and Jewish owned businesses, including a pizzeria and a pharmacy. To repel the attackers, the police used tear gas, water cannons and rubber bullets. "Is this really France in the twenty-first century?" This question was one many French Jews posed after this riot, in scenes eerily reminiscent of the wedding pogrom in Fiddler on the Roof.[88] One Jewish Sarcelles resident, who has spent his whole life in the area, remarked, "We never would have believed that this could happen in Sarcelles."[89] As a student of Jewish history, I have lost count of the number of times I have read documents of Jews saying, "it can't happen here." In this small town, it did, and many left as a result.

---

[87] Carpenter, Juliet. "The French Banlieue: Renovating the Suburbs." In The Routledge Companion to the Suburbs, edited by Bernadette Hanlon and Thomas J. Vicino. London: Routledge, 2018. p.3.

[88] Haaretz and The Associated Press. "Pro-Palestinian Protesters Raid Jewish Neighborhood Outside Paris." *Haaretz,* July 21, 2014. https://www.haaretz.com/jewish/2014-07-21/ty-article/.premium/rioters-raid-jewish-neighborhood-near-paris/0000017f-dc66-d3a5-af7f-feee348a0000

[89] Cited in Leïla Amar, "Suburbs and Antisemitism: The Case of Sarcelles - Part 2," Get The Trolls Out!, originally published in French on *Guiti News,* https://getthetrollsout.org/cmfe-articles/suburbs-and-antisemitism-the-case-of-sarcelles-part-2

Since 2000, both during and after the Second Intifada, or uprising, the banlieues have become the place in which a great many, even the bulk of antisemitic incidents in France, take place. Some of the most extreme incidents include murders, countless assaults, or even the case of a Muslim gang breaking into the home of a 19-year old Jewish woman (living with her boyfriend), stating, "You must have cash here because you are Jews," before brutally raping her. These are not daily experiences, but they do reflect a worsening problem in the banlieues which have been brewing in recent years. That said, in the banlieues, there is also the everyday difficulty of being a Jew.

In an essay for Vanity Fair, Marie Brenner, spoke to an 18-year-old Jewish girl living in Paris. This girl, who was about to be a student in England, asked Marie "Is it true that if I lived in America, I could wear a tiny Star of David necklace or a sweatshirt from Technion university?" Upon hearing this, Marie responded with a question of her own, "What would happen if you wore it in this neighborhood? Do you think you would be physically attacked?" To which the student said, "I would be made to feel angoisse."[90] This feeling of angoisse, or disquiet, is a common experience for Jews in Paris and its suburbs. For many who have displayed their Jewish identities in public, they have been on the receiving end of abuse, harassment, and sometimes worse. In an article for the New York Times, Adam Nossiter refers to a Jewish woman who recently left a banlieue, as she would experience harassment from her neighbors who would "spit when [she] walked in the street," when they saw her Star of David necklace.[91] Experiences like this, since 2000, have become increasingly common. It is why Jews in these banlieues (and elsewhere) feel compelled to keep their identity as hidden as possible.

These suburbs have not only been the place in which most antisemitic incidents happen, they have also provided a fertile ground for extremism. As we shall see in the next chapter, a vehement and conspiratorial hatred

---

[90] Brenner, Marie, "The Troubling Question in the French Jewish Community: Is It Time to Leave?" *Vanity Fair,* July 8, 2015. https://www.vanityfair.com/news/2015/07/anti-semitism-france-hostage-hyper-cacher-kosher-market

[91] Nossiter, Adam. "They Spit When I Walked in the Street: The 'New Anti-Semitism' in France." *The New York Times,* July 27, 2018. https://www.nytimes.com/2018/07/27/world/europe/france-new-anti-semitism.html

of Jews, alongside a Gallophobia, a hatred of France (and of the West more broadly, defined as anti-westernism), is passed on to younger Muslim generations. As such, it should come as no surprise that these places, and the young people within, are so disconnected from not only France, but the values which France, and the wider western world, embodies. And consequently, those within the banlieues who subscribe to these beliefs have found alliances with various anti-democratic movements. All of which, however, share the view that the Jew is the eternal enemy. Perhaps this should be described as the allure of Jew-hatred.

In France, a notable case in point is the 2014 jour de colère, or Day of Wrath, in late January of 2014. What began as a protest against Francois Hollande's socialist government, especially after it drew up plans to legalize same sex marriage, wound up becoming a large, public Jew-hating fest. A coalition of far-right groups, with Muslims from the banlieue and far-left activists, were clamorously chanting, amongst other things, "Jew, France is not yours," and "Europe paedo criminal Zionist satan."[92] Not only is this demonstration significant because it exposes the way in which antisemitism and other warped isms intersect, but also because it exposes how seemingly irreconcilable movements can stand together in their shared contempt for Jews. Those on the far-right, some of whom were performing Nazi salutes, were willing to stand by Muslims, some of whom were performing the Quenelle – invented by a black, ultra-left comedian. A peculiar and nauseating concoction, but one which exists based upon Treitschke's popular declaration in 1879, "The Jews are our misfortune!." Just like the antisemitic demonstrations of the past, this one was against what these nutty factions saw as the evil Jewish hegemony, the source of all things bad. As shall be explored in the next chapter, antisemitism is the prevailing thread in all movements with totalitarian ambitions.

In the French context, however, this is not something new. Commenting on French antisemitism under Drumont, Pierre Birnbaum reminds readers, "it should be recalled that Drumont's movement represented a populism that brought together far left and far right alike, in

---

[92] Birnbaum, P, "Day of Wrath," trans from (2015). Jour de colère. *Revue d'histoire moderne et contemporaine* (Paris, France: 1954), 62-2/3(2), 245–259. https://doi.org/10.3917/rhmc.622.0245

which white supremacists took part, along with Guedists and sometimes even socialists, who had no scruples about being involved in a large scale anti-Semitic movement that overwhelmingly drew its inspiration from the far right."[93] Those who reject liberal-democratic values cannot resist the allure of Judenhass, and exhibit a readiness to get into bed with all sorts of characters, even those they loathe.

Nevertheless, what has been discussed has profoundly affected the Jewish communities of these areas. In addition to a range of security measures, a number of Jewish families have left. Adam Nossiter cites the pollster, Jerome Fourquet, who co-authored a book, 'Next Year in Jerusalem, French Jews and anti-Semitism.' Forquet gives us the data on these shrinking Jewish communities. He says, "In Aulnay-sous-Bois, the number of Jewish families dropped to 100 in 2015 from 600 in 2000; in Le Blanc-Mesnil, to 100 families from 300; in Clichy-sous Bois, there are now 80 Jewish families, down from 400; and in La Courneuve, there are 80 families, down from 300."[94] Many Jews have moved to the 17th Arrondissement, a wealthy and bohemian area of Paris. Nossiter also refers to Ouriel Elbilia, a rabbi in this area, who claims Jews have moved because "they feel threatened in their neighborhoods." He adds that his brother, a rabbi in Clichy-sous-Bois, told him, "there are practically no services anymore because the community has emptied out."[95]

After visiting the 17th Arrondissement, I was impressed. It is a progressive and diverse area. And yet there is a worry among French Jews that even this is a temporary refuge. Sadly, I think they are right. Like Sarcelles, indeed, like anywhere, it can happen there, too.

For the Jews of both Malmö and the Banlieues, their right to live in peace and dignity, like every other group, has been compromised, as a direct consequence of the delusions of our liberal-minded leaders. As we shall see in the next chapter, when looking at the nature of contemporary antisemitic attitudes and demographic forecasts, this is set to get worse. It

---

[93] Birnbaum, Pierre. "The French Radical Right: From Anti-Semitic Zionism to Anti-Semitic Anti-Zionism." In *Anti-Semitism and Anti-Zionism in Historical Perspective: Convergence and Divergence,* edited by Jeffrey Herf. London: Routledge, 2013.
[94] Nossiter, 2018.
[95] ibid.

is well within the realms of reason to suggest that more places within the region will look like Malmö and the Banlieues.

Final Remarks

This chapter has argued that, despite the best intentions of Western European leaders, this 'New Europe' — which emerged, to no small degree, as a consequence of Jewish suffering — has allowed for the return, resurgence, and indeed reincarnation, of a plague we thought would never again gain traction in our midst. In what has been discussed, doubtless the absurd and pernicious charges of racism and Islamophobia will be levelled against myself and others who make this critique of a system which has failed Jews, and as we shall see, civilization itself. Making such baseless comments may be politically convenient, and conducive to achieving the applause of self-congratulatory progressives, but in the long run, to ignore what has been discussed, is to endanger us all.

With that, we must now explore the sources of this hatred. As I explain in the next chapter, this is complex, multifaceted, and requires analysis. It is by no means straightforward. But by grappling with these varied sources, we are in a better place to discuss effective and credible solutions, if indeed there are any.

Chapter Two:
Where is this hatred coming from?

There is a crisis of antisemitism within our Muslim communities. Not in small pockets, but in disproportionate numbers, Jew-hate has become endemic, systemic, and rife. And it is getting worse. Of course, as underscored in the introduction, this does not mean all Muslims are antisemitic, nor is it to say that this a problem only for Muslim communities. Such an assertion would be demonstrably and palpably false. Yet, while anti-Jewish poison traverses oceans and continents, transcends community boundaries, and unites the most hostile of enemies, in the Western European context, we can no longer ignore that amongst Muslims in the region, negative and dangerous attitudes towards Jews are markedly, disproportionately, and despairingly high.

Before exploring why this is the case, it should be said that the recent intellectual, social, and political climate, has made it a gargantuan challenge to discuss racism among non-white and/or non-European people. In recent years, particularly within certain scholarly, left-wing, and self-proclaimed "anti-racist" circles, there have been concerted efforts to not only downplay, but deny the very idea that non-white people have the capacity to be, dare I say it, racist. In fact, the claim is vexingly and ludicrously dismissed as racist itself. And when those in such circles do, on the rare occasion, concede that racism is not the sole property of white heterosexual men, the eternally damned West is still to blame. To such ideologues, the West is guilty not merely by its past wrongdoings, for which they argue there is no redemption, but by its very existence.

This kind of pathology, of course, is self-abnegation and self-abasement to the point of naked racism. The late Manfred Gerstenfeld, a pioneer in the field of antisemitism studies, described such refutations as 'humanitarian racism,' meaning, "the conviction that people of color are only victims and thus are not responsible for their own fate."[96] Although this 'bigotry of low expectations,' (the view that we expect nothing better from non-white people), may be cloaked under the guise of progressive politics, it is fundamentally dehumanizing, for at the core of our humanity, is our individual capacity for both agency and responsibility. How else are we to describe those who deny this to people who are non-white?

Above all, this travesty of what is evidently true both exonerates the victimizers and further endangers the victimized. In our case, if Jew-hatred among Muslims is not treated in the same way we would treat similar expressions from the far-right, such lethal views go unopposed. This first came to my attention back in the June of 2019. Four activists, including my mother and I, went to stand outside the Cambridge Union when the Malaysian Prime Minister, Mahathir Mohamad, was invited to speak. Yes, I know, we are big on activism in my house! We sought to warn the queuing audience of what this man stood for, amongst other things, Holocaust-denial and encourage those in the audience to challenge him accordingly. After what had been a successful afternoon, we all agreed that had this been a populist or far-right European speaker, the four of us would have been joined by many, perhaps even hundreds, more. When, for instance, Marine Le Pen, an alleged racist and antisemite, spoke at the union a few years earlier, hundreds were outside in protest.[97] Those activists were proudly chanting, amongst other things, "Nazi go home," and "No Nazis welcome here." For sure, there was condemnation from some of those sources when the Malaysian Prime Minister was invited, but nothing comparable to the outrage when Le Pen came to town. And this leader, in contrast to Marine Le Pen, has publicly endorsed antisemitism–he even did so that day at the union by stating that he has Jewish friends, but "they are not like the other Jews, that's why they are my friends,"

---

[96] Gerstenfeld, Manfred. "Muslim antisemitism in Europe." *Journal for the Study of Antisemitism* 5, no. 1 (2013): 195-230.
[97] Press Association. "Protesters greet Marine Le Pen at Cambridge Union." *The Guardian,* February 19, 2013. https://www.theguardian.com/world/2013/feb/19/protesters-marine-le-pen-cambridge

resulting in laughter from this highbrow, educated Cambridge audience.[98] Of course, Le Pen is not alone in facing abusive crowds, but the striking differences between these two incidents highlights the rank hypocrisy of those who pride themselves on their commitment to both anti-racism and anti-fascism.

Such double standards do not simply manifest in an apathy bordering on indifference, it leads to scholarship and research being dismissed and covered up. In his article, *The Denial of Muslim Antisemitism*, Neil Kressel, a US-base scholar, begins by detailing what happened, back in 2006 to Professor Pieter van der Horst of the Dutch, Utrecht University. A member of the well-regarded Royal Netherlands Academy of Arts and Sciences, and a specialist in early Christianity and Judaism, this scholar sought to give his farewell address on the fascinating subject of "the myth of Jewish cannibalism." The lecture he planned was going to explore this antisemitic trope from its pre-Christian origins to contemporary anti-Jewish blood libels in the Arab world. The university, says Kressel, had no issue with his treatment of ancient Greeks, Christians, or modern Europeans. However, the rector of the university, as a consequence of a report released by a committee of deans and scholars in the field of human rights, told this professor that he had twenty-four hours to remove all references to Muslim antisemitism. Allegedly, three grounds were provided for this decision: fear of violence, fear that this would undermine the institution's efforts at bridge-building between Muslims and non-Muslims, and fear that the lecture fell below the university's scholarly standards. As a result of the mounting pressure, this scholar, one of considerable repute, wound up editing his address.[99]

The reasons given for this episode, some of which shall be explored in the next chapter, are outrageously misguided. This example, along with others, demonstrates how within our own social ecosystem, it has become

---

[98] "Cambridge Union Audience Laughs at Anti-Semitic 'Joke' by Malaysian Prime Minister." The Telegraph, June 17, 2019. https://www.telegraph.co.uk/news/2019/06/17/cambridge-union-audience-laughs-anti-semitic-joke-malaysian/
[99] Kressel, Neil J. "The denial of Muslim antisemitism." *Journal for the Study of Antisemitism 2*, no. 2 (2010): 259+. Gale Academic OneFile https://link.gale.com/apps/doc/A267715829/AONE?u=anon~20c22d5&sid=googleScholar&xid=73663808

extraordinarily hard, and in some cases out of the question, to discuss these issues. As Kressel rightly points out, "Most people in the West are quite ready to denounce Jew-hatred when it comes from Nazis and other long-dead antisemites," however, he adds, "there is deep resistance to straight-speaking, unobstructed analysis of far more dangerous hostility to Jews-- when it comes from Muslims and Arabs."[100]

A refutation which is often levelled in the discussion surrounding antisemitism amongst Muslims is that they cannot be antisemitic since they, like Jews, are semites, too. In the same vein as Gerstenfeld's 'humanitarian racism,' this absurdity leads to the absolution of Muslim bigots since, according to this line of argument, only non-semites can be accountable for expressions of anti-Jewish racism. If a fellow semite says or does something anti-Jewish, indeed antisemitic, it doesn't really count. It is anything but antisemitic.

On several fronts, this argument, which crops up far too often in discussions on this matter, does not hold up. Firstly, the concept of semites describes a group of shared languages, not, contrary to this ahistorical interpretation, a distinct ethnic or racial group. The late eminent historian, Bernard Lewis, in his *Semites and Anti-Semites*, a work to which I shall return, identified a logical fallacy of the rebuttal that Muslims cannot be antisemitic. He remarked, "The logic of this would seem to be that while an edition of Hitler's Mein Kampf published in Berlin or in Buenos Aires in German or Spanish is anti-Semitic, an Arabic version of the same text published in Cairo or Beirut cannot be anti-Semitic, because Arabic and Hebrew are cognate languages." And he correctly reasoned, "It is not a compelling argument."[101] This kind of non-sequitur leads to the second point, the term 'anti-semitism,' popularized by the German racist, Wilhelm Marr, was intended to mean Jews, and only Jews. It took the fictious idea that Jews constituted a discernible racial group, and an omnimalovelent one at that, and attacked them accordingly. This is why, in recent years, the hyphen has been dropped; since the term semite, in its racial usage, has no scientific or credible basis. Indeed, even the Nazi

---

[100] ibid.
[101] Lewis, Bernard. *Semites and Anti-Semites: An Inquiry into Conflict and Prejudice.* New York: W.W. Norton & Company, 1986. p.16.

Foreign Ministry in 1936 made a point of clarifying that the Nuremberg Laws pertained to Jews, and not to any soul who happens to be from the Middle East. Adding to this, Jeffery Herf observed that before the Berlin Olympic Games, Egyptian and Iranian diplomats sought an answer from German officials that their race laws would not affect their people, with the Iranian Ambassador to Berlin declaring, "there was no doubt that the Iranian, as an Aryan," was "racially kindred" with the German people.[102] In response, Herf notes, that the German Foreign Ministry that the Nazis did not make a distinction between "Aryans and non-Aryans" (though of course they did), but between "persons of German and related blood on one hand and Jews as well as racially alien on the other."[103] Islamist forces, back then, were pleased by this distinction, but today have craftily but guilefully made this term a part of their own outreach strategies. But even if Muslims are Semites, and therefore to the last criticism of this fatuous usage of the term, being a part of a semitic group does not preclude members of this group from being antisemitic. Taking this argument to its logical conclusion, if Muslims cannot be racist against Jews, the latter cannot be prejudiced against Muslims. No one can reasonably make such a claim. This refutation is worse than a nonsense. It is an exculpation to the point of giving permission for such ideas to become further entrenched in these communities.

Nevertheless, although there are those who wish to deny the realities of this crisis, the evidence for it is overwhelming. Despite the fact only a minority of Muslims go out and commit acts of antisemitic abuse, harassment and violence, to see those individuals as bearing no relationship to their communities, is delusional in its own right. Rather, Muslim perpetrators of antisemitism, more often than not, are a product of these communities in which anti-Jewish thinking has become commonplace, accepted, and usual. If you don't believe me, the data is pretty revealing.

---

[102] Herf, Jeffrey. *Nazi Propaganda for the Arab World: With a New Preface.* New Haven: Yale University Press, 2011. p.21
[103] ibid.

Some Data

Across many parts of the Islamic world, there is a widespread problem of Jew-hatred. This was revealed in a 2011 Pew survey, which explored Muslim-Western relations. The report noted that while Jews are largely viewed positively in the West, the data is "dismal in the Muslim world." In numbers, "about 9 per cent Muslims in Indonesia, 4 per cent in Turkey, 4 per cent in the Palestinian territories, about 3 per cent in Lebanon (3%), 2 per cent in Jordan, 2 per cent in Egypt, and 2 per cent in Pakistan express favorable opinions of Jews."[104] This is reaffirmed by an unprecedented worldwide 2014 Anti-Defamation League (ADL) survey, which investigated global antisemitic attitudes. Noting that more than 26 per cent of surveyed adults are strongly attached to antisemitic attitudes, this is most acute in the Middle East and North Africa, where 74 per cent of those surveyed agreed with at least six out of eleven antisemitic statements. On a country by country level, the index results are even more chilling; 87 per cent in Algeria, 75 per cent in Egypt, 93 per cent in Iraq, 81 per cent in Jordan, 87 per cent in Libya, 80 per cent in Morocco, 74 per cent in Saudi Arabia, 86 per cent in Tunisia, and 69 per cent in turkey, all top the scale of the index used by the ADL.[105] Globally, while no less ubiquitous, antisemitic attitudes, particularly of an extreme conspiratorial flavor, are most pronounced in the Muslim world.

Measuring attitudes in the European setting, however, is a challenge. In his incisive 2015 article, Antisemitic Attitudes among Muslims in Europe: A Survey Review, Gunther Jikeli rightly points out that "few representative surveys have been conducted to establish levels of antisemitism among Muslim European," adding that this "leads to false generalizations about Muslims, on the one hand, and, more frequently, the denial of an increased level of antisemitic attitudes among Muslims, on

---

[104] Pew Research Center. "Muslim-Western Relations: A Global Perspective." Washington, DC: Pew Research Center, 2011. https://www.pewresearch.org/wp-content/uploads/sites/2/2011/07/Pew-Global-Attitudes-Muslim-Western-Relations-FINAL-FOR-PRINT-July-21-2011.pdf. p.22.

[105] Anti-Defamation League. "ADL Poll Over 100 Countries Finds More Than One-Quarter of Those Surveyed Infected with Anti-Semitic Attitudes." Press release, May 13, 2014. https://www.adl.org/resources/press-release/adl-poll-over-100-countries-finds-more-one-quarter-those-surveyed-infected

the other."[106] Yet, while there should be more data in this regard, from what is available, the results are very instructive.

Let's begin with Jikeli, and his monograph, *European Muslim Antisemitism: Why Young Urban Males Say They Don't Like Jews*. His meticulous investigation, which interviewed 117 ordinary Muslim men in London, Paris, and Berlin, all of whom from different educational, ethnic, cultural, and religious backgrounds, sought to discover the extent to which anti-Jewish stereotypes and feeling exist amongst this small cross-section of Muslim men in Europe. In interviewing these individuals, he discovered that there are four main types of anti-Jewish hostility, namely, 1) classic antisemitism (including both conspiracies and stereotypes), 2) antisemitism related to Israel, 3) antisemitism with direct reference to Islam, and 4) anti-Jewish hostility without rationales. He found that, though there are positive examples of those who rejected this, the "majority of interviewees displayed resentment against Jews in at least one way or another."[107] He even found that "Negative attitudes towards Jews were often openly exhibited, at times aggressively so, including calls for violence against Jews and intentions to carry out antisemitic actions."[108] Perhaps the most concerning revelation was the extent to which this problem exists among young people. In fact, he pointed out that "negative views of Jews have become the norm in some young Muslims' social circles."[109] When such attitudes gain traction amongst the youth, particularly in this cyber era, how on earth can these warped ideas be challenged? The more cross-generational this crisis becomes, the more it seems unlikely, if not impossible, to possibly make any meaningful change.

In any event, another important study came in 2006 from the Pew Global Attitudes Project. It asked Muslims and non Muslims in a number

---

[106] Jikeli, Günther. "Antisemitic Attitudes among Muslims in Europe: A Survey Review." ISGAP Occasional Paper Series, no. 1. New York: Institute for the Study of Global Antisemitism and Policy (ISGAP), 2015. https://isgap.org/wp-content/uploads/2015/05/Jikeli_Antisemitic_Attitudes_among_Muslims_in_Europe.pdf. p.5
[107] Jikeli, Günther. *European Muslim Antisemitism: Why Young Urban Males Say They Don't Like Jews*. Bloomington: Indiana University Press, 2015. p.271
[108] ibid.
[109] ibid.

of countries if they have "favorable or unfavorable opinions of Jews." Although only a single question was asked, it found that Muslims in France, Germany, and Spain were twice as likely as non-Muslims to harbor negative views of Jews. In the case of Britain, British Muslims were seven times as likely. In fact, this survey found that Muslims were even three to ten times more likely to cleave to "very unfavorable" views of Jews than non-Muslims did in France, Germany and Great Britain.[110]

Such disturbing findings are further corroborated in a 2013 international survey, also made some important revelations. The well-regarded WZB Berlin Social Science Center undertook a major study, led by Rudd Koopmanns, focused on religious fundamentalism and out group hostility (attitudes towards Jews, homosexuals, the West, Muslims/Christians) amongst native-Christians and Muslim-immigrants in Germany, France, the Netherlands, Belgium, Austria and Sweden. In Germany, the study found that 28 per cent of Muslims and 10.5 per cent of Christians agreed with the statement "Jews cannot be trusted." In France, this was much higher – with 44 per cent of Muslims, and 7 per cent of Christians agreeing with this.[111] As we shall see, Koopmanns details the relationship between antisemitism and other, equally nefarious, ideas.

For now, though, many of the studies exploring this issue have looked at antisemitic attitudes within schools. Returning to Germany, in 2010, perhaps the most detailed survey was undertaken by Jürgen Mansel and Viktoria Spaiser, which sought to understand antisemitic attitudes amongst 2,404 high school students from different backgrounds in Bielefeld, Cologne, Berlin, and Frankfurt. It found that anti-Jewish attitudes related to Israel, religious antisemitism, classic antisemitism, and false equations between Israel and the Nazis were considerably higher

---

[110] Pew Research Center. "Muslims and the West: How Each Sees the Other." Washington, D.C.: Pew Research Center, June 22, 2006. https://www.pewresearch.org/global/2006/06/22/i-muslims-and-the-west-how-each-sees-the-other/

[111] Cited in Koopmans, Ruud. "Religious Fundamentalism and Out-Group Hostility Among Muslims and Christians." Berlin: WZB Berlin Social Science, June, 2013 Center. https://www.wzb.eu/system/files/docs/sv/iuk/ruud_koopmans_religious_fundamentalism_and_out-group_hostility_among_muslims_and_christian.pdf

among students, and specifically Arab students.[112] Another such study in Germany, this time commissioned by the German Ministry of the Interior, which focused on radicalization of young Muslims, sought to discover the level of anti-Jewish sentiments among 200 German-Muslims, 517 non-German Muslims, and a representative sample of 200 young non-Muslims in 2009 and 2010.[113] Asking if the respondents agree or disagree with the statements – "Israel is exclusively to be blamed for the origin and continuation of the Middle East conflicts" and "It would be better if the Jews would leave the Middle East," it found that about 25 per cent of both German and non-German Muslim participants agreed with both these antisemitic ideas. And less than 5 percent of non-Muslim Germans agreed.[114]

A few years later, in 2022, a study by the Konrad Adenauer Foundation added to this worrying picture, by finding that Muslims in Germany likely to agree with antisemitic than the general population. In a survey of 5,511 people, including 500 Muslims, people were asked, over the phone, whether they agree with certain antisemitic tropes. It found such attitudes to be rare, with a mere four per cent agreeing with the idea that "Jews are sneaky," and six per cent agreeing with the view that "rich Jews are the actual rulers of the world." And only four per cent of those surveyed believe that Israel has no right to exist. Interestingly, this report found that differentiators between age-groups, gender, location, made "almost no systematic difference" to the results. Being of a Muslim background, found this report, made you more predisposed to adopting antisemitic ideas. It notes, "on average, people of Muslim faith show significantly higher agreement values [with antisemitic tropes] than Christians and non-denominational people," adding that three times as many Muslims agree that Jews are "sneaky" and four times as many believe Israel should not exist. According to the report, the great difference in attitudes was most clear on the question of whether "rich Jews are the actual rulers of the world," with 26 per cent of Muslim respondents

---

[112] Cited in Jikeli, European Muslim Antisemitism, p.43.
[113] ibid.
[114] ibid.

agreeing with this claim.[115] It is fantastical that in Germany, of all places, Judenhass has surreptitiously returned through the back door. But, as this data shows, it isn't as popular amongst native Germans any longer; this problem is far more pronounced within our Muslim communities. And by no means is this solely a German problem; amongst Muslims the region, whether young or old, antisemitism is an alluring, potent, and yes, sexy, force.

The glaring state of this continental plague is further evidenced in a 2013 book, authored by Mark Elchardus, a Flemish sociologist. He dedicated a chapter to antisemitism in Dutch-language schools in Brussels. This looked at the attitudes of students from 14 years old. He found that 55-50 per cent of the Muslim students could be considered antisemites, as opposed to 10 per cent of the non-Muslim students.[116] Indeed, he found that antisemitic attitudes were unrelated to low educational levels or social disadvantage. Sticking to Dutch-speaking environments, a different 2013 study in the Netherlands interviewed 937 teachers to establish teacher experiences of antisemitism and Holocaust denial and/or distortion among students. It found that both are more present within schools that have a higher percentage of students of Turkish and/or Moroccan backgrounds, both of which are largely Muslim. In numbers, schools with under 5 per cent of students from Turkish or Moroccan backgrounds, 28 per cent of teachers reported problems with regards to antisemitism or their students diminishing the Holocaust once or more in the preceding year. This figure was 43 per cent in schools where these students made up more than 25 per cent of the student body.[117]

Given what was noted in the previous chapter about Malmo, you won't be surprised to discover that this has also reached Scandinavia. In Denmark, a 2009 study by the Institute for Political Science at Aarhus

---

[115] Hirndorf, Dominik. "Antisemitische Einstellungen in Deutschland: Repräsentative Umfrage zur Verbreitung von antisemitischen Einstellungen in der deutschen Bevölkerung. Monitor Wahl-und Sozialforschung. Berlin: Konrad-Adenauer-Stiftung" e.V., Juli 2023. https://www.kas.de/documents/252038/22161843/Antisemitische+Einstellungen+in+Deutschland.pdf/cead70cb-a767-65f8-82a1-5f3537c409d1?version=1.0&t=1689845078953

[116] Cited in Jikeli, European Muslim Antisemitism, p.44.

[117] Jikeli, Europea Muslim Antisemitism, p.45.

University interviewed 1,503 immigrants from Turkish, Pakistani, Somali, Palestinian, and former Yugoslavian-states backgrounds, as well as 300 ethnic or native Danes. Antisemitic stereotypes, the data found, are up to 75 per cent more common amongst immigrants and amongst ethnic Danes.[118] It also found that anti-Jewish attitudes are more widespread among Muslims than Christian immigrants. For the latter, Sweden, in a 2009 survey of 4,674 upper-secondary students found that 38 per cent of a Christian, and 55 per cent of those of a Muslim background, exhibit negative attitudes towards Jews.[119] Although antisemitism remains endemic in the native population, again, it is disproportionately present amongst Muslims.

And then, of course, is my neck of the woods, Blighty. A 2020 Henry Jackson Society (HJS) paper written by Rakib Ehsan, entitled, Muslim Anti-Semitism in Contemporary Great Britain, found, amongst other things, that "when compared with their perception of other faith groups, British Muslims have the least favorable attitude towards Jewish people." In late 2019, HJS commissioned the polling organization, Savanta ComRes, to undertake a survey of 750 British Muslims. Eshan's paper noted that 18 per cent of the population at large believe that Jews have disproportionate influence over business and finance. For British Muslims, however, 34 per cent of surveyed Muslims were of the view that Jews have too much influence over the global banking system. Moreover, 15 per cent of the population at large felt Jews have disproportionate influence in politics. Eshan pointed out that 33 per cent of the British Muslim respondents were of the view that Jews have too much control over the global political leadership. Speaking of dual loyalty, the report states that 24 per cent of the general population believed British Jews were more loyal to Israel than to the UK. The same figure for British Muslims is 44 per cent. the report, contrary to popular belief, identified that British Muslims who are university-educated, are more likely to believe that British Jews are more loyal to Israel than the UK, coupled with holding

---

[118] Cited in Jikeli, European Muslim Antisemitism, p.44.
[119] Cited in Jikeli, Günther. "Antisemitic Attitudes among Muslims in Europe: A Survey Review." *ISGAP Occasional Paper Series,* no. 1. New York: Institute for the Study of Global Antisemitism and Policy (ISGAP), 2015. p.19.

the belief that Jews have too much global control. Specifically with regards to this charge of dual loyalty, the report found that 55 per cent of respondents who attend Mosque at least three to four times a week believe in Jews are more loyal to Israel than the UK. The figure for British Muslims who very occasionally or never attend a Mosque is 34 per cent.[120] More studies will need to be undertaken in the UK, but antisemitic attitudes amongst British Muslims are higher, by some distance, compared to the rest of the population.

Of all countries in Western Europe, however, the situation in France is particularly dismal. The Fondapol studies have been critical, indeed indispensable, in our understanding of antisemitism in the nation that is home to the largest Jewish population in Europe. The 2022, An Analysis of Antisemitism in France, made the point that "According to our data, 15% of Muslims admit to experiencing antipathy for Jews, a proportion 10 points higher than that measured across the French population."[121] It further noted that the false notion of Jewish control of the media is a belief held by 54 per cent of Muslims (60% over the age of 50), which is thirty points higher than the national average. Further, the idea that there is Jewish control in the economy and finance is shared by more than one out every two Muslim people.[122] Like the study conducted by Koopmans, Fondapol's research has rubbished the idea that antisemitism among Muslims is specifically attributable to social or economic discontents. Rather it found that these attitudes are particularly high amongst graduates of higher education, as well among those who frequently attend places of worship. Importantly, 61 per cent of Muslims who visit the Mosque every week subscribe to the idea that "Jews have too much power in the areas of the economy and finance," compared with what is still a high 40 per cent

---

[120] Rakib Ehsan, *Muslim Anti-Semitism in Contemporary Great Britain* (London: The Henry Jackson Society, 2020) https://henryjacksonsociety.org/wp-content/uploads/2020/08/HJS-British-Muslim-Anti-Semitism-Report-web-1.pdf
Edit Query
HJS-British-Muslim-Anti-Semitism-Report-web-1.pdf
HJS-British-Muslim-Anti-Semitism-Report-web-1
[121] Reynié, Dominique, et al. *An Analysis of Antisemitism in France*. Paris: Fondation pour l'innovation politique, March 2022. https://www.fondapol.org/en/study/an-analysis-of-antisemitism-in-france/
[122] ibid.

of those who are non-observant.[123] There are other similar studies, but this one offers an important insight into the extent of anti-Jewish thinking which disproportionately afflicts Muslim communities and individuals.

Above all, these various studies matter because they shed on why this crisis needs to be understood beyond the barbaric actions of a few wrong'uns in our Muslim communities. This is much more than a radical few. And, indeed, such disquieting results further underscore why we must not see this as a parochial problem, one between Jews and Muslims alone. In her article for the Fathom Journal, *Intersectionality and Antisemitism – A New Approach*, the German sociologist, Karin Stögner, pointed out that "antisemitism is permeated by sexism, racism, and nationalism, while reflecting the economic class relationship in a completely delusory and distorted way, masquerading as a critique of capitalism," adding, "antisemitism can be understood as the example par excellence of an ideology shot through with the marks of other ideologies."[124] Meaning, the worldview of antisemites is intimately connected to sexist, racist, and classist thinking, as well as, a rejection of the 'other' This intersectionality of ideologies, as Stögner put it, was noted in a 2014 Fondapol survey. It found, among other things, that "although age, qualifications and income are possible factors in individuals' expression or approval of antisemitic views, these opinions are much more consistently linked to a set of interconnected perceptions and political views."[125] To illustrate this further, Fondapol made use of Theodore Adorno's 1950 concept of the 'authoritarian personality,' which provided both a psychological and sociological explanation for the development and propagation of antisemitic, indeed totalitarian, ideas. The survey identified a clear correlation between those who subscribe to antisemitic ideas, regardless

---

[123] ibid.
[124] Stögner, Karin, "Intersectionality and Antisemitism: A New Approach." *Fathom*, [May, 2020]. https://fathomjournal.org/intersectionality-and-antisemitism-a-new-approach/
[125] Dominique Reynié, *Antisemitic Attitudes in French Public Opinion: New Insights*, trans. Caroline Lorriaux and Michael Scott (Paris: Fondation pour l'innovation politique, November 2014). p.35.

of faith, and those who believe in authoritarian notions.[126] Meaning, the negative attitudes towards Jews are an instructive barometer of where people stand on a whole host of other social matters, including, women, democracy, homosexuality, sexual freedom, and more. In that sense, then, all of you, Jew and non-Jew, should be disturbed. For this is not about attitudes to Jews. In a way, that's only the tip of the iceberg. This is about attitudes to the values which underpin our way of life.

This intersectionality is particularly evident within our Muslim communities. If we return to Rudd Koopmans, his 2013 study found that "religious fundamentalism is by far the strongest predictor of hostility against gays, Jews and, respectively, Muslims (for Christians) or the West (for Muslims)."[127] Despite the need for more research in this regard, what was particularly striking about his findings was that, as well as religious fundamentalism being far more prevalent among Western European Muslims than Christians, this is by no means marginal amongst the former. In numbers, taking first and second generations, close to 60 per cent agree that Muslims should return to the roots of Islam, 75 per cent believe there is only one possible interpretation of the Quran – which is binding for every Muslim, and a hefty 65 per cent believe that religious rules are more important to them than the laws of the country in which they reside.[128] Although the were some variations according to cultural and age differences, and although large numbers of Muslims reject extremism, this was not the only study which revealed concerning rates of fundamentalist thinking among the region's Muslims. This is significant since it means our assessment of Muslim antisemitism must not be divorced from how this is symptomatic of, and inextricably linked to, a startling problem of normalized extremist (or, as noted in the introduction, Islamist) thinking from within our Muslim communities. This is why this issue matters for more than just Jews – it has implications for everyone, particularly those

---

[126] Dominique Reynié, *Antisemitic Attitudes in France: New Insights,* trans. Caroline Lorriaux and Michael Scott (Paris: Fondation pour l'innovation politique, November 2014), p.40.
[127] Koopmans, Ruud. "Religious fundamentalism and out-group hostility among Muslims and Christians in Western Europe." *Berlin: WZB Berlin Social Science Center,* 2014. https://bibliothek.wzb.eu/pdf/2014/vi14-101.pdf. p.21.
[128] ibid, p.11.

concerned with the future of women's rights, gay-rights and for the very integrity of democratic society.

With this, we must now address the sources of this crisis. Although there is no one root of this problem, there are, I believe, three overarching factors, which adumbrate how we have ended up here: 1) historical developments, 2) communal antisemitism, and 3) anti-Israelism and its dangerous alliances. By wrestling with how this has come to be, scholars and those in relevant governmental authorities will have a better idea of what can be done, if anything, to stop this worrying trend. As James Baldwin put it, "Not everything that is faced can be changed; but nothing can be changed until it is faced."[129]

Section One: Historical developments

This book explores that which has been dubbed the 'new-antisemitism.' To wit, in Western Europe today, Islamist antisemitism has largely replaced the traditional, Christian, and European expressions of this hatred. While it is true that for Western Europe this particular form of Jew-hate is novel, historically speaking, it is not. Rather, as this section shall detail, the emergence, development, and proliferation of this venom in the Islamic world must to be understood beyond the reductive approaches to history which hold that 'Jews and Muslims lived in peace until the emergence of Zionism,' and/or 'European colonialism is solely to blame for the roaring success of antisemitism in the Islamic world.' These ideas may be popular on Twitter, or to those who endeavor to repudiate the proposition that their ardent loathing of Israel has anything to do with antisemitism. But the truth, as ever, is more complex. Although these factors have served to exacerbate anti-Jewish hostility, antisemitism in the Muslim world has roots which predate these identifiable culprits.

The late eminent historian, Bernard Lewis, in an exchange with the journalist, Fareed Zakaria, stated, "People often note that in the late 1940s and 1950s, hundreds of thousands of Jews fled Arab countries," but added, "they rarely ask why so many Jews were living in those lands in the first

---

[129] James Baldwin. In *Oxford Essential Quotations,* edited by Ratcliffe, Susan. : Oxford University Press, https://www.oxfordreference.com/view/10.1093/acref/978 0191843730.001.0001/q-oro-ed5-00000730

place."[130] From 1948 until the early 1970s, more than 850,000 Jews fled (often forcibly) their homes in Muslim lands. Jewish civilization had existed in the Middle East and North Africa (MENA) region, uninterrupted, albeit not always prosperously, for the best part of 3,000 years. A thousand years before the emergence of Islam. Today, though there are some Jews who remain in Islamic territories, the largest community of which is in Iran (numbering approximately 8,500), the Islamic world is largely Judenfrei.

However, it would be a travesty of historical truth to view the Jewish experience in Muslim lands as one of constant strife and challenge. In his 1986 *Semites and Anti-Semites*, Bernard Lewis, rightly pointed out that "Jews have lived under Islamic rule for fourteen centuries, and in many lands, and it is therefore difficult to generalize about their experiences." However, he says that while Jews were never free from discrimination, "there is nothing in Islamic history to parallel the Spanish expulsion and Inquisition, the Russian pogroms, or the Nazi Holocaust."[131] Although the Holocaust needs to be understood transnationally, the general point he is making is an important one. He pronounced, contrary to popular belief, that the Jews, as dhimmis or protected people, were more protected than fellow Jews living under Christendom, since they were able to benefit from the legalized protections of various caliphs, or religious leaders. He said this only changed for these Jews when nationalism, imported from Europe, became a major force in the Islamic world. That said, Lewis also recognized that, "there is also nothing to compare with the progressive emancipation and acceptance accorded to Jews in the democratic West during the last three centuries." Indeed, he pointed out that even though "their situation was never as bad in Christendom at its worse," it was never, "as good as in Christendom at its best."[132]

Also taking note of this complexity was the late Sir Martin Gilbert in his 2010 work, *In Ishmael's House: A History of Jews in Muslim Lands*. As one of the most reputable historians of the past one hundred years,

---

[130] Zakaria, Fareed. "Anti-Semitism Has Spread Through the Islamic World Like a Cancer." *Washington Post,* February 14, 2019.
[131] Bernard Lewis, *Semites and Anti-Semites: An Inquiry into Conflict and Prejudice* (New York: W.W. Norton & Company, 1986), p.121.
[132] ibid, p.122.

Gilbert described with sensitivity and detail the contents and discontents of Jewish life under Islamic rule. Like Bernard Lewis, he noted, "for Jews living in Muslim lands, times of suffering and danger have alternated with times of achievement and fulfilment." He continued, "from the time of Mohammed until today, Jews have often found greater opportunities, respect and recognition under Islam than under Christianity."[133] However, he rightly identified that although Jews have made profound contributions in Islamic lands, Jews "have also been subjected to the worst excesses of hostility, hated, and persecution."[134] In sum, as articulated by both Bernard Lewis and Martin Gilbert, Jewish life under Islamic rule was not straightforward.

Evaluating the various interpretations to Jewish life under Islamic rule, Neil Kressel correctly evaluates, "that Jews, under Islam, were treated considerably better much of the time than Jews in Christian Europe—but, also, that such a conclusion unfortunately is not saying all that much."[135] In other words, despite the fact that many Jews had legalized protections under Islam, this did not mean Islamic rule was a beacon of tolerance and respect. While Bernard Lewis was right in that dhimmitude gave Jews (and other monotheists) recognized protections, it is also appropriate to recognize this was a legalized form of discrimination, and Jews, and other "protected" peoples were, at best, second-class citizens. These discriminatory measures varied at different times, and according to different rulers, however, amongst many other restrictions, dhimmis could not ride horses or camels, synagogues and churches could not be higher than a Mosque, often Jews had to wear signs (in fact, the original yellow star used by the Third Reich, was first a yellow belt or fringe used by Caliph Haroun-al-Rashin (807 CE) in Baghdad), Dhimmis had to pay a special tax for protection (the Jizzya), a Jew could not overtake a Muslim on public street, and much more. In every avenue of

---

[133] Gilbert, Martin. *In Ishmael's House: A History of Jews in Muslim Lands.* United Kingdom: Yale University Press, 2010. Pp 31-32.
[134] ibid, p.31.
[135] Kressel, Neil J. "Muslim Demonization of Jews as 'Pigs and Apes': Theological Roots and Contemporary Implications." In *Global Antisemitism: A Crisis of Modernity, Volume IV: Islamism and the Arab World,* edited by Charles Asher Small, 67-80. New York: ISGAP, 2014.

life under Muslim rule, those residing in such lands had their lives, in some measure, determined by the authorities of the time. It was a system of control which, while not innately murderous or destructive, affected the totality of, even on the microscopic level, the life of the dhimmi. Being "protected" was by no means the guarantor of the freedoms with which so many associate Islamic rule. And so, even prior to the persecution and expulsion of Jews in the 20th century from Islamic lands, life, for many, was arduous. To say the least.

It is important to state, however, that some historians depart from the claim that Jew-hatred was a major problem in Islamic lands prior to the advent of colonialism in the 19th century. The likes of Bernard Lewis, for instance, argues that although Jews were often held in contempt, sometimes treated with condescension, and could be on the receiving end of discrimination, antisemitism was not a tectonic force in the Islamic world until the emergence of these colonial influences. Going further, he argued that textually speaking, Jews were regarded with an "unimportance," which, again, only changed when external circumstances in the Islamic world changed, i.e. the European and Christian colonizers imported antisemitism to the Muslim world.[136] Also cleaving to this view is Bassam Tibi, a leading expert of Islam and Islamism. Despite recognizing the pervasiveness of negative perceptions of Jews, or Judeophobia in traditional Islam, he argued in his *The Islamization of Antisemitism*, that "the Islamists equate what has been Islamized with what is authentic, but Islamized antisemitism is not authentic to Islam. Rather, antisemitism is alien to Islam."[137] To put it another way, what is seen today has no legitimacy in either Islamic theology, or in Islam's 1,400 year history.

Others, of course, do not make the same assessment. The likes of Andrew Bostom, for instance, a medical scholar, submits in his magnum corpus, *The Legacy of Islamic Anti-Semitism, from Sacred Texts to Solemn History*, that "Islamic antisemitism is as old as Islam." In this view, Jew-

---

[136] Bernard Lewis, Semites and Anti-Semites, 1986.
[137] Tibi, Bassam. "From Sayyid Qutb to Hamas: The Middle East Conflict and the Islamization of Antisemitism." Working Paper No. 5. New Haven: Yale Initiative for the Interdisciplinary Study of Antisemitism (YIISA), 2010. https://isgap.org/wp-content/uploads/2011/10/bassam-tibi-online-working-paper-20101.pdf. p.8.

hatred was a part of Islam from its inception, and is foundational in the relationship Islam has had to Jews. Indeed, the likes of Bat Ye'or and Philippe Simonnot have suggested that the roots of antisemitism are grounded much more in the internal affairs of Islam than the external influence of colonial forces. The focus ought to be, so this argument goes, on the cultural and theological motivations for why anti-Jewish rhetoric has become such an omnipresent force in the Muslim world, even amongst those whose neighbors, business partners, and friends, were (and, in some cases, are) Jewish. Otherwise, so they might ask, how might we account for some of the violent episodes against Jews before a single colonial boat arrived?

Both sides of this debate present interesting, but ultimately, problematic arguments. Although Jew-hatred did exist in the Islamic world prior to Europe's expansion, what came to be, and what exists today, is of a different breed. The essentialist view of history, as ever, diminishes from the important complexity of this subject. While instrumentalizing both Islamic literature and history, antisemitism in the Muslim world is distinctly European in its conspiratorial flavor. By the same token, it is equally reductionist, even another such example of 'humanitarian racism,' to hold Europe as the sole guilty party. This may be a voguish line of argument, but much more significance needs to be placed on the role of traditional anti-Jewish feeling and anti-Jewish vocabulary in Islamic life, which existed well before the political, intellectual, and cultural expansion of Europe, into the Middle East and Africa. Since this factor, as we shall see, provided the indispensable terrain for what would become this 'Islamization of antisemitism.' As such, most compelling, is the middle ground argument articulated by Matthias Küntzel, a German political scientist, in his article *Islamic Antisemitism: Its Genesis, Meaning, and Effects*. 'He posits that antisemitism in the Islamic world is "a fusion of two sources: the anti-Judaism of early Islam and the modern antisemitism of Europe."'[138]

---

[138] Küntzel, Matthias. "Islamic Antisemitism: Its Genesis, Meaning, and Effects." *Antisemitism Studies 2,* no. 2 (2018): 235-253. https://muse.jhu.edu/article/718393. p.236.

Acknowledging this fusion, it is important to examine this 'Islamization of antisemitism,' and thus, recognize its proliferation across the Muslim world. Firstly, though, a definition for this term needs to be established. In short, it is the marriage of European anti-Jewish ideas with parts of Islamic theology and literature. It is worth dwelling on a few such examples.

This fusion is evident in several places, but most notably is the 1937 manifesto, *Islam and Jewry*, published in Cairo. The author of this work is not clear, with some attributing this to the derangements of the Grand Mufti El-Husseini. The Nazis, in particular, made this claim. In fact, this became an important part of their propaganda campaign. As the historian, David Motadel put it, "Berlin made explicit use of religious rhetoric, terminology, and imagery and sought to engage with and reinterpret religious doctrine and concepts," adding that "sacred texts such as the Qur'an . . . were politicized to incite religious violence against alleged common enemies." Summarizing, Motadel notes, "German propaganda combined Islam with anti-Jewish agitation to an extent that had not hitherto been known in the modern Muslim world."[139] While its author is unknown, it is clear that this document was the first of its kind. It brought together instances of Mohammed's dealings with Jews with European ideas of Jewish malevolence. In its own words, the text concludes with the following pronouncement:

> The verses from the Qur'an and hadith prove to you that the Jews have been the bitterest enemies of Islam and continue to try to destroy it. Do not believe them, they only know hypocrisy and cunning. Hold together, fight for the Islamic thought, fight for your religion and your existence! Do not rest until your land is free of the Jews.[140]

This 31-page diatribe, which would later be published and disseminated by the Third Reich, was, as Matthias Küntzel details,

---

[139] Motadel, David. *Islam and Nazi Germany's War.* Cambridge, MA: The Belknap Press of Harvard University Press, 2014. Pp. 76,97.

[140] Cited in Mohamed Sabry, "Islam-Judentum-Bolschewismus (Berlin: Junker & Dünnhaupt, 1938), 22, translated from the German version of "Islam-Judentum. Aufruf des Großmufti an die Islamische Welt im Jahre 1937.

pioneering in several ways.[141] Firstly, Mohammed's struggle with the Jews, which for centuries was treated by Islamic literature as a minor episode in his life, was now given profound significance, and arguably became a central theme. Secondly, traditional Judeophobia in the Islamic world was enveloped with a range of non-Islamic European themes. As Küntzel puts it, "converging with European racism, the Jews were attributed a certain unchanging nature with negative characteristics."[142] This meant, like European antisemites, Muslim ones saw the Jews as not merely bad, but a distinct and significant a threat to Islam. It is no source of stupefaction, therefore, that these Islamic ideologues asserted, "Do not rest until your land is free of the Jews." However, this was more, says Küntzel, "reminiscent of the policies of the Nazis than the attitudes of Mohammad."[143]

Another notable instance of this fusion comes from crucial figure in the history of the Muslim Brotherhood, as well as one of the key architects of Islamism, Sayyid Qutb. In his pamphlet, *'Our Struggle With the Jews,'* Qutb asked: "Who tried to undermine the nascent Islamic state in Medina and who incited Quraish in Mecca, as well as other tribes against the foundation of this state?" He answered, "It was a Jew!" Qutb asked, "Who stood behind the fitna-war and the slaying of the third caliph Osman and all the tragedies that followed hereafter?" He answered, "It was a Jew!" Qutb asked, "And who inflamed national divides against the last caliph and who stood behind the turmoil that ended the Islamic order with the abolition shari'a?" Guess who? "It was Ataturk, a Jew!" Indeed "The Jews always stood and continue to stand behind the war waged against Islam. Today, this war persists in the Islamic revival in all places on earth."[144]

For Qutb, the war with the Jews was not recent development. It began from the inception of Islam and has continued uninterrupted. Adding to his bellicose preachings, he said, "The Jews perpetrated the worst sort of obedience (against Allah), behaving in the most disgusting aggressive manner and sinning in the ugliest way. Everywhere the Jews have been

---

[141] ibid.
[142] ibid.
[143] ibid.
[144] Qutb, Sayyid. "Ma'rakatuna ma'a al-Yahud" [Our Battle with the Jews]. 10th legal printing. Cairo: Dar al-Shuruq, 1989. p.33.

they have committed unprecedented abominations. For such creatures who kill, massacre and defame prophets one can only expect the spilling of human blood and any dirty means which would further their machinations and evilness." As such, he reasoned, "The Jews will be satisfied only with the destruction of this religion (Islam)."[145]

One final, but certainly not last example of this fusion, is Hamas' charter. Article Seven of its Covenant of 1988 borrows from the Hadith, in which violence against Jews is called for, "when the Jew will hide behind stones and trees. Then stones and trees will say: O Moslems, O Abdulla, there is a Jew behind me, come and kill him." Indeed, the same genocidal manifesto, in Article 22, declares that "Jews were behind World War I ... [and] were behind World War II ... There is no war going on anywhere without having their finger in it." Here, as Küntzel observes, we see the Jews as both weak and cowardly, as well as a conspiratorial group, set on world domination. As he correctly concludes, "European antisemitism becomes recharged by the religious and fanatical basis of radical Islam, while the old anti-Judaism of the Qur'an, supplemented by the world conspiracy theory, receives a new eliminatory quality."[146]

Such examples, if you needed them, demonstrate the way in which European antisemitism was incorporated into the worldview of Islamic antisemites. And they are by no means exhaustive. The joining of these two polarities did not happen overnight. Rather, as Bernard Lewis correctly observes, this occurred in a series of phases, beginning with Christian minorities in Islamic lands and ending in the translation, publication, and dissemination of antisemitic literature – often translated directly from European sources.[147] A useful way of understanding the development of antisemitism in Islamic lands is the 'burning-house' analogy put forward by the leading Holocaust historian, Doris Bergen, in her work, *War and Genocide: A Concise History of the Holocaust*. She

---

[145] Qutb, Sayyid, "Our Struggle with the Jews." Cited in: Bostom, *The Legacy of Islamic Antisemitism: From Sacred Texts to Solemn History,* 357. Cited from: Nettler, Ronald L. Past trials and present tribulations : a Muslim fundamentalist's view of the Jews, (Oxford 1978).
[146] Küntzel, 2018, p.237.
[147] See Lewis, Bernard. *Semites and Anti-Semites: An Inquiry into Conflict and Prejudice.*

noted that for a house to burn down, "you need the dry timber, the spark and favorable weather."[148] Although her analogy was describing the prerequisites of the Nazi Holocaust, this is also useful for our purposes. For the "dry-timber" was the historic, or traditional Islamic Judeophobia; the "spark" was the consequence of European colonialism; and the "favorable weather" was the external political and social developments in the Islamic world, particularly the emergence of Jewish nationalism. It was a combination of these three things which created the perfect storm for Judenhass to be such a potent, central, and deadly force, in the Islamic world.

The issue of Palestine, perhaps more than any other, has been the "favorable weather," or the fanning of the flames, which has allowed Jew-hatred to spread from the Islamic intelligentsia and/or elite to wider audiences. Through the mediums of state media, be that television, literature, school-books, or even school curriculums, the perception that Israel, like Jews, is the source of all evil, has become not merely a popular belief, but in many quarters, the standard. This pernicious inversionism, in which Jews have gone from victim to victimizer, has twisted the imaginations of many. If there ever was a Holocaust, which is widely denied and/or distorted anyway, particularly so in the Muslim world, the Jews, as collectivized in Israel, are real ones deserving of the Nazi epithet. They are the real enemy. For this reason, as Lewis explains, since 1967, when Israel defeated three large Arab armies, "Nazi-type anti-Semitism came to dominate Arab discussions of Zionism and Judaism as well as of the state of Israel."[149] Over the years, this has been compounded by the lack of intellectual inquiry, the suppression of free-speech, and crucially, the absence of Jewish communities, in a great many Muslim nations. Such warped ideas cannot be challenged, nor is there any incentive or itch to do so, when the powers that be deprive their people of all the important mechanisms of understanding the power of manipulation and deceit. When one hears about the perfidious Jew, has never met one, and the evil of the Jew is flaunted as if it were as true and unquestionable as the Pope's

---

[148] Bergen, Doris L. *War & Genocide: A Concise History of the Holocaust*. Vancouver, B.C.: University of British Columbia Crane Library, 2017. p.14.
[149] Lewis, *Semites and Antisemites,* p.240.

Catholicism, no wonder such disconcerting statistics and attitudes exist. It is, to put it crudely, the bleeding obvious.

Yet, contrary to popular belief, Jew-hate to the tune of anti-Zionism did not begin in the June of 1967. Rather, although Israel's astonishing victory in those six days gave it a new lease of life, as pointed out by Matthias Küntzel, the first instance of Arab opprobrium of Zionism coupled with conspiratorial antisemitism, was evident in the Bludan Conference, held in Damascus, in the September of 1937. This conference, notes Küntzel, was important because it was the beginning of a pan-Arab movement united in opposition to Zionism, and secondly, because it was vital in taking the *Islam and Jewry* pamphlet to wider Arab audiences.[150] Spearheaded by the notorious antisemite, and keen Hitlerian, The Grand Muffti, Amin El-Husseini, who could not attend in person, but did fund the conference, Bludan was a gathering of Arab leaders and representatives from across the Middle East. Closed off to the public, and even to journalists, except for a Nazi press officer, one British spy managed to stealthily creep in. In his report, he described the conference as "a manifestation of Judeophobia," adding in the annex of his work that the *Islam and Jewry p*amphlet was given to each person in attendance, especially to members of the Palestine Defense Committee.[151] The inference being that Anti-Zionism in the Arab world, from its political beginnings, was indistinguishable from the antisemitism raging in continental Europe. It was as infectious, deranged, conspiratorial, and inciteful, as that seen in Berlin or Vienna. As Bernard Lewis points out, "in some Soviet, Arab, and latterly also other Islamic polemical writings, "Zionist" simply means "Jew," and therefore anti-Zionist means anti-Jew."[152] The distinction may be a popular one, but in actuality, it is one of semantics. Same hate, different name.

But why instrumentalize religion in this way? On this, Küntzel's reasoning is instructive as it is irrefutable. By using this pamphlet, the intention was to "theologize" this territorial conflict in order to dissuade others in the Arab world more predisposed to accepting territorial

---

[150] Küntzel, Matthias. *Islamic Antisemitism: Its Genesis, Meaning, and Effects.* p.239.
[151] cited in ibid, pp 240-241.
[152] Lewis, Bernard, *Semites and Anti-Semites*, p.19.

compromise with the Jews, particularly in light of the 1937 Peel Commission, which suggested a division, much more in the favor of Arabs, in Palestine.[153] Indeed, the Arabic publisher of I*slam and Jewry,* Mohamad Abdel Taher, drew a connection in his short preface between this pamphlet and the 1937 Peel Commission, stating, "[Muslims and Arabs] should know about Jews just now while the Jews seek to create a state by eliminating Muslims and Arabs."[154] A Jewish-state is not just an encroachment on Islamic territory, although that is a sin deserving of a severe punishment, but a state destined on destroying Islamic civilization, and with it, the wider world. The assimilation of European views of imagined Jewish power, together with theological interpretations of why Jews are deserving of scorn, have become foundational in the well of anti-Zionist discourse in the Muslim world. For this reason, the most popular strain of anti-Zionism, while cloaked with the pretexts of liberation and human-rights, are not about territory nor equality, as widely claimed. This may be enticing to the modern palate, but ultimately, sinister. But more on this in section three.

For now, although this analysis of Islamic antisemitism is far from panoramic, it has shown how, and why, anti-Jewish attitudes have gone from the peripheries to a significant worldview in much of the Islamic world. And like its European counterpart, this Islamist conviction is rooted in a psychosis that the Jews are behind a variety of cunning, but no less diabolical, plots. However, given this historical analysis reveals the way in which antisemitism has become the norm in the Islamic world, it begs the question: why would Western European leaders allow such significant migration from this part of the world knowing that friendly attitudes towards Jews are, alas, few and far between? Describing this as 'indirect state antisemitism,' Manfred Gerstenfeld pointed to a policy of allowing large numbers of people to arrive from countries in which Jew-hatred is commonplace, with no measures in place to challenge such noxious ideas on arrival. Knowing full well many are arriving from countries in which Jew-hate is rife, successive governments across the region have decided to ignore, even occasionally confute this reality, in the pursuit of diversity.

---

[153] Küntzel, Matthias. *Islamic Antisemitism: Its Genesis, Meaning, and Effects.* p.244.
[154] cited in ibid.

And doubtless, just as Gerstenfeld, and others have predicted, this has had a marked impact on the landscape of antisemitism in Western Europe.[155]

On that note, we turn to section two, where we see the impact of such attitudes on the region's Muslim communities.

Section Two: Communal Antisemitism

Historical developments have paved the way for antisemitism in the Islamic world, be that in Muslim-majority nations or amongst Muslims in Western Europe, to become deep rooted, widespread, systemic, and institutionalized. So much so that rooting this out is, perhaps, an insurmountable task. Nevertheless, in our case of Western Europe it is important to see how these historical developments have led to both a vocabulary and culture of Jew-hatred within these communities, and how this is leading to disproportionate levels of Muslim perpetrators of antisemitic abuse, harassment, and violence.

There are multiple agencies from which antisemitism continues to be disseminated and reinforced. A concern which many have correctly raised, however, is the lack of research and data, that aims to quantify the impact each factor has on this crisis. Accordingly, given the nature of this complex issue, it is important to establish a framework that can be used to clearly understand these various elements, and the way in which they interact. Therefore, I have categorized the sources of communal antisemitism in the region into three subheadings, namely, social, institutional, and digital. Together, these three factors provide an insightful tour d'horizon behind the power and influence of anti-Jewish sources in our Muslim communities.

1. Social

In the view of Pierre Andre Taguieff, when discussing the "new-antisemitism," we ought to reintroduce the term "banalization," for, he explains, "it is exactly as if many different attitudes and manifestations of Judeophobia had become banalized, as if they fitted so well into the

---

[155] Gerstenfeld, Manfred. "Muslim antisemitism in Europe." *Journal for the Study of Antisemitism 5,* no. 1 (2013): 195-230.

ideological scenery that they were no longer perceptible."[156] Although he mulls upon various reasons behind this, it is the case that particularly within Muslim communities, so much are anti-Jewish expressions uttered liberally and without any real thought, they have become a part of the common vernacular for many of those who reside in these communities. This, of course, extends well beyond France. From conspiracies to vilification, and from contempt to statements of violent incitement, anti-Jewish feeling is not a thing of the fringes. In the interactions between Muslims in various settings, it is a troubling standard.

Let's, however, begin with France. A leading sociologist, Michel Wieviorka, in his first-rate study of European antisemitism among Muslims, studied the French areas of Trois-Ponts in Raoubaix (north of France) and Sarcelles, an area we considered in the previous chapter. Both areas have a significant Muslim population, with only the latter having a visible Jewish community. Nevertheless, this study, concentrating on "disenfranchised youths" (many of whom are Muslim), found that antisemitism in both areas was expressed bluntly, and sometimes, publicly. It was found that the term 'Juif' and 'feuj' (Jew) were widely used as insults. A notable observation was that the use of this racist language put pressure on other youths to also partake in anti-Jewish rhetoric.[157] And similar findings have been replicated in other studies of this kind, too.

In fact, Jikeli's own study of 117 ordinary Muslim men, Jikeli found influence of friends and peers to be a vital portal of antisemitism. He noted, "most interviewees were no exception to this rule, and many of the respondents referred to the antisemitic views of friends and classmates, which are usually accepted and questioned."[158] What was particularly concerning, however, was that, "antisemitic actions by peers are often trivialized and justified."[159] One interviewee, Bilal from Paris, condemned an attack by a fellow student in his school on a Jewish member of staff

---

[156] Taguieff, Pierre-André. *Rising from the Muck: The New Anti-Semitism in Europe*. Chicago: Ivan R. Dee, trans, Patrick Camiller, 2004. p.3.
[157] Wieviorka, Michel. *The Lure of Anti-Semitism: Hatred of Jews in Present-Day France*. Translated by Kristin Couper Lobel and Anna Declerck. Leiden: Brill, 2007.
[158] Jikeli, *European Muslim Antisemitism,* p.217.
[159] ibid, p.219.

because she is a woman, but gave a possible justification for attacking Jews, in other, more general circumstances. This assault was connected to what he sees as a general Muslim hatred of Jews. Terrifyingly, this young man believes that if a Jew wearing a kippah (skullcap) came to his neighborhood, he would be attacked. He even said that when he witnessed a Jew being insulted on the street, "sometimes, I say it's well done."[160] As Jikeli rightly summarized, "Bilal is accustomed to violence against Jews from his peers and partly justifies and endorses it."[161] No doubt, this creates the necessary conditions for those with violent intentions to find reason for putting their rage to chilling ends.

However, peers and friends are the tip of the iceberg. The leading French historian of Jews in Arab lands, Georges Bensoussan, landed himself in court for hate speech after he declared in a radio interview with Alain Finkielkraut, "in Arab families, antisemitism is suckled on the breast of the mother." This aroused the attention of many intellectuals, with some anti-racism groups accusing him of stirring up racism, and others claiming he has the right to make such statements, even if they are invidious.[162] In the end, he was acquitted of this charge, but this statement does highlight an uncomfortable state of affairs: negative attitudes towards Jews are both given and reinforced in the home, and by implication, the family.

If we return to Jikeli's study, he notes that "interviewees mentioned, some approvingly, that their parents and other members of their family possessed antisemitic views, while others distanced themselves from such views."[163] There is good reason for this. A number of Muslim families reside in Western Europe as first, second, or third generation immigrants, coming from places in which antisemitism, as previously detailed, is mainstream and is the norm. Hardly astonishing, therefore, why these attitudes have become so woefully pervasive in these communities. For the home, as the transmitter through which traditions are passed down to the next generation, is a major source of conspiratorial tropes, deranged

---

[160] ibid.
[161] ibid.
[162] Sitbon, Shirli. "French Historian Georges Bensoussan Sued Over Arab 'Hate Comment.'" *The Jewish Chronicle,* February 3, 2017. https://www.thejc.com/news/world/french-historian-georges-bensoussan-sued-over-arab-hate-comment-lzzw0iar
[163] Jikeli, *European Muslim Antisemitism*, p.223.

obsessions with Jewish power and wealth, dehumanizing religious depictions of Jews, and all other delusional and devilish ideas surrounding Jews and our apparent conniving ambitions for world domination and subversion.

One deplorable case of this is Mohammed Merah, the 23-year-old Jihadist, who murdered three paratroopers, a Jewish school teacher, and three Jewish schoolchildren in 2012. In a brave admission, Abdelghani Merah, Mohammed's brother, remarked in a book he later co-authored, *Mon frère, ce terroriste* (My brother, the terrorist), that the Merah home was rife with Jew-hate. As children, they were taught, "Arabs are born to hate the Jews,"[164] and that "In the Merah household, we were brought up with hating Jews, the hatred of everything that was not Muslim."[165] When they were children, they asked to put a Christmas tree up, and the father, according to Abdelghani, objected, and explained that his belief was grounded on the theological myth that a, "Jew wanting to kill the Prophet hid himself behind a pine tree."[166] From a young age, this murderous antisemitism was clearly present. It wasn't banal in this case. It was aggressive and potent. Indeed, as experts on this family put it, the "Merah's familial milieu was a crucial channel for the transmission of a radical ideology that was built on the historical Islamic anti-Jewish polemics."[167] As a matter of fact, Abdelghani was himself violently attacked by his younger brother, Abdelkader Merah, whom he described as a "tumor," when he discovered that Abdelghani was dating a woman with slight Jewish origins, and refused to break up with her.[168] At the hands of his own brother, who was jailed for thirty years for his complicity with Mohammed, he sustained multiple stab wounds. His own brother. The

---

[164] Cited in Andre, Virginie, and Shandon Harris-Hogan. "Mohamed Merah: From Petty Criminal to Neojihadist." *Politics, Religion & Ideology* 14, no. 2 (2013): 307-319.
[165] Cited in Rodan-Benzaquen, Simone. "Muslim Anti-Semitism Threatens France's Democracy." *Fondapol.* November 19, 2017. https://www.fondapol.org/dans-les-medias/muslim-anti-semitism-threatens-frances-democracy/
[166] ibid.
[167] Cited in Lee, Benjamin, and Kim Knott. *Ideological Transmission I: Family. Center for Research and Evidence on Security Threats* (CREST), 2017. https://crestresearch. ac.uk/resources/family-ideological-transmission/
[168] Lichfield, John. "How My Hate-Filled Family Spawned Merah the Monster." *The Independent,* November 13, 2012. https://www.independent.co.uk/news/world/europe/how-my-hatefilled-family-spawned-merah-the-monster-8307341.html

antisemitism of Mohammed Merah, Abdelkader Merah and their sister, Souad Merah, who left with her children to Syria, did not emerge from thin air. Mohammed, along with his other siblings (except for Abdelghani), to borrow from Bensoussan, sucked the hatred from their mother's breast.

Like antisemites over millennia, they did not just regard Jews as the embodiment of evil, but they were raised to see Jews as the source of everything that is evil. Or, in their case, to regard Jews as the very antithesis of Muslims and Islam, and to regard their Abrahamic cousins as an enemy which must be tenaciously fought, and never, under no circumstances, to be appeased or propitiated. It will come as no surprise that none of Mohammed's siblings had a damascene conversion like Abdelghani. Afterwards, Souad proudly asserted that "Mohamed had the courage to act. I am proud, proud, proud ... Jews, and all those who massacre Muslims, I detest them."[169] She was not the only one. Abdelghani notes that "when the medical examiner brought [his] brother's corpse home, people came over. They cried tears of joy." He added, "They said that he had brought France to its knees. That he did well. Their only regret was that he had not killed more Jewish children."[170]

Although extreme, this example reflects the way in which negative anti- Jewish attitudes have the capacity to inspire deadly actions. A lexicon of dehumanization, or nonviolent violence, produces the likes of Merah and Nemmouche. In fact, no. It is more. It is the necessary precondition for their inhumanity. It is for this reason that we must understand the influence of Islamism beyond Islamists. And this has long been true of historic antisemitism. While it only takes a minority, even a tiny minority to commit horrific crimes, such people emerge from a place in which hatred is embedded in the society around them. Indeed, as ever in the history of persecution, things never begin with the machines of murder and destruction. It all begins in the realms of ideas and words. In the context of Islamist antisemitism in Western Europe, not much has changed.

---

[169] ibid.
[170] Cited in Simone Rodan-Benzaquen. "Muslim Anti-Semitism Threatens France's Democracy."

What happens in the home is, of course, heavily determined by external social interactions. The two that I shall turn to in a moment are both the influence of Islamic intuitions, as well as the role of social media. For now, though, it's worth seeing how non-Islamic institutions have also become a breeding ground for anti-Jewish poison amongst Muslims. One such place, of many, is schools.

Here, anti-Jewish attitudes are communicated and reinforced from multiple sources, not least by teachers and peers. In her 2022 analysis of antisemitism in 1,314 British schools across the country, Charlotte Littlewood, an Associate Research Fellow for the Henry Jackson Society, found amongst other things, that there has been a "173.3 per cent rise in antisemitic incidents of pupil misconduct, bullying, or harassment reported in schools over the last five years, with a 29.13 per cent rise in recorded antisemitic incidents in schools between 2021 and 2022."[171] Moreover, over the past five years, more than a thousand incidents have been uncovered, with 79 incidents reported to the police.[172] To make matters worse, Littlewood found that only a meagre 47 of schools which responded, or 3.40 per cent, have a policy to which specifically refers to antisemitism.[173] What happens in the playground, in the classroom, or anywhere else in the school building, is positively fundamental in the formation of attitudes and ideas amongst young people. There is, as this one survey illustrates, a worrying situation in schools across the country. But, again, this problem seems to disproportionately affect young Muslim pupils.

Addressing schools, Jikeli cites many examples of students encouraging one another to participate in anti-Jewish activity. One extreme example includes the assault of a Holocaust survivor in Berlin by Muslim pupils. The interviewee, Ismail, stood next to his friends while they assaulted, screamed, and spat on this survivor. As Jikeli notes, no sanctions were reported, and the survivor had to return at a later date, when it was safe to speak. Describing this disgraceful affair, Suleiman, who was

---

[171] Littlewood, Charlotte. "Antisemitism in Schools." Center on Social and Political Risk, Henry Jackson Society, 2022. https://henryjacksonsociety.org/wp-content/uploads/2022/07/Antisemitism.pdf. p.1.
[172] ibid, p.3.
[173] ibid.

also present, said, "In school, there was a Jew. After that he really looked differently, because we threw him out from school [laughs] [. . .]. He came in, he was spat at by the Arab students, beaten, and then he ran away quickly."[174] Such contemptible displays are rare, but could not have happened without the influence of those around the violent students in question. And in a study of the Muslim schools in the UK, published in 2009, some of the estimated 166 Muslim schools teach the rejection of Western values and a hatred of Jews. It found that many of these schools display varying degrees of affiliation to various extreme groups, such as Wahabis, Salafis, Deobandis and the Muslim Brotherhood.[175] These are schools. But the point stands: when dehumanizing talk is regular and routine, and many of those who participate have little to no contact with Jews, the breeding ground for violence becomes palpable in the same measure it becomes all the harder to push back against it.

At this stage, it is important to return to an observation made in the previous chapter: virtually all Islamist perpetrators of antisemitic murder have spent time in jail. This common denominator is important, though most work has overlooked this all too crucial stage on the road to murderous barbarism. Those guilty of these crimes were, to begin with, imprisoned for a variety of petty (and some non-petty) crimes, not, as you might expect, for violence, terrorism, or extremism. Rather than rehabilitate them, the experience of prison served either to radicalize those miscreants or to immensely contribute to their radicalization process. Explaining why, Noemie Bisserbe, a specialist in French politics, argued that the presence of Islamist ideologues and terrorists in prisons has meant that vulnerable Muslim inmates, susceptible to extremist rhetoric, have fallen to the influence of these dangerous convicts. As she correctly avers, in the French context, this has deteriorated due not only to the increase in Islamist returnees from Syria and elsewhere, who are being put into prison and do influence their fellow inmates, but also the disproportionately high levels of Muslim prisoners; with some estimating that around 50 to 60 per

---

[174] Jikeli, *European Muslim Antisemitism,* p.208.
[175] Cited in ibid, p.54.

cent of the prison population in France being Muslim.[176] The factors behind disproportionate levels of criminality in the French Muslim community are varied and complex, with economic hardship, social alienation, and the entrenchment of Islamist thinking, all playing an important role. Such an analysis goes beyond the scope of this book, as does an appraisal of the various attempts both to deradicalize, and to isolate the extremist influencers, within the prison. However, as we know in France, and Western Europe, efforts have not been particularly effective, or as she puts it, they've been, "piecemeal and sluggish."[177]

To show how possible and easy it is to be radicalized in prison, it is worth citing an example from Haras Rafiq, a leading expert and consultant on extremism. In an interview in the Financial Times about this very issue, Rafiq described how a British Muslim, who found himself in prison as a result of a brawl, came out an Islamist. According to Rafiq, this man, before prison, was entirely irreligious, and he neither fasted nor prayed. In prison, he was afraid, and he sought "to explore his faith for answers and to become a better person." Doing this, "He got straight in with the Islamist gang." Much like other cults, Rafiq observed, they started very political, racial indoctrination: "Brother, you are innocent, it's really the corrupt judicial system that sent you in for being a Muslim. The only way is to be part of our gang." Rafiq identified that they gave him much literature on the idea of 'us and them,' which he says, is the first point of recruitment. He came out an Islamist, but, interestingly, "didn't realize he had been radicalized."[178] Somehow, he would revert to a more moderate position, but for most others, this does not happen. They remain radical.

Returning to a more 'moderate position' was certainly not the case for the people I looked at in Chapter One. It is necessary to highlight some examples of how significant the prison-experience was in the radicalization of those who subsequently became murderous antisemites. For instance, Mohammed Merah, although raised to hate Jews, first found

---

[176] Bisserbe, Noemie. "European Prisons Fueling Spread of Islamic Radicalism." *Wall Street Journal*, August 1, 2016. https://www.wsj.com/articles/european-prisons-fueling-spread-of-islamic-radicalism-1470001491
[177] ibid.
[178] Burgis, Tom. "The Making of a French Jihadi." *Financial Times*, January 26, 2015. https://www.ft.com/content/a7fd3d50-a302-11e4-9c06-00144feab7de

himself in jail for robbing a woman off her handbag. He arrived to prison, and was, according to a prison guard who knew him "just a kid banging on his cell's door shouting for his PlayStation."[179] This would all change, say the French authorities, who declared that he was radicalized while serving his sentence. After serving, he travelled to the Middle East, where he claimed to be taught by an al-Qaeda instructor. Another case is Mehdi Nemmouche, who murdered four at the Jewish Museum in Brussels. Unlike Merah he was more violent, being sent to prison for armed burglary. However, he, too, once he left jail, was flagged for extremism, and ended up travelling to Syria, where he worked as a sadistic prison guard for ISIS. The prison process, again, being a vital stage in the process of becoming a terrorist. One last, but particularly abhorrent case, is Amédy Coulibaly, the man who in 2015 murdered four at the HyperCacher supermarket in Paris. He, like Nemmouche, in 2004, found himself in prison for armed robbery. In 2008, as part of a documentary on prisons, Coulibaly told Warda Mohammed, a French journalist that "Prison changed me." He went on to say, "I learnt about Islam in prison. Before that I wasn't interested, now I pray," and added, "Just for that, I'm glad I went to prison."[180] Coulilbaly, along with Chérif Kouachi, one of the brothers in the shooting at Charlie Hebdo, were mentored by Djamel Beghal, who was jailed in 2001 for plotting to blow up the US embassy in Paris. According to Jean-Charles Brisard, a former advisor to France's chief of antiterrorism prosecutor as well as expert on al-Qaeda, "Beghal was the real mentor, a scholar who taught them about religion, about jihad," and reasoned that for both, "the time in prison was crucial."[181] This is not an exhaustive list, but reflects the significance of this factor in all anti Jewish murders in recent years: prison, for many, was a turning point, and they, unlike the man Haras Rafiq wrote about, remained loyal to their extremist ideals.

---

[179] Bisserbe, Noemie. "European Prisons Are Incubators of Terror." *The Australian*, August 2, 2016. https://www.theaustralian.com.au/business/wall-street-journal/european-prisons-are-incubators-of-terror/news-story/b338701529f3d7c2fd0d03b8025a7007
[180] Cited in Noémie Bisserbe "European Prisons Fueling Spread of Islamic Radicalism."
[181] Cited in Tom Burgis. "The Making of a French Jihadi."

There are, of course, other institutions which need analysis. As part of our efforts to combat this issue, more research needs to be undertaken to establish the significance of these social structures in the dissemination of Jew-hate. What, however, has been discussed demonstrates the way in which expressions of antisemitism penetrates various places in which Muslims interact. It has become normalized. Now, we must consider the way in which antisemitism has become endemic in important Muslim institutions and organizations in Western Europe.

2. Institutionalized Jew-hatred

The comparison between Islamism and white supremacy is often made. They are both, so people claim, insignificant and marginal, even in their own communities, and should not be used as a stick to attack all Muslims or Christians. And certainly, the latter part of this assertion is correct. But the comparison between the two is barefaced distortion. While exponents of white supremacy tend to operate out of their cluttered bedrooms (I know, I am no one to talk), their supremacism and murderous racism, though not to be overlooked, do not command even a fraction of the influence Islamist forces carry within large sections of our Muslim communities. One is fringe, almost desperately fringe, and the other, sadly, is, not so fringe.

A number of important Muslim organizations in Western Europe have ties, either directly or indirectly, to Islamist entities, and/or Islamist influencers. In his study, Jikeli listed a number of these disconcerting affiliations, and as the years go by, the number of such organizations is increasing. Some of these exist in cyberspace, and have large numbers of followers on social media. Others, by contrast, have ties, perhaps even influence, over Mosques, schools, community centers, and more. Although far from representative of all Muslims in Western Europe, they play a part, to varying degrees, on the attitudes of their Muslim constituents. This, alone, reveals why this issue needs to be understood beyond the actions of a few troubling actors. It reaches the very heart of our Muslim communal life.

Returning to Jikeli's interviews, he found that these and other organizations play an important part in the anti-Jewish activities of

Muslim activists. In the UK, the Islamist organization, Hizb ut-Tahir, is, according to Jikeli's interviewees, active. One interviewee from London said, "They put up stalls and stuff, in markets, and they distribute leaflets." This person added, "they're probably the most active of all the groups in East London."[182] A fellow interviewee, Hussein, said that this organization's view vis-à-vis Zionism is in line with their own thinking. He said, "Perhaps you can have a link to Huzb ut-Tahir… they're kind of, the way like we're thinking about Zionists."[183] In other words, the way many members of our Muslim communities feel towards Zionists is naked, conspiratorial disdain. It is not a mere objection to the policies of the state. It is driven by this fusion of theological anti-Jewish polemics, along with European conspiracies, all about insidious Jewish power. A sublime cocktail for what we see today. Other interviewees in London identified the leaflets they receive from Muslim organizations urging the boycott of Israeli companies as being the reason why they believe Jews are "rich and run all the big companies."[184]

Yet this doesn't end here. There are Islamic religious institutions which have also become vehicles of antisemitism. We know that from the Fondapol Study of 2022 that the attendance at places of worship is linked to beliefs in anti-Jewish prejudice. The more religious and devout one is, the more likely one is to cleave to particular negative attitudes of Jews. In numbers, the survey found 61 per cent of Muslims who visit the mosque every week subscribe to the belief that "Jews have too much power in the areas of the economy and finance," whereas a less significant, but still high 40 per cent of those who do not attend, agree with this statement.[185] This is not always the case, as evidenced by some of the findings in other reports, but we know that there is an issue of anti-Jewish discourse which exists in many religious intuitions, be that Mosques, Madrasas, cultural centers, and more, across the region. What a religious leader, almost always a man, will say, is said in a position of authority. And if such an authority is inclined towards some Islamist ideals, no wonder his

---

[182] Jikeli, *European Muslim Antisemitism*, p.240.
[183] ibid.
[184] ibid.
[185] Dominique Reynié, , et al. *An Analysis of Antisemitism in France*. Paris: Fondation pour l'innovation politique, p.6.

congregation, which includes impressionable young folk, will take what is said as not simply the truth, but a truth of divine providence.

This is particularly acute in the British setting. Ex-Islamist and author, Ed Hussein, estimates that up to 50 per cent of British Mosques are run by the Deobandis, an Islamist movement which played an important role in the birth of the Taliban in Afghanistan.[186] This is along with a number of seminaries and schools. That is, important, even core Islamic institutions in Britain, and beyond, receive money from organizations and entities which are, by their nature, antisemitic, anti-democratic, and extreme. Particularly disconcerting was an investigation Jikeli cited, which looked at the available literature in UK mosques, Islamic schools, and Islamic cultural centers. Many such institutions, especially Mosques, contain books which preached hatred against Jews and the West, antisemitic conspiracy theories, even positive reference to The Protocols of the Elders of Zion.[187] If this material is readily available, coupled with the teachings of some warped clerics, then be in no doubt why a growing number of devout individuals find antisemitism not just acceptable, but in some cases, a duty.

The Mosque, like any other religious center, is not a place for just prayer and reflection. It is also a place of community and a center of discussion. In his interviews, Jikeli took note of the fact that "interviewees reported that the Israeli-Palestinian conflict is a constant theme of discourse in Mosques and among Muslims gathering there, and that this discourse often contains strong anti-Israel or anti-Jewish subject matter."[188] Jikeli cites the study undertaken by Anke Schu, a German social-scientist, who also conducted a study on anti-Jewish attitudes. She quoted one of her interviewees, a young Turkish man in Germany, who said, "The Jews shall all die." Asking why he thought this, he replied, "I remember I was once in the mosque and […] [the imam] recounted that Jews in earlier times and turks – and Arabs were always in conflict […]

---

[186] Cited in "Author Reveals How Mosques in UK Enforcing Radical Islam Among Muslims." *OpIndia,* June 24, 2021. https://www.opindia.com/2021/06/author-reveals-how-mosques-in-uk-enforcing-radical-islam-among-muslims/
[187] Cited in Jikeli, *European Muslim Antisemitism,* p.54.
[188] Ibid, p.239.

and [...] fighting each other. And that's why."[189] It is not hyperbole to suggest that given the presence of antisemitism within a number of religious institutions, as well as the burgeoning menace of 'Islamist thinking' in these communities, sentiments of this kind, in our Muslim communities, are not the exception to the rule.

Sadly, Islamic schools and/or Madrassas, Islamic evening or weekend schools, have also become an important distributor and reinforcer of anti-Jewish ideas. A leading expert in Islamism in Europe, and a Senior Fellow at the Investigative Project on Terrorism, Abigail R Esman, wrote a detailed article of the most disturbing realities in these places. This issue, Esman notes, has been excessive in the Netherlands. She cites a report from the Dutch newspaper, HRS Handelsbald and television news show, Nieuwsuur, which both found that at least half of the independent Koran schools in the Netherlands were run by Salafists, known for disseminating extremist messages to their students.[190] The study found that "teachers at these schools have praised sharia-based legal systems, warned children to stay away from "enemies" (gays and non-Muslims), and reject Western (and therefore, Dutch) culture completely."[191] The report even found that one Imam told his students, "You can better congratulate someone for a murder than wish them a Merry Christmas."[192] This radicalization in such schools exist across all age groups, including primary school children. Despite the protestations from the Dutch Education Minister at the time of this report, few, if any other, senior people in government were prepared to speak out.

This problem exists throughout across our region. One other notable case is in point is Belgium. Esman found that "more than half of all public school students in Brussels and Antwerp are enrolled in religious Muslim schools, with as many as 81 per cent in the Antwerp region of Borgerhout."[193] At least one school, the Plura C school, had a connection

---

[189] Cited in ibid, p.239.
[190] Esman, Abigail R. "Europe Grapples with Independent Quran Schools." *Investigative Project on Terrorism*, January 11, 2023. https://www.investigativeproject.org/9310/europe-grapples-with-independent-quran-schools
[191] ibid.
[192] ibid.
[193] ibid.

to a group with alleged links to extremism. A report into this school found that it "would become an extremist vector in the Limburg educational environment, in accordance with the supporting ideology that goes against the principles of human rights and other foundations of the rule of law."[194] Unlike the Swedish and French governments which have closed some extreme educational institutions down, this one remains open. And as rightly pointed out by Belgium's Education Minister, "I can see no way in which such a school can contribute to integration and a harmonious society … We do the children and parents no service [by permitting] them."[195] Will these positive and encouraging sentiments lead to action? That remains to be seen, but the failure to deal with this poison, particularly when it comes to malleable youths, will only serve to exacerbate this crisis of antisemitism, as well as that of integration, we see across the region.

As ever, though, more studies will need to be undertaken to see the extent to which these organizations and institutions influence anti-Jewish attitudes. Even if, however, they are not so influential, they are contributing, at least in some measure, to this epidemic of Jew-hatred. The point must be reiterated, though, that this problem is not comparable to some preacher in the Westboro Baptist Church. This problem is deep-seated in many core Muslim institutions of Western Europe.

There are those who call for the closure of these institutions which push such radical ideas. And some Mosques and other institutions in the region have been closed. For reasons I shall now detail, this may have little effect given that this crisis has now gone well beyond the confines of religious congregations, meetings, and in-person social interactions. Finding a hospitable environment on the internet, especially on social media, renders this crisis of antisemitism, perhaps, impossible to contain, much less resolve.

3. Media

This is a topic deserving of its own book. Not wishing to diminish from the enormity of this topic, I shall be terse, and defer to the expertise of those much more qualified. Nevertheless, what is clear, is that while

---

[194] ibid.
[195] ibid.

not particular to Islamist extremism, social media, along with other forms of media, has given rise to Islamist voices who are able to reach much larger audiences over the internet and beyond. This has added an entirely new, but most perturbing element to this crisis. For what happens in the elusive online market of ideas cannot be effectively challenged or monitored. Making use of all media, and speaking to the grievances held by many, these voices, many of which with a large following, have become influential, particularly (though not exclusively) amongst vulnerable and disenfranchised young Muslim men. When this material is unprecedently accessible, it begs the question, can there even be a push back?

What is known, however, is that the internet, not only social media, is identified by the ADL Global 100 survey as a primary means through which anti-Jewish attitudes amongst Muslims is shared and reinforced. And if that is not enough, it found Muslims who get their information about Jews from the internet are much more likely to harbor antisemitic views than those who get their information from non internet sources. This includes, antisemitic ideas surrounding the Israeli-Palestinian conflict, conspiracy theories about Jewish involvement in the attack on the Twin Towers on September 11th (9/11), Jewish power in the media and in America, and more.[196] Without dwelling on this topic too much, what occurs online has considerable, potentially the most significant, influence over the dissemination of antisemitic ideas, including Muslims.

That said, this prejudice is not only being passed through virtual sources. The media, be that on print, the news, or online, has reinforced these attitudes. There are many such examples of this, however, for brevity, I shall look at one example, television media. Discussing this, Jikeli found that the television is "one of the most important sources cited for antisemitic beliefs about the Israeli-Palestinian conflict, as well as for stereotypes of rich Jews and Jewish control over large companies, and for conspiracy theories."[197] He pointed out that given many older generations are watching television from their home countries, the culture of

---

[196] Cited in *Anti-Defamation League*. "ADL Global 100: A Survey of Attitudes toward Jews in over 100 Countries around the World." New York: *Anti-Defamation League*, 2014. http://global100.adl.org/public/ADL-Global-100-Executive-Summary.pdf
[197] Gunther Jikeli, *European Muslim Antisemitism*, p.229.

antisemitism which exists, is often transmitted down to their children and to subsequent generations. The significance of these non-European channels varies on the basis of linguistic comprehension, but negative imagery of Jews (in particular Israel) is, as Jikeli points out, arguably are very important. Of course, Western-media has contributed to this with its own misguided and distorted reporting of the Israeli-Palestinian conflict, not to mention, the use of certain media outlets instrumentalizing anti-Jewish tropes in their reporting of Israel. Describing what he sees on various reporting of Israel, and speaking for many, Suleimann in Berlin, in an interview with Jikeli, said, "For example on TV, what I see there, may hatred of this people becomes bigger and bigger."[198] In fact, some say what is shown leads to violence against Jews. One French respondent, Hamza, describing the portrayal of Israel on French television stated, "It's because of the media, on tv, what happened […] after the game PSG/Tel Aviv," in which antisemitic violence broke out after a fixture between Paris Saint-German (PSG), and Hapoel Tel Aviv.[199] Clearly, therefore, what people can see has the potential to lead to real anger and violence.

The emergence of new media puts into question the efficacy of silencing extreme voices in institutions, be that Mosques, schools, or prisons. Even if these places are closed down, or radicals denied a physical platform, what good is that when all this stuff can be accessed in your bedroom? If anything, this underscores the importance of sunlight as the best disinfectant, the importance of free speech as a means of identifying, and in turn countering, extremist ideas. By keeping an eye on these places, rather than allowing individuals to find hate in an unrestricted cyberspace, we will, at least in some measure, be better placed to push back against the manipulation and grooming of extremist inclined preachers and influencers.

Regardless, social media companies are going to work judiciously to ensure their platforms are not being used to incite and inspire violence, particularly when it comes to malleable young and disgruntled men. I am no expert with regards to how we best limit the influence of online radicalization, but when the arena of the online world has changed the way

---

[198] ibid, p.231.
[199] ibid, p.231.

in which anti-Jewish, anti-Western thinking is passed down, the approach of yesteryear, if there ever was one, is no longer fit for purpose.

Section Two of this chapter has considered where this hatred is coming from in Western Europe. It has considered the roles of social interactions, institutionalized racism, and poisoned digital agencies, which have allowed antisemitism to proliferate throughout our Muslim communities, with little to no resistance. Beyond the complexity of this issue, what remains blindingly obvious, is that so long as nothing changes to deal with these communal sources, then no matter how robust our borders, how hardline our policies of integration, or how vociferous the statements from politicians, nothing will improve. As we shall see, the antidote to this crisis is difficult and multifaceted, but like with any worsening situation, necessary and urgent.

This work has explored the issues which have led to the development of antisemitism among Muslims in Western Europe. What now needs to be discussed is the elephant in the room, the issue of Israel and Palestine. It is this issue which is rightly and wrongly said to be the real reason for why antisemitism is seemingly out of control amongst Western European Muslims.

Section Three: anti-Israelism and its extreme alliances

As noted in the introduction, there are many who regard anti-Jewish feeling and activity amongst Muslims to be the sole consequence of Zionism, and the actions of its progeny, the State of Israel. As elaborated in the first section of this chapter, however, anti-Jewish feeling amongst Muslims pre-dates both factors. Although it can be said that baseless conspiracies about the Jewish-State is one of most significant modes through which antisemitism amongst Muslims is expressed, there exists, as discussed in the first section, a historical tradition of animosity towards Jews within the Islamic world that long predates the events of 1948.

Before we turn to the role of Middle Eastern politics, I feel compelled to give the usual, albeit platitudinous, disclaimers. Criticisms of Israel and her government are not, on their own, antisemitic. If they were, scores of Israelis, many of whom regularly protest, lambast, lampoon, and vituperate their government, would be antisemites. One can make criticisms of all aspects of Israeli society and government, and do so without apology, without being an antisemite. In fact, as with any democratic state, it is a necessary function to hold the government of the day accountable. But there is a line. When criticism goes from proportionate to wholly disproportionate, holding Israel to a singular standard which no other nation on earth is held to, and even denying that state, the place upon which Jews worldwide depend on for their safety and dignity, the right to exist, your motivations become, at best, suspect, and at worst, plain, repackaged, Jew-hate. Reminiscent of Sartre's work decades earlier, Taguieff views the Zionism targeted by anti-Zionists as "an imaginary construct, a fiction." For this reason, he claims, "If Zionism had not existed, the "anti-Zionists" would have invented it," adding, "they did in fact reinvent it, constructing a totally repulsive entity out of rumors, prejudices, stereotypes, and legends, an entity mean to be totally rejected and ultimately suppressed."[200] Indeed, over the years, thanks to the influence of the Soviet propaganda machine, rhetoric around Israel has become redolent of the beast of the past. The conspiracies surrounding the Jewish State, which have become present in all communities, but especially our Muslim communities, has given post-Holocaust antisemitism a new lease of life.

It would be honest to acknowledge that, although the conflagration of 1967 was a major turning point in the way it led to the popularisation of conspiratorial anti-Israelism, there were clear traces of this beforehand. The following examples, from leading Nazis, reveals how Zionism was, even in the days before the State of Israel, greeted with diabolical suspicion. In 1922, Alfred Rosenberg, an infamous Nazi ideologue, in his, 'Der staatsfeindliche Zionismus' (Zionism, The Enemy of the State), argued that Zionism was not about Jewish national liberation, but world Jewish domination. Agreeing with this, Adolf Hitler in Mein Kampf suggested that, "While the Zionists try to make the rest of the world believe that the national consciousness of the Jew finds its satisfaction in the creation of a Palestinian state, the Jews again slyly dupe the dumb Goyim." He added, "It doesn't even enter their heads to build up a Jewish

---

[200] Taguieff, Pierre-André. *Rising from the Muck: The New Anti-Semitism in Europe.* p.19.

state in Palestine for the purpose of living there; all they want is a central organization for their international world swindle."[201]

Does this ring a bell? These attitudes, plucked straight out of Nazi literature, have become pervasive globally, but especially within the Islamic world. The former King of Morocco, Hassan II, rightly pointed out: "The hatred for Israel is the most powerful aphrodisiac in the Arab world."[202] Although there has been much progress since the Abraham Accords, or, the beginning of normalization agreements between Israel and several Muslim states, the potency of anti-Israelism remains a present and uniting force across the *Umma*. The objection to this, of course, is that Israel is to blame. If it did not treat the Palestinians so appallingly, so this argument goes, this would not exist. Yet while no state in war, particularly one fighting for its very survival, will be free of mistakes and errors, anti-Israelism in the Muslim-world exists beyond a purported concern for the welfare of their Palestinian brothers. To appreciate the depth of its feeling one must see its existence outside a mere reaction to the actions of the Israeli state. There is something, if you will, distinctly metaphysical about this war on Israel's legitimacy.

Both Zionism and Israel represent the very negation of dhimmitude, and for that matter, the idea that Jews can be self-governing in territory which was once conquered by Islam. The belief that Jews must be subordinate to Muslims under Islamic rule, particularly in this land, remains a powerful feeling in the Islamist orbit. In an important sense, Jewish self-determination on that land serves to refute the traditional perspective that Jews are weak, defeated, and a people that must submit themselves, as dhimmis, to the rule and (potential) magnanimity of Islamic rulers. Indeed, in Islamist thought, this young state, by its very existence, has converted the image of the Jew from subject to subjugator of Muslims. The war against Israel is thus, to no small extent, driven by the all-consuming rage in opposition to Israel's raison d'etere - encapsulated in

---

[201] Cited in Hitler, Adolf. Extracts from *Mein Kampf.* Yad Vashem. https://www.yadvashem.org/docs/extracts-from-mein-kampf.html

[202] Cited in Bruckner, Pascal "There's No Such Thing as Islamophobia." *City Journal.* Summer, 2017 https://www.city-journal.org/article/theres-no-such-thing-as-islamophobia

the Hatkikvah, its national anthem - "To be a free people in our land. The land of Zion and Jerusalem."

Make no mistake: the desire for statehood, and the commensurate wish for Palestinian dignity, should not be considered antisemitic pursuits. And they are not. However, it has become apparent that this cause has become indistinguishable from a much more shady pursuit: the destruction of the Jewish-state, and in its stead, the emergence of an Islamist theocracy between the Mediterranean sea and the Jordan river. Although liberals have a tendency to deny this, all they need do is listen to the various utterances of Islamic rulers and scholars, not to mention the chants heard at global Palestine demonstrations. For in the Islamic world, there is little, if any, distinction made between Israeli, Zionist, and Jew. Amongst scores of Muslims, the Palestinian cause has been the cause of all causes, which has transcended all cultural, religious and political divides. It is the cause par excellence that has succeeded in galvanizing Muslims from all backgrounds to rally behind the Palestinian flag. But this cause is about much more than a claim to a land, one the size of Wales. It is also taking a stand against what it regards to be a malefic, eternally damned, colonial minded Western hegemony, which is perceived to be the very reason as to why not only Israel exists, but why all things antithetical and indeed harmful to the Islamist worldview exist. Accordingly, the seemingly insoluble war against Israel is emblematic of a much wider Islamist war launched against the Jewish rights, as well as the very legitimacy of the West and its values.

However, a requisite component of this burgeoning anti-Israelism is that these dangerous views have been koshered and enabled by non-Muslim actors. In a 1974 interview, Jean Genet, the prolific left-wing French author opined, "Why the Palestinians? It was perfectly natural that I should be attracted not only to the most disadvantaged people but also to the one that most fully crystallizes hatred of the West."[203] This quotation best encapsulates why, in Western Europe, this anti-Israelism has been permitted to blossom. It has found an ideological (as well as political) alliance with large sections of the left which, in various political, social,

---

[203] Cited in Bruckner, Pascal. *The Tyranny of Guilt: An Essay on Western Masochism.* Translated by Steven Rendall. Princeton: Princeton University Press, 2010.

and academic settings, has legitimated and indulged this genocidal ideology. In the view of this millenarian far-left ideology, the Palestinians are the new proletarian; they, above anyone else, are the people which demand the attention of all revolutionary left-wing movements. In a sense, they are the new Jews: the victims of an oppressive system which must be brought down only through revolution, or by any means of resistance. Including terror. The struggle is no longer against the evil machinations of capitalism, but against the diabolicalities of Zionism, which, in their eyes, is the First Cause of all that is destructive to mankind. In forging an alliance with the bloodthirsty, racist, sexist and homophobic cause of Islamism, leftist sophists have had to relinquish their long-standing and universalist convictions on the rights of those they have traditionally defended, especially Jews. The once politics of progress which once stood by secularism, universal suffrage, liberty, now demonstrate an unwavering fidelity to movements responsible for suffering and terror. And yes, we are supposed to believe these are the movements of progress.

What is central in in this strange partnership between Islamism and the hard-left, often dubbed the 'red-green alliance,' is a shared loathing for all things Western, and Israel, as a Jewish force, is ultimately perceived to be the defining essence of this irredeemable satanic Western hegemony. The Islamist call to destroy Israel has been lent, by virtue of its support by the cognitive dissonance of the 'tolerant' Left, an air of social and intellectual acceptability. One needs to look no further than at various social-liberation movements, universities, as well as the activities of prominent left-wing politicians in the region to see this alliance in action. Perhaps unsurprising, therefore, that both view the evisceration of the West in a positive light. One anti-Western ideologue, Serge Latouche, a professor of economics, suggested that "the death of the West will not necessarily be the end of the world," but, he added, "the condition for the blossoming of new worlds, of a new civilization, a new era."[204] While this statement is not calling for Jihad, or any kind of violent retribution against the West, this particular utterance is reminiscent of one made by an Islamist: the destruction of the West, as a democratic community of nations, will present an opportunity for a new order to take charge. In many

---

[204] ibid.

cases, though not necessarily in the case of Latouche, the end of the Jewish State is an indispensable step in this process, perhaps, even, its precondition. Too often in these minacious circles, anti-Israelism, as well as being a fashionable cloak for Jew-hatred, is a crucial démarche towards the end of the West.

The university space is the epicenter of this unholy alliance. I've had my own experience of this, witnessing Palestinian events on campus, in which religious Muslim students' team-up with rainbow-flag-waving leftists, whom agree on nothing, except vilifying and delegitimizing Israel and the West. On this, they are soulmates. One vivid memory takes me back to 2017, at the School of Oriental and African Studies (SOAS), in which a range of far-left organizations turned up, including the socialists and the risible 'Gays for Palestine,' both of whom stood beside religious Muslim staff and students, in opposing the presence of the Israeli ambassador (incidentally, the same students excoriate the IHRA definition of antisemitism because of concerns this undermines freedom of speech. All speech is equal, but some speech is more equal than others.) At this demonstration, one far-left, white-male, proudly exclaimed, 'Victory to Hamas; Victory to Hezbollah.' These Islamist organizations, if this needs saying, are explicitly genocidal, homophobic, racist, and no different from any white-supremacist, Neo-Nazi organization (although these Islamist groups command political influence). All the while, this individual, who presumably purports to stand up for the rights of minorities and oppressed, saw that these fascist groups could be, to borrow from Jeremy Corbyn, his 'friends.' Such noisy hard left students not only are the 'useful idiots' of religious fanaticism, but they, as the well-intentioned progressives, hold the gates open for barbarism to enter untrammeled. And anyone who challenges them, or their cause, is, vituperatively and scurrilously maligned as a racist.

This Molotov–Ribbentrop Pact of our age has indeed been reinforced by many far-left academics who devote much of their time, in some cases all of it, to educating their students about the evils of Zionism and Israel. As such, there are some university campuses, particularly the likes of SOAS, which young Jews increasingly avoid. I will never forget the May of 2021, during that bloody conflict, in which the president of my Jewish

Society at UCL sent a message to our WhatsApp group suggesting that "if anyone is returning to campus over the next few days and can work remotely instead I strongly encourage you to stay away from UCL." This was the first university in Britain to have admitted Jews, and yet, due to the hostility generated by far-left and Muslim students at a time of great tension in the Middle East, Jewish students were being encouraged by their peers, understandably, to stay away for their own safety. Although the president did reassure students that security was going to be extra vigilant, this is not normal. Indeed, nothing that has been discussed can be regarded as tolerable or normal. It is a damnable and unforgivable indictment on not only our education system, but the society which produces this kind of intellectual bigotry.

We must remember, however, universities are not only places of higher education. These centers of learning are also businesses. The reality is that many institutions around the world are in receipt of money from overtly antisemitic sources. The Institute for the Study of Global Antisemitism and Policy (ISGAP) in their 2020 paper '*Examining Undocumented Foreign Funding of American Universities: Implications for Education and Rising Antisemitism,*' found that, in the past few years, "totalitarian Middle Eastern regimes, terrorist organizations, foundations, and affiliated private corporations have funneled billions of dollars to American universities with a view to promoting an environment that encourages the demonization of Israel and the Jewish people within the curriculum and on campus."[205] Of the billions which have been poured in from Middle Eastern states to US universities, most of which are in the Gulf, "Qatari donors account for 75% of Middle Eastern donations… while the Qatar Foundation accounts for virtually all the donations from the Persian Gulf kingdom."[206] Moreover, "these funds have a significant impact on campus attitudes, including the emergence of an antisemitic culture and BDS activities at some of the most important universities in

---

[205] Small, Charles Asher, and Michael Bass. "Examining Undocumented Foreign Funding of American Universities: Implications for Education and Rising Antisemitism." Vol. 2. New York: *Institute for the Study of Global Antisemitism and Policy* (ISGAP), September 2020. https://isgap.org/wp-content/uploads/2020/09/ISGAP-Report-Volume-II-3.pdf. p.6.
[206] ibid, p.5.

the United States." As such, this ISGAP report found that within the United States alone, there is "a direct correlation between the funding of universities by Qatar and the Gulf States and the active presence at those universities of groups that have been proven to foster an aggressive and hostile antisemitic atmosphere on campus..."[207] This is to say, antisemitism has risen to prominence not because of a change in the intellectual climate. But because there are actors beyond our shores who are funding it.

Alas, there is no similar study of the situation in the European context. However, we know there has been Qatari involvement in universities outside of the United States. For instance, in their 2015 paper, *Gulf-funding of British Universities and the Focus on Human Development*, published in the Middle East Law and Governance journal, Jonas Bergan Draege and Martin Lestra, noted that between 1997 and 2007, Gulf entities gave UK institutions around £70,000,000.[208] Indeed, Abudulkhaleq Abdula, a scholar from the UAE, stated, "UK universities are the oldest Gulf think-tanks in the world."[209] As such, Madawi al-Rasheed, a Saudi critic and scholar, suggested, "They [Gulf donors] are creating a sphere of influence at universities ... It's an indirect influence, rather than a direct one."[210] And they are influencing our institutions. The venality of our universities has a range of implications, not only in terms of antisemitism, but in contributing to what studies have found to be an outbreak of radicalization on campus.

More studies will need to be undertaken to evaluate the extent to which this problem exists in Western Europe, however, it is the case that there are universities or sections within these institutions, which are influenced by these antisemitic, anti-democratic, extremist donors. This not only brings into question the very integrity of academic freedom but as a consequence of taking this money, many universities, across our region

---

[207] ibid, p.5.
[208] Cited in England, Andrew and Simeon Kerr "Universities challenged: scrutiny over Gulf money." *Financial Times,* Dec 13, 2018. https://www.ft.com/content/fa6d15a4-f6ed-11e8-af46-2022a0b02a6c
[209] ibid.
[210] ibid.

and beyond, suffer from an institutionalized, and funded problem, of antisemitism.

There are those who pooh-pooh this being a mere proclivity for eccentric leftist scholars, rendering what occurs in the university space as inconsequential. In fact, in 2015, Boris Johnson, who was Mayor of London at the time, in a characteristically humorous speech he gave in Israel, dismissed the BDS campaign against Israel by suggesting that "the supporters of this so-called boycott are really a bunch of, you know, corduroy-jacketed academics." He continued, "They are by and large lefty academics who have no real standing in the matter and I think are highly unlikely to be influential on Britain. This is a very, very small minority in our country who are calling for this."[211] While it may be only a minority (perhaps a hefty minority) of academics who believe in a boycott of Israel, antisemitism in the academy is not to be sneered at. Historically speaking, the fictitious notions of racial hierarchies and heredities -which would be used by the Nazis to justify their genocidal actions - emerged in the academy, in the arena of intellectuals. In other words, the place these falsehoods had in scholarly circles gave the Nazi creed, centered on a belief in Aryan-supremacy, legitimacy and acceptability. Indeed, even when the Nazis came to power, though there was some resistance in the universities, notably the White Rose movement, Nazism was a seductive force to a large number of students and scholars.

It was rightly pointed out by George Orwell that, "there are some ideas so absurd that only an intellectual could believe them." In our case, anti-Israelism is the refashioning of a very old bug. The intellectual reverence lent to this ideology provides those who work towards such destructive ends with a justification, indeed a motivation, for their actions. And as the historical record demonstrates, when intellectuals make Jew-bashing sexy, this leads to deadly consequences.

So far, only the far-left and Islamism has been considered. But the far-right also joins this party. What has been described as the 'triple-threat,' describes the three major security risks to Britain and Europe: the far-right, the far-left and Islamism. The common denominator for these three groups

---

[211] Cited in Neumann, Jonathan. "Boris Johnson, BDS." *Commentary,* November 12, 2015. https://www.commentary.org/jonathan-neumann/boris-johnson-bds/

is their shared hatred for Jews. It has become apparent that certain far-right movements have been willing to compromise on their racist, white supremacist policies to team up with the radical-left and Islamists, in the war against both Israel and Jews. Although far-right anti-Israelism is less common than similar sentiments expressed from the left, an interesting case in point is Nick Griffin, who has a conviction for incitement to racial hatred, and former leader of the racist British National Party. This convicted racist declared his support for Jeremy Corbyn, a self-proclaimed anti racist, when it emerged that the far-left leader of the Labor Party stated a few years earlier that British Zionists, "having lived in this country for a very long time, probably all their lives, they don't understand English irony..."[212] It is no coincidence that Griffin offered his support for Corbyn. It is the shared loathing for Jews and/or Israel that brings these extremes together.

There are other such examples of this 'unholy' trinity of Jew-hatred. For our purposes, though, the assault upon Israel, which is perhaps one of (if not the most) common expressions of Muslim antisemitism has found support and thus been reinforced across the political spectrum, mostly, though, from the far-left. As such, the implacable hatred of the Jewish nation is not only the most enticing aphrodisiac in the Islamic world, but has found a home across all political extremes which use this issue to undermine the basic human-rights and dignity of Jews, the people who knit together these forces of hate. Indeed, in particular, the ideological support bestowed upon Islamism has meant that its aims go unchallenged. The disturbing levels of Muslim antisemitic actions we see, in the name of Palestinian activism, has occurred precisely because of its permissibility in these outside circles. And this, as ever, is a threat to not only Jews, but the very fabric of our civilization.

---

[212] Tapsfield, James, "Former BNP chief Nick Griffin praises Corbyn over slur on 'British Zionists,'" *Daily Mail,* October 6, 2018, https://www.dailymail.co.uk/news/article-6094457/Go-Jezza-Former-BNP-chief-Nick-Griffin-praises-Corbyn-slur-British-Zionists.html

The Troubling Future

This chapter has considered the various sources of contemporary Islamist inspired antisemitism in Western Europe. It refutes the all-too-often made arguments that this hatred exists as a mere reaction to socioeconomic issues, discrimination, and/or a response to Israel's treatment of the Palestinians. Rather, though it can be said these factors add fuel to the fire, they are not, as this chapter has argued, the genesis of what has become the greatest threat to Jewish life in the region. Rather, its roots run much deeper, and the sources of contemporary Muslim antisemitism are multifaceted.

However, before concluding, it's worth seeing how this could get worse before it gets better. One study, undertaken by Pew in 2017, looked at what the Muslim population of Europe might look like by 2050. It offered three different potential scenarios of future Muslim population forecasts in the continent. In one such scenario, it suggests that even if "all migration into Europe were to immediately and permanently stop – a "zero migration" scenario," this would still mean "the Muslim population of Europe still would be expected to rise from the current level of 4.9% to 7.4% by the year 2050." In a "medium" migration scenario, it points out that high levels of refugee flows will stop, "but that recent levels of "regular" migration to Europe will continue," and as such, "Muslims could reach 11.2% of Europe's population in 2050." In a third scenario, a "high migration scenario," predicts that the high levels of migration seen from 2015 onwards will continue indefinitely. Consequently, in this case, "Muslims could make up 14% of Europe's population by 2050 – nearly triple the current share, but still considerably smaller than the populations of both Christians and people with no religion in Europe."

Although this report notes that it is impossible to predict future migration levels, this study, with its three different scenarios, "provides a set of rough parameters from which to imagine other possible outcomes." If we look at specific countries in Western Europe, we can see just how significant these changes would be. Some notable examples include, for instance, Germany, in which the Muslim population in the high migration scenario could grow from nearly 5 million in 2016 to almost 17.5 million 2050, and to 8.5 million and almost 6 million in the medium and zero scenarios respectively. In Sweden, the Muslim population in the high migration scenario could grow from 810,000 in 2016 to almost 5 million, and to 2.5 million and 1.13 million in the medium and zero scenarios respectively. In the UK, the Muslim population in the high-migration scenario could grow from 4.13 million in 2016 to almost 13.5 million in 2050, and to nearly 13.1 million and nearly 6.6 million in the medium and zero scenarios respectively. In France, although figures are harder to establish here due to the French state not recording religious attachments, the Muslim population in the high-migration scenario could grow from nearly 6 million in 2016 to 13.21 million in 2050, and to nearly 12.7 million and nearly 9 million in the medium and zero scenarios respectively.

Interestingly, and perhaps importantly, this study also found that, "while Europe's Muslim population is expected to grow in all three scenarios – and more than double in the medium and high migration scenarios – Europe's non-Muslims, on the other hand, are projected to decline in total number in each scenario." It added, "Taken as a whole, Europe's population (including both Muslims and non-Muslims) would be expected to decline considerably (from about 521 million to an estimated 482 million) without any future migration. In the medium migration scenario, it would remain roughly stable, while in the high migration scenario it would be projected to grow modestly."[213]

What is clear, Islam in Europe is growing, and is the fastest growing global religion. And although Muslims are not a monolith, and have diverse communities, like any other minority, the growth of this population, certainly has implications for our purposes. Put simply, if nothing is done to address the issues this book explores, with forecasts predicting a definite population growth, this will become a crisis so impregnable that Jews may be forced to reassess their place in the countries they have made home. Indeed, to make matters worse, this population growth also serves to further dissuade politicians and policymakers from involving themselves in fixing this crisis. If anything,

---

[213] Pew Research Center. "Europe's Growing Muslim Population." November 29, 2017. Accessed March 6, 2025. https://www.pewresearch.org/religion/2017/11/29/europes-growing-muslim-population/

may actually lead to politicians in Europe to adopt policies hostile towards Israel, and by implication, Jews. But more on this in the next chapter.

For now, the crisis of Jew-hatred in our Muslim communities needs to be faced. The culture of not grappling with this crisis is not only a betrayal to Jews, the very people to whom Europe swore never-again, but also to its commitment to liberalism, democracy, and the rule of law. If there is to be a future for that which we hold dear, our leaders must be willing to confront the harsh truths this chapter has explored.

Before considering what can be done, we must first try to understand why this has been permitted to happen in the first place. In other words, why has this intolerance been tolerated?

Chapter Three:
Why are we here?

Our diversity, the cornerstone of our humanity, is not to blame for this crisis. There has been a lamentable failure to manage our cultural-differences; and that failure is one of government across Western Europe. We are here because those in power have been negligent to the same degree as they have been well-intentioned in trying to engineer a utopia (a word we would do well to remember translates as 'no place'). And with each year that passes, with their continued reluctance to deal with the issues this book has raised, our elected representatives, entrusted with the welfare of all, are guilty of harming the very societies they are sworn to protect.

Before exploring this further, we must examine the seismic transformation of Europe after 1945. Various post-war developments, not least in the realms of democratic processes and human rights, have made our societies more open, stable, and liberal. But in addition to this social and political progress, Western Europe has witnessed an astonishing change in migration and demographics.

The region, of course, has always had its minorities, as well as migration to its shores, including that from the Islamic world. This was happening well before the twentieth century. What happened in the post-war period, however, was markedly different from previous years of migration, both quantitatively and qualitatively, that is, in terms of both the numbers of those who have since arrived, and the places from which they came.

Since the end of the war, there have been several waves of migration to Europe, which included various cultural and ethnic groups, many of whom have been of Muslim background, albeit from vastly different places. Over the years, those who left their countries of origin did so for multiple reasons, including for economic opportunities, refuge, family considerations, and some for an amalgamation of these and other reasons. Most of those who came, particularly because of decolonization, arrived as so called "guest-workers," or people that would come to Europe, and when the demand for their labor would cease, they would return home. In practice, to the surprise of European leaders, most did not return. They remained and made these countries their new home. Even when this program came to an end in the early 1970s, migration from former colonies, amongst other places, continued. This was hastened as a result of laxed laws on family reunification, which many were understandably eager to make the most of, and in doing so, re-established their families in this continent.

Overall, although it is hard, even impossible, to quantify the exact figures of those who have arrived over the past eighty-odd years, as well as the fact that there are country-based variations, migration over the years, notably from Islamic nations, has increased by several million. The speed of change on the demographics front, particularly from the latter part of the previous century, has been both exponential and unprecedented. The change in many towns and cities across Western Europe, demographically speaking, has been major. And done, I hasten to add, without any democratic consent from the people who reside in affected areas.

Speaking in 2015, the then German Chancellor, Angela Merkel, in a speech she gave about the European migration crisis, asserted, in the face of much criticism, that Germany should take in those fleeing Syria and the Middle East. With her words of "Wir schaffen das," we can manage this, between 2015 and 2020, five million asylum seekers arrived into Europe, with 40 per cent of which settling in her country.[214] Notwithstanding the various issues which have arisen out of this policy, Merkel's statement is indicative of a particular negligence which has existed in Europe over the years: a well-intentioned, but misplaced view, that Western European governments can manage large numbers arriving to our nations, at an

---

[214] Nöstlinger, Nette "Revisiting Merkel's refugee pledge: Has Germany 'managed it?'" *Politico EU* Dec, 2021. https://www.politico.eu/article/angela-merkel-refugee-pledge-we-can-manage-it/

unparalleled pace, coming from places in which the cultural attitudes are vastly different, even antithetical to our own.

The point needs to be reiterated, however, that having a society which makes space for difference does not, necessarily, lead to cultural conflict, and a break down in social cohesion. So long as it is managed responsibly, a multicultural society enriches nations and serves to strengthen their democracies. The very idea of what the Germans describe as *Willkommenskultur*, or a welcoming culture towards cultural difference, which is at the heart of multiculturalism, is not, in principle, a bad idea. For we find a profound wisdom in diverse crowds. Yet we have not made the most of difference. Far from it.

From 1945, our region's policies towards migration and multiculturalism have been chiefly driven by economic and practical considerations rather than the ostensibly obsolete notions of shared culture, identity, and values. But not all that is 'good' can be quantified in terms of its economic benefit. Do we want migrants only for their labor, or do we want those to come here to be a part of our collective future and story? Liberal elites, who have been at the forefront of Western Europe's migratory policies, have little interest in this question. The territory of non-financial interests is not a burning issue on their agenda. If anything, it is an inconvenience; and one which stands in the way of progress. But their failure, indeed negligence, to take this issue seriously, has led to societies in which people of all backgrounds live in the same place, side-by-side, but not really, it seems, together. And the clear absence of this sense of togetherness, compounded by unprecedented and unsustainable rates of migration to Europe, has provided the necessary preconditions for divisions, inequalities, a burgeoning rejection of liberal-democratic ideals, and an emboldening of right-wing populism in the region. This negligence has unwittingly imperiled the positions of such liberal elites, as well as those targeted by illiberal forces.

For the avoidance of doubt, our leaders and those in other relevant authorities are not oblivious to this reality of multiculturalism, nor to the resurgence of Jew-bashing, and the extent to which this threatens Jewish life in Western Europe. Even though I have presented a variety of studies that attest to the seriousness of this problem, I haven't told governments and state officials anything new. They know full well. And so, their pitiful efforts cannot be excused by ignorance. Nor should the contents of this chapter be used to get those responsible off the hook. It has been under the watch of successive liberal-democratic governments that this worsening tide of antisemitism and extremist thinking has gone unchallenged. This chapter explores what has disincentivized those in elected positions from taking action, but is not, in any way, a justification for their self-induced political impotence.

Therefore, the question to which we must now turn is why governments have been so derelict in their duties to all their citizens. As with the previous chapter, a culmination of the following factors explains this, namely: 1. The Politics of Fear; 2. The Politics of Numbers; and 3. The Politics of Identity (or lack of it). A blend of these three has rendered those who represent us to be not merely negligent, but through their own reluctance, complicit. This chapter argues that so long as these factors remain in place, liberal-democratic governments will continue to move away from the ideas and values which they readily defend. With that, let us turn to the first of these factors.

Section One: The Politics of Fear

While in a seminar, a professor encouraged a class discussion about Islamism in Europe. To vivify the sullen mood which had gripped the classroom, I raised the point that in order to challenge this militant ideology, we need to recognize that while far from synonymous, it does have some connection to Islam. For making this perfectly legitimate observation, made by many, a non-Muslim student, with rage in their voice, tempestuously asserted, "this debate needs to end now." The professor, without any hesitation, agreed and moved swiftly on with the class – without really engaging with the point I had just made. Although disappointed, I remained uncharacteristically schtum, and got on with making notes, or, at least, pretended to do so. But at the end of class, this student decided that the debate hadn't really ended, and pursued me down the corridor, and then out of the building, frequently describing me and my views to be "Islamophobic."

For even daring to talk about some of the issues we see in the Islamic world today, to their easily offended sensibilities, my words were racist. In response to this idiotic charge, I pointed out that, as a Jew, who has his ancestry in Eastern-Europe, I am more than prepared to speak out against the weaponization of Christian ideas which provided the foundations for the suffering of my ancestors. Therefore, "why," I asked, "is that not Christianophobic?" In response, they spoke of societal power structures, which necessarily privilege white-people, or the idea that because Muslims are non-white (which is not necessarily true; Islam, is a religion, not a 'race'), talking about these issues is inherently racist. But what this interaction demonstrates is how a seemingly well-educated, progressive-minded individual refuses to even discuss the very real issues within Islam. In the name of well-intentioned progressivism and anti-racism, to that individual and others who share their views, that discussion cannot even take place. To even discuss it, so they think, is to lend credence to racist forces. And, therefore, to avoid this cardinal sin, we must keep quiet.

There are plenty such examples which speak to this, but I begin with this anecdote since it led me to ask why those, who would be the first to speak out if the perpetrators of hate and similar crimes were Christian (specifically, white Christian men), exhibit a deafening silence in the face of Islamist crimes? A factor which plays a critical role is this reluctance, and this negligence, is a deep-rooted, two-fold fear. Firstly, that of being regarded as an Islamophobe, which has been synonymized with racism, the most reprehensible ideology invented by man. Secondly, that of retribution, which might result from daring to do something that runs the risk of upsetting Islamist sensibilities. These, as we shall see, are all legitimate concerns. But such concerns have given rise to a societal disinclination to talk about some of the difficult realities we see in modern Islam. And this fear has reached the highest levels of government.

With regards to this fear of being labelled a racist, in one sense, it is a testament to the huge strides we have made that this heinous creed is so widely frowned upon. Yet inasmuch as we are far less tolerant of intolerance, our hyper-awareness of racial-sensitivities has led to an over-correction, which itself has created confusion, distortion, and profound misunderstanding, particularly when it comes to the much-needed conversations about Islamism. In the name of Islamophobia, a term scarcely used before the 1980s, issues we see within our Muslim communities, both globally and in Europe, are ignored and swept under the carpet. For who, after all, wants to be accused of racism?

Before we explore this further, to be clear: there are, tragically, criminal and deplorable acts of abuse, harassment, and violence against Muslims because they are Muslim, which is deserving of the label anti-Muslim hatred. Indeed, in recent years, there have been an alarming number of these incidents, perpetrated by the far-right, on Muslim individuals and places of worship. This poison of anti-Muslim-hatred is a loathsome and murderous doctrine, as witnessed in Christchurch back in 2019, which must be met with the full force of the law. For the sake of ensuring our liberal societies remain liberal, we cannot afford to be complacent. And it is, in part, for this reason why I joined the Association of British Muslims, the oldest Islamic organization in the UK, as its Head of Research and Policy. I wanted to work with my cousins and those of all faiths in calling out this ideology, in its multiple and varied forms.

However, contrary to popular opinion, anti-Muslim-hatred is not Islamophobia. Speaking of the latter, the venerable French philosopher and public intellectual, Pascal Bruckner, who has written extensively on this subject, points out that this term "was a clever invention because it amounts to making Islam a subject that one cannot touch without being accused of racism."[215] He reasons that when Islamophobia became popular in the 1980s, particularly after the Rushdie Affair, it was, and has since been used, as a strategy of Islamists to dismiss any perceived "dishonoring of Islam," which includes critiques, satire, or dissent, as expressions of racism. Appealing to the post-modernist anti-racist forces, which continue to this day, this term has led many to view Islam, a religion, as having a racial component, and therefore, it follows; to challenge Islam or its orthodoxies is to make a racially prejudicial assertion. Of course, such statements can be bigoted, but not necessarily nor always, and most do not even come close, even if Islamist spokespeople pretend otherwise. If anything, the opposite must be emphatically vindicated: holding Islam to the same standards as any other organized religion is essential in not only ensuring a cohesive and just society, but in challenging a perception,

---

[215] Pascal Bruckner, *The Tyranny of Guilt: An Essay on Western Masochism,* p.48.

which does seem to have merit, that these serious issues are hushed up in our Muslim communities.

Nevertheless, this false conflation between challenging ideas and race hate, has become a trend which seems unstoppable in certain circles. There are many such examples which attests to this, but here, I shall focus on two egregious cases of the pernicious and unconscionable efforts to undermine free expression.

The first takes us back to my time at school, when I first noticed this attempt by well-intentioned liberals to advocate, albeit not in explicit terms, for blasphemy laws. At this Orthodox Jewish High School, in which Jewish pupils are the minority (more on this further down), an external organization came into speak about racism, antisemitism, and so called 'British-values.' During this talk to a group of spotty and bedraggled, but suggestible teens, I recall their representative turned to the subject of Islamophobia, and declared that the cartoons used by Charlie were indeed racist. This figure of authority sullied this publication and those who were murdered by suggesting that although the attacks were wrong, they were the architects of their own bloody fate for what they injudiciously dismissed as racist caricatures. Even then, I realized either they were plain ignorant, or intentionally silent on the fact that this magazine has a long-established record of mocking everyone, and its best work has been in its derision of the Pope and Marine Le Pen. Upon hearing these asinine remarks, and knowing them to be an insult to those who paid the price for free expression, I could not bite my tongue, and be the servile teen my classmates wanted me to be. With seething haste, I retorted vociferously, "Offending a religion is not the same as racism," because "you can't be racially prejudiced against ideas and values." But the visitor, adamant to shut me down, said words to the effect of, "but Muslims find it offensive, so therefore, it's racist!" This protracted argument was not, I should tell you, held cordially or with decorum. My then precocious and pugnacious disposition was overwhelmed with unmistakable indignation that someone, with the apparent credentials to promote 'anti- racism' in schools, would suggest that blasphemy is tantamount to an expression of racism. But this was not an isolated incident. Throughout the Western world, and especially in the Anglosphere, for publishing what many saw as blasphemous, Charlie had become the new Der Stürmer. That's right: a publication fit for Nazi Germany.

With a disarming incisiveness, such arguments, nonsensical though they are, were rubbished by Robert McLiam Wilson, a journalist at the magazine. In his article for The Guardian, entitled, *The Scurrilous Lies Written About Charlie Hebdo,* he quips, "If Charlie Hebdo is racist then it's not very good at it." He not only observes Charlie's continued and interminable assault upon the populist right, but also the "routine and constant support of Charlie on the part of SOS Racisme, France's main anti-racism campaigning group." Indeed, he continues, "And know too that justice minister, Christiane Taubira, the "victim" of the infamous monkey cartoon, was so wounded and offended that she gave an extraordinary, moving speech at the funeral of one of the murdered cartoonists."[216] On those grounds, this magazine is certainly not to be found on the coffee tables of Nick Griffin or Jean-Marie Le Pen. One would have to find a pretty confused, or low-grade racist, to approve of Charlie's material.

However, not only are these charges absurd, but they are also exceedingly dangerous. When McLiam Wilson first became a journalist with Charlie, after the shootings, he described what it was like walking into the new office of the magazine:

> *A few days ago, I went into the new, secret-location, super-secure offices of Charlie. Being Northern Irish, security was not unfamiliar to me but this was on a different level. It was the villain's lair in one of the dumber Bond films, hermetically sealed, massively protected. And yet inside was a typical small magazine set-up – not many people, untidy kitchen, debatable dress sense. And a bunch of gentle, humble, funny people that I adore. As always when I see Charlie people en masse, there's a giant disconnect. I see a troupe of nerdy sweethearts surrounded by concentric rings of titanic security. They look like kittens in a bunker. I'm tempted to say that this is now the world they live in. But that's not what is*

---

[216] Wilson, Robert McLiam. "Charlie Hebdo: scurrilous reports by non-French speakers." *The Guardian,* January 3, 2016. https://www.theguardian.com/commentisfree/2016/jan/03/charlie-hebdo-scurrilous-reports-by-non-french-speakers

interesting. The point is that this is now the world you live in.[217]

The intellectual and cultural vilification of Charlie has provided those murderous fanatics with the permission they could not do without. In the mind of those kind-hearted, yet obsequious and supercilious anti-racists: yes, the actions of those Islamists are wrong, but their vexation and desire for vengeance are not illegitimate. Their victims had it coming. It was their own darn fault. This magazine, so they say, is racist. The haughtiness of these people knows no bounds. Such an inversion and perversion of truth has contributed to the rotten and terrifying circumstances journalists and workers at this publication continue to find themselves living under. Those we would entrust to stand up for the voice of dissent have given those fanatics who viciously persecute any form of 'blasphemy' a cover, a respectability, even a justification, for their calculated wickedness. Such lies are not only cruel, unjust, and supremely idiotic, but they also underpin the violent scenes we see throughout the West.

Another such example of this conflation between blasphemy and racism takes us, once again, to France. This time, to the case of Mila, who back in 2020 said some rather disobliging things about Islam. Sixteen at the time, Mila (last name not published), like many her age, took to social media to livestream details about her life, including about her sexuality. She is a lesbian. While interacting with her audience, a grown man, watching her live-stream, made unsolicited sexual advances, which Mila outright rejected. Feeling aggrieved, the man invoked 'Allah' and Islam to cruelly dehumanize this child. Horrified by him describing her as a 'dirty whore,' 'dirty-lesbian,' amongst other things, Mila posted on her Instagram story some extremely distasteful words about Islam.[218] In her various comments, many of which even the most provocative amongst us might regard as too incendiary, she did not target individuals or groups. Her comments were strictly about a religion, a faith, for which people can convert to, or apostasies from. The very point of liberal democracy, if there

---

[217] ibid.
[218] Willsher, Kim. "Macron wades into French girl's anti-Islam row, saying blasphemy is no crime." *The Guardian,* February 12, 2020. https://www.theguardian.com/world/2020/feb/12/macron-wades-into-french-girls-anti-islam-row-saying-blasphemy-is-no-crime-mila

ever was one, is to allow for all kinds of views, even those which we deem excessive and unpalatable, to be expressed, about any faith. We may find words offensive, but to state the obvious, we do not have blasphemy laws in our countries. And if anyone wanted to prosecute someone for making a similar remark about the Torah, my holy book, my position, which was articulated by Maajid Nawaz, would remain the same: "no idea is above scrutiny and no and no people are beneath dignity."[219] In any case, these remarks went viral, and in the weeks which ensued, her posts elicited over 100,000 hate messages, including death-threats and rape-threats. For this, she and her family had to endure 24-hour police protection, and she had to withdraw from school.

Naturally, Mila's life was wrecked by this wretched ordeal. Not only have the usual avenues and experiences open to people of her age been cut off, but to top it all off, she continues to live, in perpetual fear of falling to an assassin's gun. But this has never stopped her. Throughout this tumult, and to this very day, she displays a fortitude which few could muster. Indeed, in a subsequent TV interview did for Le Qotideien, she responded to the charges levelled against her, stating, "I am not a racist, not at all. You can't be racist about a religion," adding, "(I)said what I thought, I am completely in my rights. I don't regret it at all."[220] In all of this, she never expressed antipathy towards people, but to a religion. Does being rude, offensive and defamatory towards a religion, which is a set of values and ideas, constitute a form of racism? It may be provocative, wounding, and inflammatory, but this is distinct from racism, which is a hatred of, and a feeling of superiority towards, those with different immutable features and/or qualities, some of which are real, some of which are imagined. This is much deeper than a disliking or a vilification of a belief, or even a system of belief. And it's much more dangerous.

Many did not see things her way. Out of the over 100,000 abusive and threatening messages she received, just 13 individuals found themselves on trial. Of these, 11 defendants were given suspended sentences, and only

---

[219] See Harris, Sam, and Maajid Nawaz. *Islam and the Future of Tolerance: A Dialogue.* Cambridge, MA: Harvard University Press, 2015.

[220] "Free speech vs Islamophobia: A teenager fuels debate in France." *Al Jazeera,* August 10, 2021. https://www.aljazeera.com/news/2021/8/10/mila-affair-free-speech-islamophobia

some would have to pay fees to the teenage and legal fees. What was extraordinary was that not all those convicted were Muslim. In fact, a number said they were atheist! Yes, even those who those who proclaim to have no faith, and reject God, joined an Islamist bandwagon to traduce her, and see her become the next Samuel Paty. One of those, who works in a school, posted on Twitter not only his wish for Mila to die, but stated he felt as though he could make these remarks with impunity because he is "white and a nonbeliever."[221] At the time of the affair, a senior member of the French Council of the Muslim Faith (CFCM), Abdallah Zekri, told French radio, that this young woman had, "asked for it" (the threats), adding "You reap what you sow," although the leading authority at the organization distanced himself from this sentiment.[222]

This is what McLiam Wilson meant when he said, "the point is that this is now the world you live in." A state in which our progressives, with all their supercilious self-serving piety, deem it laudable and noble not only call out, but abuse, intimidate, and threaten those who do that which is seen to be disrespectful towards religion. But not all religion. This standard, it seems, is only applied to Islam, which, for many, has become the exception to the rule on what can be scrutinized and challenged.. The irony of leading figures who purport to fight for the equality of Islam is that they, in fact, want this faith to be treated uniquely, not equally. If they sought the latter, they would apply the same standard had these remarks been expressed about Judaism, Christianity, or Hinduism. Had they been, she might have had some abuse on social media, but she would not fear for her life as she does now. This would not have happened had the violent thugs threatening this young woman been without the permissibility, the koshering, of their fanaticism. They have flourished because the torchbearers of sanctimonious progressivism have gone from archnemesis to enabler of religious totalitarianism. The once-liberators from the

---

[221] Breeden, Aurelien. "France Holds Trial Over Online Harassment of Teen Who Criticized Islam." *The New York Times,* July 6, 2021. https://www.nytimes.com/2021/07/06/world/europe/france-online-harassment-trial.html

[222] Agence France-Presse. "French teenager put under police protection after Instagram anti-Islam rant." *France 24,* February 4, 2020. https://www.france24.com/en/20200204-french-teenager-put-under-police-protection-after-instagram-anti-islam-rant

shackles of religious orthodoxy have given the theocrats of our time an impetus to advance their illiberal cause.

Above all, these instances demonstrate the insidious weaponization of an anti-racist politics by the guardians of our progressive milieu, which has not only emboldened Islamist forces, but has, in the process, diminished the enormity of racism to its victims, past and present. If only this human evil were a criticism, dislike, or hatred of an ideology. If it were, perhaps millions would not have been enslaved, dehumanized, and murdered in its eternally grotesque name. But this failure to distinguish between legitimate views on ideas and hatred of people, has given Islamist ideologues, and their progressive minded allies, the momentum they need to suppress dissent. For Islamophobia, in the name of anti-racism, has become a crucial tool of Islamists who wish to make Islam immune from, and impervious to, any kind of intellectual scrutiny and challenge. And our well-intentioned progressives have not just fallen for it. They have made it popular and mainstream.

For this reason, Bruckner identifies Islamophobia as "a clever invention," since it succeeds in giving radicals a new alibi: opposition to blasphemy and dissent is justified on the grounds that such acts are not only heretical, but they are indeed racist. In turn, this has given traditional exponents of rights and liberties, especially those on the left (though not exclusively), a justification to maintain an unpardonable silence with regards to Islamism. This explains why various "defamation of religions," which is a fancy way of describing blasphemy laws, have been pushed by various organizations wishing to enshrine such anachronistic ideas into modern, secular, and even international, law. But not only is there taciturnity. There is complicity. Those who are charged with defending our liberties have joined in with Islamists by falsely charging those who do speak out, even those of a Muslim background, of occidentalist, racist thinking. And anyone guilty of this must be silenced.

Summarizing what this term had set out to achieve, Salman Rushdie, who we shall return to, in memoir which followed his Satanic Verses (1988), stated:

> *Something new was happening here: the growth of a new intolerance. It was spreading across the surface of the Earth, but nobody wanted to*

know. *A new word had been created to help the blind remain blind: Islamophobia. To criticize the militant stridency of this religion in its contemporary incarnation was to be a bigot. A phobic person was extreme and irrational in his views, and so the fault lay with such persons and not with the belief system that boasted over one billion followers worldwide. One billion believers could not be wrong, therefore the critics must be the ones foaming at the mouth.*[223]

Critically engaging with ideas, especially those which emanate from a religious tradition, should be widely encouraged in our secular Western-culture. It was, after all, a consequence of Judaism and Christianity undergoing major intellectual criticism, that it was able to, for the most part, reconcile its theology and ideas with modernity. But Islamists, with the support of their non-Muslim progressive allies, have denied this right to Islam. As Rushdie elucidates, to even contemplate doing this, in the eyes of many, is to be bigoted. In turn, the disruptive thinkers within our Muslim communities suffer vituperation and marginalization, and concomitantly, those menacing Islamist voices have been inspired to a disquieting degree.

What is clear is that Islamophobia, and the use to which Islamists and progressives have put it, serves to stifle any reckoning with the issues of contemporary Islam, especially antisemitism. The issues which exist within our Muslim communities are often ignored because the consequence of being charged with Islamophobia is not worth the abuse and aggravation which often follows. In the UK, we saw this when it came to the state and law enforcement failing the victims of Pakistani grooming gangs in parts of England. As we know from reports and studies, these gangs have been responsible for sexually assaulting several thousand, predominantly young and white working-class British girls. Speaking of this, the secretary to a 2022 Independent Inquiry into Child Sexual Abuse report, correctly asserts that "We need to break the culture where people are worried that they might be accused of being racist just because they record factual information."[224]

---

[223] See Rushdie, Salman. *Joseph Anton: A Memoir.* New York: Random House, 2012.
[224] Cited in Dearden, Lizzie. "Fight against grooming gangs hindered by fear of being branded racist, says official." *The Independent,* Feb, 2022. https://www.independent.co.uk/news/uk/home-news/grooming-gangs-iicsa-racist-fears-b2007649.html

And this fear has major implications for our purposes. The nonsense of Islamophobia claims is that to discuss Islamist intolerance, in fact, makes you intolerant. For raising the issue of antisemitism, which we know is widespread in the Islamic world, I have become a bigot. Behind a veil of well-intentioned anti-racism, actual racism, as well as sexism, homophobia, and supremacist thinking, go unchallenged. It has been under the cloak of this #bekind culture, which has become the civic- religion of our time, that willful blindness has been able to blight the highest levels of government. But we cannot escape the stark reality: if Western Europe's leaders do not pluck up the necessary courage to speak about such issues, then not only will populist parties continue to rise up the polls, but they leave the targets of Islamism in an even more vulnerable position.

Notwithstanding these concerns, some have put their heads above the parapet. And not, it must be said, without great risk. Many of those who haven't maintained a meek disposition, even those who have expressed themselves through artistic and creative means, have found their lives to be irrevocably changed. Almost imperceptibly, their lives went from one of comfort and safety to one of abject fear. Here we must face a stark truth: many, perhaps even most do not speak out, because they are frightened of potentially violent and life-changing consequences if they do.

A man who knows all about this is Salman Rushdie. A year after publishing *Satanic Verses*, a fatwa, or religious decree, was issued by Ayatolah Khomeini, the then Supreme Leader of Iran, offering a $3m reward to any Muslim who would slay the head of Rushdie, and those involved in the publication of this work of literature. The ruler called "all zealous Muslims to execute quickly wherever they find them," so that "no one will dare to insult Islamic sanctity" ever again.[225] Subsequently, in addition to Rushdie needing round the clock security, the novel's Japanese translator was murdered, its Italian translator was stabbed, its Norwegian publisher was shot, and at a Turkish hotel hosting its Turkish publisher, 35 guests were burned to death.[226] Most recently, in a public lecture Rushdie

---

[225] Cited in Marshall, Paul. "Exporting Blasphemy Restrictions: The Organization of the Islamic Conference and the United Nations." Hudson Institute. https://www.hudson.org/national-security-defense/exporting-blasphemy-restrictions-the-organization-of-the-islamic-conference-and-the-united-nations
[226] ibid.

gave in New York, in the August of 2022, he was stabbed in the face on multiple occasions, leaving him permanently blind in one eye. What would be described as the Rushdie-affair, marked a profound point in the way Islam could be discussed in the West: If you offend Muslims, you not only run the risk of being falsely described with the epithet of 'racist,' but run the risk of being a victim of an Islamist assault.

The Rushdie Affair set a template and a precedent for those who dared to speak out, or worse, do something deemed as blasphemous. While writing this section, I was reminded that just over two years ago, in Batley, England, a Religious Studies teacher, who has not been named, went into hiding, along with his family. His crime? In a lesson to his pupils about blasphemy, this teacher, in his late-twenties, dared to show his students an image of the Prophet Mohammed, allegedly from Charlie Hebdo's 2015 front cover, which was used to justify the murder of 12 innocent-souls at the offices of the left-wing satirical magazine back in the January of that year.[227] He did not do this in an Islamic school, nor in an Islamic country, and certainly not in a place with any blasphemy laws. He did this in largely secular Britain, and specifically, a secular, high-achieving grammar school. He was neither endorsing nor criticizing the image; to be clear, he used this image in a pedagogical manner to show what many consider blasphemous. And critically, this image was not used in isolation. According to a 14-year-old pupil in the class, it was shown alongside images of the Pope, Donald Trump and Boris Johnson.[228] However, it was for a cartoon of a religious prophet, which he was indifferent towards, that his life thereafter become one of perpetual fear.

After becoming public knowledge, mobs of Muslim men decided to gather outside the school gates and loudly protest. A large group of men, chanting (amongst other things) 'Allahu Akbar' outside a place of learning, with the sole aim of terrifying students and staff. And, boy, did they succeed. Rather than stick by their colleague and resist this anti-

---

[227] "The UK's Charlie Hebdo Moment." *Academics for Academic Freedom (AFAF)*. Accessed March 6, 2025. https://www.afaf.org.uk/the-uks-charlie-hebdo-moment/

[228] Fuller, Phoebe, "Batley Grammar teacher showed Prophet Muhammad image next to Donald Trump, Pope Francis and Boris Johnson, pupil claims," *Yorkshire Live,* [May, 2021], https://www.examinerlive.co.uk/news/local-news/batley-grammar-teacher-showed-prophet-20558472

democratic extremism, at the first opportunity, the school suspended the young teacher. The headmaster, in the face of this thuggery, publicly stated that the school "unequivocally apologizes for using a totally inappropriate resource in a recent religious studies lesson," adding that it was a "totally inappropriate image," and that it "should not have been used."[229] Although this suspension would be later overturned, after this pronouncement, the teacher and his family, knowing what happened to Samuel Paty in the October of 2020, went into hiding. To this day, after all this time, they continue to live in a condition that one would not think possible in twenty-first-century Britain.

Be under no illusion, this incident, which threatens to destroy the life of an innocent man, stemmed from one malicious falsehood, that he, for showing an image of the Prophet, is an Islamophobe; a racist who cannot be forgiven, and must pay for his transgression. When this unsubstantiated charge was bandied around, the school not only threw him to the wolves, but their commitment to 'British values,' which apparently includes a commitment to 'personal freedoms,' seemed to fly out the window. Like others in the face of this extremist mob-madness, in the first instance, the school capitulated to this abuse and intimidation.

Although this teacher and his family have had to endure unimaginable anxiety, he has been luckier than others. Following Satanic Verses, those individuals and publications who did something to anger Islamists, whether they meant it or not, found that they encroached on dangerous and, in some cases, lethal territory. After the attacks on those connected with the publication of Satanic Verses, notable instances of reprisal include the killing of Dutch filmmaker, Theo Van Gough, the killing of those in retaliation for cartoons depicting the Prophet Mohammed, the murder and beheading of French teacher Samuel Paty on the streets of Paris for showing the same image as the teacher in Batley, not to mention death-threats and violent assaults. These and other beastly crimes, thankfully few and far between, have led to widespread fears among many, of retribution

---

[229] Sky News. "Batley Grammar School: Protest over image of Prophet Mohammed shown in class 'unacceptable,' say education officials." *Sky News,* March 26, 2021. https://news.sky.com/story/batley-grammar-school-protest-over-image-of-prophet-mohammed-shown-in-class-unacceptable-say-education-officials-12256247

for the crime of expression. And it needs to be reiterated: the same fears do not exist when it comes to challenging and/or offending other religions, including Christianity or Judaism. This standard is particular, it seems exclusive, to the Islamist sacralization of its own ideals.

Of course, however, the most depressing aspect of this ignominious situation is how self-proclaimed liberals shrink from the core principles of liberalism, which they purportedly champion. Since the Rushdie Affair, they have not only repeatedly abandoned those who dissent, but also apportion, at least some of the blame, to those individuals for the threats and life-changing circumstances many subsequently deal with. This first came to my attention while, one day, scrolling through YouTube, I came across a 2007 BBC Question Time debate, a weekly show where politicians and journalists discuss the issues of the day. This time, panelists, which included Boris Johnson and Christopher Hitchens, discussed the motion: 'Is Salman Rushdie's knighthood an insult to Muslims worldwide?' In response, the late Baroness Shirley Williams, who was a leading voice for the Liberal Democrats, a centrist party, argued that awarding Rushdie a knighthood would be "a mistake," given that "this is a man who has deeply offended Muslims in a very powerful way." And while she was unequivocal in her condemnation of the Iranian bounty, she even ventured to point out that the security given to Salman Rushdie has come at "great expense to the taxpayer." In response, the legendary secularist, Christopher Hitchens, who has also since passed on, dismissed this view as "contemptible," and asked, in good-old Hitch style, "what better way was there to spend taxpayers' money than in the interest of freedom of expression?" To be clear, the Baroness was not alone. Other liberal voices had already expressed similar sentiments. For instance, in the May 1989, when there were widespread protests against the book, including a march of 20,000 Muslims in Hyde Park where slogans of "Rushdie must die!" and an effigy of Rushdie hanging from the gallows were fluttered.[230] Even Keith Vaz, the former Labor MP for Leicester East, led his own demonstration of several thousand Muslims in his own city. The longest-serving Asian MP, himself a Catholic, called for the book to

---

[230] "Muslims in London Protest Rushdie Book; 84 Arrested." *Los Angeles Times,* May 28, 1989. https://www.latimes.com/archives/la-xpm-1989-05-28-mn-1613-story.html

be removed and described this action as "one of the great days in the history of Islam and Great Britain."[231] What, though, is most disconcerting about this Question Time exchange is that it reveals how liberals, who represent the ideology that once emancipated the West from the chains of religious control, not only gave Rushdie up, but saw him, to some extent, as responsible for the threats he received. Indeed, Baroness Williams' words point to a pattern we have seen from other like-minded voices over the years, namely, if you dare to offend Muslims, specifically Islamists, you are asking for trouble. In the words of that spokesperson during the Mila Affair, "you reap what you sow."

And, sadly, today, all over Western Europe, we are spoilt for examples of not only a stomach-churning culture of victim-blaming, but a clear betrayal of the liberal commitment to liberalism. Nowhere, however, is this victim-blaming more evident than in the UK. It is worth taking note of a few of the most striking cases.

In 2015, in a talk she gave about blasphemy and apostasy to the Atheist, Secularist, and Humanist Society at Goldsmiths University in London, Maryam Namazie, a secular Iranian dissident who campaigns for the rights of women (and others) in the oppressive Islamic Republic, was interrupted by a number of male members of the university's Islamic Society (Isoc). This protest, orchestrated by the Isoc, in Maryam's words, "began," when, "ISOC 'brothers' started coming into the room, repeatedly banging the door, falling on the floor, heckling me, playing on their phones, shouting out, and creating a climate of intimidation in order to try and prevent me from speaking."[232] Indeed, at one stage a lecturer, Reza Moradi, also a human-rights activist, claimed he was the recipient of a death-threat at the event, stating that the student in question, "looked directly into my eyes and moved his hands into a handgun shape and

---

[231] Cited in Slater, Tom, "The shameful story of Britain's backdoor blasphemy laws." *Spiked,* March 12, 2023. https://www.spiked-online.com/2023/03/12/the-shameful-story-of-britains-backdoor-blasphemy-laws/

[232] Aftab, Ali, "Muslim students from Goldsmiths University's Islamic Society heckle and aggressively interrupt Maryam Namazie talk." *The Independent,* Dec, 2015. https://www.independent.co.uk/student/news/muslim-students-from-goldsmiths-university-s-islamic-society-heckle-and-aggressively-interrupt-maryam-namazie-talk-a6760306.html

touched the middle of his forehead."[233] In all of this, what was truly astonishing, aside from there being no obvious condemnation from the Students Union, was how the Feminist Society and LGBTQ Society both released statements in support of the Islamic Society.[234] *Let that sink in.* The two societies, which you might think would spearhead the liberal cause, gave their support not to the individual voicing the plight of women and gay people in the Islamic world, but to the society that sought to silence such a voice. The President of the society was forced to resign at the time amid allegations that he tweeted, upon seeing the support from the LGBTQ Society, profoundly homophobic remarks, "Can you fag lovers get out of my mentions pls, thanks."[235] Although the society very much distanced themselves from this contemptible statement of anti-gay bigotry, the point remains: these societies, which should be outraged by the attempt to cancel a feminist and secular voice, distanced themselves from this brave liberal-dissident, and in comments so grotesque in their betrayal, held her responsible for the intimidation which inflicted upon this event. Nonetheless, Namazie would later be barred from speaking at Warwick University by the Students Union for 'inciting hatred,' however, this decision was later reversed.[236]

In 2021, we saw a similar picture during the Batley Affair. After this teacher was suspended, the Labor Member of Parliament (MP) for the area, Tracy Brabin, who resigned soon-after, in the face of this intolerable mob-pressure, condemned the threats and intimidation the teacher faced, but qualified her remarks by saying, "I welcome the school's apology" adding that she is pleased with the "recognition of the offence this has

---

[233] "Muslim students try to disrupt ex-Muslim Maryam Namazie's talk on blasphemy at Goldsmiths University." *National Secular Society.* Posted December 3, 2015. https://www.secularism.org.uk/news/2015/12/islamist-students-try-to-disrupt-ex-muslim-maryam-namazies-talk-on-blasphemy-at-goldsmiths-university

[234] Alwakeel. Ramzy Evening Standard. "Goldsmiths Islamic Society head quits in wake of anti-gay tweet claims." *Evening Standard,* December 4, 2015. https://www.standard.co.uk/news/london/goldsmiths-islamic-society-head-quits-in-wake-of-antigay-tweet-claims-a3133086.html

[235] ibid.

[236] "Another blow to free speech on campus: Warwick University Student Union bans atheist human rights activist from speaking at AHS event." *Humanists UK.* September 25, 2015. https://humanists.uk/2015/09/25/another-blow-to-free-speech-on-campus-warwick-university-student-union-bans-atheist-human-rights-activist-from

caused..."[237] In other words, while what the teacher continues to face is wrong, in the same measure, he was in the wrong to go and show that image, even though he did so legally, and for pedagogical purposes. For this MP and others who share her well-intentioned anti-racist politics, there is an equivalence of evils between the reaction and what caused this reaction in the first place. The fear of stoking up tensions led her to lend intellectual and political acceptability to those forces of terror which sought to ruin this teacher's life. Her job was to, without reservation, condemn and resist this. And she failed.

A few months after this incident, Naz Shah, Labor MP for Bradford West, a city in which copies of *Satanic Verses* were burnt by a large number of Muslim men, in a parliamentary debate about a government police and crimes bill, argued that depictions of the Prophet should be recognized as a form of 'emotional harm.'

Along with her words that such images are not 'not just a cartoon,' this Labor MP, belonging to a party with a long and distinguished commitment to democracy, stated in Parliament, "When bigots and racists defame, slander or abuse our Prophet (peace be upon him), just like some people do to the likes of Churchill, the emotional harm caused upon our hearts is unbearable."[238] In other words, if the government criminalizes the vandalization of statues, then depictions of the Islamic prophet, the work of "bigots and racists," should also be seen as a criminal act, because the offense it causes runs the risk of undermining "civil society." Again, this finds fault with the ones who challenge religious authority, not the people who incite violence. This is from a politician representing the next party to be in government, and there she is advocating laws on cartoons because of the upset it causes.

A retrograde politics has, it seems, found an important ally in members of progressive parties. What this might mean for secular liberal democracy, time will tell. For sure, though, this is setting us on a path

---

[237] Tracy Brabin (@TracyBrabin), "Please see below for my statement on the protests at Batley Grammar School," *X,* March 26, 2021, https://x.com/TracyBrabin/status/1375418637448777728

[238] Cited in Steerpike. "Watch: Labour's Naz Shah hints at blasphemy law." *The Spectator,* September 29, 2023. https://www.spectator.co.uk/article/watch-labour-s-naz-shah-hints-at-blasphemy-law/

which, not too long ago, would have disconcerted every secularist going, especially those attached to the Labor Party and the political left. However, before we consider the implications of this fear for our study of governmental negligence, there is one last example that needs to be discussed.

And so, we turn to Kettlethorpe High School, in the city of Wakefield, which is only ten miles from Batley. In the February of 2023, this school was home to an incident that highlights the extent to which our free societies have retreated and cowed in fear. In brief, four children, in Year Ten, no older than fourteen, were suspended by this secular state school. One of them, who has not been named but who suffers from Autism, brought a Quran into school, after an innocuous dare from his friends for losing a game of Call of Duty. Reportedly, when the child did this, he read the Islamic holy book out loud on the tennis courts, and afterwards, walked back into the school where another student, intentionally or unintentionally, knocked it out of his hands, causing negligible damage. That's it. Contrary to some of the false claims, this book was not spat on, burnt, or in any way, broken. And yet, not only were the four boys involved immediately suspended, but the police were called in, presumably by their school, for an investigation.[239]

Upon becoming aware of this, a local Labor councillor, Usman Ali, went on to Twitter to describe this event, on a now deleted tweet, as "provocative action," stating that it needed to be dealt with "urgently by all the authorities, namely, the police, the school, and the local authority."[240] Well, the authorities heeded Mr Ali's call. Although the school found that there had been "no malicious intent," the police spokesperson for this incident, Chief Inspector Andy Thornton, said that this was going to be recorded as a "non-crime-hate-incident," adding that

---

[239] LBC. "Police record 'hate incident' after autistic boy drops Quran in school corridor." *LBC,* March 1, 2023. https://www.lbc.co.uk/news/police-hate-incident-autistic-boy-quran-school/

[240] Cited in Evans, Stephen, "We need to normalize blasphemy," *National Secular Society,* February 28, 2023, https://www.secularism.org.uk/opinion/2023/02/we-need-to-normalise-blasphemy#:~:text=Her%20point%20was%20about%20the,and%20purpose%20of%20free%20speech

the young man in question was given "words of advice by an officer."[241] Again, let us reiterate, nothing happened to the book, and even if it did, there are no laws in Britain, or anywhere in Western Europe, which prevent anyone from maltreating a religious text, or holy book, even if I think all books should be treated with respect. For no book is, by its very nature, holy, and thus deserving of extra protection. Regardless, this affair begs the question: would the police have done the same had the boys used a Bible rather than a Quran? In this current climate, it is safe to say almost certainly not.

Notwithstanding this double standard, in an effort to calm things down after the boy who had brought in the Quran became the target of various Muslim death-threats, a meeting was arranged at the local Mosque, where the boy's mother, wearing a headscarf, addressed a local audience, along with the headteacher, Muslim leaders, and the Chief Inspector. Here, pleading for her son, the mother said that the boy was left "absolutely petrified," and that she does not "want anybody to be prosecuted because of the stupidity of my son and his friends."[242] There you have it – a mother pleading for her fourteen-year-old son so he does not become a victim of some Islamist violent assault, or god forbid, worse. A preposterous and odious situation, but what few discussed was the way in which community leaders spoke about this incident.

As if things could not get any more monstrous, there was, it seemed to me, a woeful lack of condemnation and denunciation, in unequivocal terms, of the threats towards this child by the panelists. In the case of both the Chief Inspector and the headteacher, the people you would expect to be most vocal, aside from emphasizing that that people should not take the law into their own hands, and that this should be dealt with through the proper channels of law and order, they said few words of consequence. Instead, both, but especially the head teacher, kept referring to this event

---

[241] Cited in Daily Mail. "Boy who dropped a copy of Quran at Wakefield school left 'petrified' by death threats." *Daily Mail,* March 1st, 2023. https://www.dailymail.co.uk/news/article-11809601/Boy-dropped-copy-Quran-Wakefield-school-left-petrified-death-threats.html

[242] Cited in Slater, Tom. "When a Wakefield boy brought a Koran to school." *Spiked,* February 27, 2023. https://www.spiked-online.com/2023/02/27/when-a-wakefield-boy-brought-a-koran-to-school/

as "a very sad day," since his school, he underscored, is built around "respect and kindness." Most likely aware of what had taken place at the Batley Grammar School two years earlier, he made it clear to his audience, "rest assured, this is a very serious matter and we have acted quickly... and we will continue to investigate and explore what has gone on....If more consequences have to follow that will be the case."[243] Adding to this, the Chief Inspector remarked this incident should lead to "longer learning," and more "awareness around all faiths."[244] As a law-enforcer, his duty, strangely enough, is to enforce the law, and disrespecting religious beliefs, as tasteless as such actions can be, do not constitute hate-crimes. They may offend, trigger, or upset a number of people, but a crime, it is not. Nevertheless, also wanting to attenuate tensions, a councilor present at the meeting, Akef Akbar, stated that "passions do flare" in response to the death threats against this child, adding that the mother "to her credit[...]understands the situation and has advised the police that she does not want any of these children [who sent threats to her son] to be prosecuted, and she only asks that her son is not harmed."[245] The imam present, insisting that retributive violence would not be acceptable, and is a violation of Islamic law, qualified his assertion by stating, "Any Muslim in Wakefield, Halifax, where I'm from, Bradford, Dewsbury, United Kingdom, or outside the United Kingdom, will never tolerate the disrespect of the holy Koran," adding that, "We will sacrifice our lives for it." Hearing this, the police officer was just nodding along – as if what he was saying was acceptable. The imam even said, "Had it been, for example, a teacher who had disrespected the holy Koran, had it been, let's say, an adult that had thrown the holy Koran, then the matter would be different. We probably wouldn't be sitting in the [mosque] right now.

---

[243] Cited in both 1. Daily Mail. "Boy who dropped a copy of Quran at Wakefield school left 'petrified' by death threats." *Daily Mail,* March 1st, 2023.https://www.dailymail.co.uk/news/article-11809601/Boy-dropped-copy-Quran-Wakefield-school-left-petrified-death-threats.html 2. Facebook, "Kettlethorpe High School Quran desecration 'a sad day,'" Facebook video, 5Pillars, 26 Feb, 2023 https://www.facebook.com/watch/?v=915596312819361
[244] ibid.
[245] See Facebook, Jamia Masjid Swafia. " COMMUNITY MEETING IN RELATION TO THE QUR'AN INCIDENT." *Facebook* video 24th February, 2023. https://www.facebook.com/masjidswafia/videos/220999650384772

We'd probably be standing outside that school and voicing our concerns."[246] Again, the chief inspector or any other leader there did nothing to question to this. They kept silent. They said gornischt.

This incident, at the time of writing, is the most recent example of liberal-minded individuals, this time with the responsibility of a child's welfare, failing to stand up for his rights in a liberal-democratic society. Instead, like the other examples given, in the face of Islamist intimidation, they were scared shitless. And the only one who paid the price for this was the victim, a fourteen-year-old, who may, heaven forbid, have to live in fear for many years to come.

What, though, such examples demonstrate is how those who are widely regarded to be the guardians of liberalism, in the face of potential Islamist retribution, both abandon and blame those that allegedly dishonor Islam for all the misery and commination which comes their way. Although not always explicitly argued, too often the accusation of 'they were asking for it' is peddled at those that do dissent and/or offend. Yet, those who engage in such victim blaming exhibit an ignorance of their own culture and its tradition of free expression. After our May 11th ordeal, with which this book began, it was said to me that 'you were asking for trouble; it's your fault.' But why should our small group, which democratically and peacefully countered a large mob spouting hatred and threatening violence, be blamed for our near-lynching experience? In retrospect, our only crime was being too few in number, not for exercising our right to freedom of speech and expression. To treat any idea or organized religion as immune from being countered, ridiculed, or offended, is tantamount to making its adherents exempt from the standards with which other people and ideas are treated. This serves not only to 'other' those concerned from societal standards, itself a racist proposition, but does exactly what fanatics want us to do: through the breathtaking stupidity of our own benevolence, we make their ideals untouchable, unimpeachable, immutable.

---

[246] Tom Slater, "When a Wakefield boy brought a Koran to school." https://www.spiked-online.com/2023/02/27/when-a-wakefield-boy-brought-a-koran-to-school/

This fear of a backlash, however, like that of being accused of racism, has crept into government and law enforcement. Such a fear plays a crucial role in the negligence of Western European authorities in dealing with the issues we see in our Muslim communities, particularly antisemitism. An instructive example that illuminates this problem emerged in the nearly three-hour French Presidential debate of 2022. Here, Emmanuel Macron, the incumbent President, captured the attitude of successive Western Europe leaders. Discussing the Muslim Hijab or headscarf, his opponent, Marine Le Pen, was far from opaque when she declared, if elected, this would not be permitted to be worn in public. She dismissed this religious clothing, worn by millions, incorrectly in my view, as "a uniform imposed by Islamists." In response, Macron, "What you're saying is very serious. You are going to cause a civil war. I say this sincerely"[247] What is significant about this interchange is not the Hijab. In fact, while Le Pen's views on this matter are misguided and misinformed, what Monsieur Macron had said in response points to a situation that very few politicians, not least himself, are at all interested in conceding: policy-makers and law-enforcement are panic-stricken to tackle the issues we see because of what might happen in response.

This has consequently created a dilemma for policymakers: should they prioritize protecting targeted groups, even if it means risking social disorder, or avoid the issue altogether? For the most part, authorities have opted for the latter. After all, if those with the power to make a change were serious in their intent to rid Western Europe of Jew-hate, they would have to stop treating this issue as if it is just the responsibility of a few pariahs in our Muslim spaces. We know from Chapter Two the extent to which anti-Jewish ideas have become normalized and accepted amongst those of a Muslim background. To have any chance of tackling this, we require a cultural, intellectual and political shift, which rises beyond the facile claim that this is just a fringe phenomenon in these communities. Yet, as we have seen above, there is a genuine prospect that dealing with this crisis comprehensively runs the risk of sparking social disorder and

---

[247] Daily Mail. "French presidential debate sees Macron accuse Le Pen of being in the grip of Russia." *Daily Mail,* April 21, 2022. https://www.dailymail.co.uk/news/article-10736853/French-presidential-debate-sees-Macron-accuse-Le-Pen-grip-Russia.html

violence. As such, this prospect removes any incentive, if any existed to begin with, for dealing with what is a distinct threat to our liberal-democratic societies and to the Jewish community in particular.

Throughout this whole section, we have seen how the politics of fear has led to a state in which our authorities are deprived of any real appetite to deal with this crisis of antisemitism in our Muslim communities. The willy-nilly use of racist accusations, as well as fears of potential social disorder and violence, has created a state in which our authorities step back and allow this madness to go on, and over the years, to get worse. Speaking in 2015, Lord Carey, the former Archbishop of Canterbury, in an article for the Sunday Times, opined "A de facto blasphemy law is operating in Britain today. The fact is that publishers and newspapers live in fear of criticizing Islam."[248] This fear exists everywhere in the region – and it has achieved exactly what it set out to achieve from the moment this politics of fear began to form after the Rushdie Affair: to keep good and well-intentioned people silent. And, therefore, it is no aberration that those whom I have charged as being neglectful have been so.

Is it right to ask, what it will take for those in positions of power to summon the courage needed to tackle these problems? Indeed, what will it take for those concerned to even admit there is a problem? We shall return to these questions in the next chapter. For now, however, we must turn to another factor which drives this negligence: the politics of numbers.

Section Two: Politics of Numbers

It is always heartening to hear Western European leaders on Holocaust Memorial Day, and on other occasions, reiterate their commitment to fighting antisemitism. It makes us feel validated and heard. But, admittedly, this feeling has a short lifespan. The cheerless fact is that this poison, particularly in its Islamist form, is on the rise. And so, either our authorities are good at talking the talk but failing to put the matching policies in place, or that such policies are unfit for purpose. In reality, both are true – and yet, a factor which has underscored the failure of successive governments, has been the political significance of numbers in the

---

[248] "Carey: UK fears criticizing Islam," *The Times,* Jan 2015, https://www.thetimes.com/article/carey-uk-fears-criticising-islam-k35j5hx7dfl

formation of policy. For such considerations, especially since Jews are so few in number, provide governments a convenient and necessary pretext to ignore, much less deal with, the themes I have addressed.

While it is the case that our leaders insist that we Jews are an integral part of this 'New Europe, ' in the realpolitik, this does not translate into anything substantive. In Western Europe, Jews number just shy of a million, or 0.5 per cent of the region's inhabitants. In a population of almost 200 million, that's a tiny number; and, in places, it continues to get smaller. We are a tiny bunch (and yet, somehow, we perfidiously control everything.) Although the political and social clout Jews exercise may be outwardly important, it is not enough to warrant the necessary action from elected- politicians to deal with the scourge of Jew-hatred. Indeed, though Badiel was right to say that in many anti-racist circles, 'Jews Don't Count,' it is also true to say, specifically for a growing number of the region's politicians, they don't count Jews. Because they do not need to.

Western Europe's Muslim communities, conversely, the political realities are different. While a diverse and heterogeneous minority, this population is growing, making Islam the fastest expanding religion on the continent.[249] This has led many of those mainstream politicians, particularly on the left, to shy away from taking decisive action vis-à-vis Muslim antisemitism. There is, after all, genuine concern over what this might do to their political influence and standing amongst Muslim voters. And it is this support which, in many places, they cannot afford to lose.

Consequently, it should be asked, with both current and forecasted population data, what political incentive is there, on the part of those mainstream politicians and their parties, to change their tune, and deal with this crisis? My argument is that given the inestimable importance of number- based considerations, this disincentive will continue for the foreseeable future. In fact, there are social-democratic and socialist parties that, in accordance with these demographic realities, propose policies and make use of a rhetoric which speaks to the attitudes of many Muslim voters, who have become electorally indispensable.

---

[249] Cited in, "How Islam Became the Fastest-Growing Religion in Europe" *Time*, January 2015, https://time.com/3671514/islam-europe/

One country that best epitomizes this development is Sweden. In R Amy Elman's insightful research on contemporary antisemitism in Scandinavia's largest country, she cites Mikael Tossavainen, a historian, who felt that the silence (bordering on indifference) of Swedish authorities, needed urgent attention. In his study, *The Denied Hatred: Anti-Semitism among Muslims and Arabs in Sweden*, he explained "Unlike the anti-Semitism that traditionally finds expression in Nazi circles—[antisemitism among Arabs and Muslims] is not mentioned or in any way stressed in the public debate. On the contrary, it is actively hushed up, excused or even denied in the media, and the political, academic and intellectual establishment."[250] When looking at the record of Swedish authorities, Tossavainen makes an important observation. We have not only seen successive politicians in the country fail to even speak about antisemitism among Muslims, but like in the politics of fear, some have even blamed Jews for the threats and violence that they have been subjected to.

As detailed in Chapter One, Malmö is a city which has been at the epicenter of these antisemitic incidents. A small pro-Israel gathering in the city center, following Operation Cast Lead, in 2008, was met with violence and vitriol. This group, which set out to express sympathy with "all civilian victims," and sang to the tune of peace and co-existence, was drowned out by a large anti-Israel mob, intent on causing harm to this small public expression of support for a democratic nation. To such an extent, after thirty-five minutes, the police were forced to intervene, and bring this gathering to an abrupt and untimely end.[251] According to Elman, "when twice as many stone and bottle-throwing counter-demonstrators arrived," there were chants of "Hitler, Hitler," "Juden Raus," (Jews out) "Bloody Jews," and "Itbach al yahoud" (death to Jews in Arabic).[252] The police, it should be stressed, did not disband those who were causing the violence and a breach of the peace on public streets, but those who

---

[250] Cited in R. Amy Elman. *The European Union, Antisemitism, and the Politics of Denial.* p.85.
[251] See both ibid, p.96; Paulina Neuding, "Sweden's 'Damn Jew' Problem," *Tablet Magazine,* April 5, 2012, https://www.tabletmag.com/sections/news/articles/swedens-damn-jew-problem
[252] Elman, *The European Union, Antisemitism, and the Politics of Denial.* p.96.

peacefully came together in accordance with the law. One might expect the mayor of the city to take a perspicuous stance against this. Well, think again! The mayor of this city, representing the center-left Social Democrats, equivocated and declared, "We accept neither Zionism nor anti-Semitism. They are extremes that put themselves above other groups, and believe they have a lower value"[253] In fact, not only did the mayor go on to criticize the Jewish community for not taking a strong enough position against Israel's position in Gaza, as if the actions of Israel could be legitimately used to justify attacks on Jews around the world, but held those demonstrators responsible, stating, "Instead they choose to have a demonstration at the main square, which can send the wrong signals."[254] A similar incident occurred at the 2009 Davis Cup tennis match between Israel and Sweden. To prevent yet another breakout in disorder, the Swedish authorities requisitioned various anti-riot vehicles and helicopters, as well as a thousand police officers. At the time, a "Stop the Match" demonstration took place, which included Islamists, neo-Nazis, and leftists, and the Swedish authorities claimed they could not keep safe the 4,000 spectators to this match. As Elman uncovers, however, "the authorities reneged on the strong police presence necessary to ensure protection to athletes and their spectators, a position that fell short of previous enhanced efforts requested by the EU to combat hooliganism."[255] Indeed, a left wing council member stated that the mere presence of Israelis is a, "a provocation against Arabs living in Malmö."[256] The match did go ahead, albeit behind closed doors, and the Mayor, again, stated, "Don't forget...this isn't a match against just anyone. It's a match against the state of Israel."[257] In such a view, the antisemitism that raged on the streets was not without justification. The authorities, be that the police or

---

[253] Cited in "Swedish Jews Raise Issue of Malmö Mayor's Anti-Semitic Comments With Social Democratic Party Leader." *World Jewish Congress,* December 5, 2012. https://www.worldjewishcongress.org/en/news/swedish-jews-raise-issue-of-malmo-mayor-s-anti-semitic-comments-with-social-democratic-party-leader
[254] Paulina Neuding, "Sweden's 'Damn Jew' Problem," *Tablet Magazine.*
[255] Elman, *The European Union, Antisemitism, and the Politics of Denial.* p.95.
[256] ibid.
[257] Paulina Neuding, "Sweden's 'Damn Jew' Problem," *Tablet Magazine.*

elected officials, decided it is better to appease the victimizers rather than protect the victims of this antisemitic thuggery.

The propensity of Swedish politicians to find excuses for violent extremism did not begin nor end here. If we go back to 2006, the Stockholm Great Mosque, one of the largest in the country, was found to be in possession of antisemitic material in its bookshop. This material wasn't mildly antisemitic; it was grossly dehumanizing and even explicitly violent and murderous. The then-Chancellor of Justice, Göran Lambertz, decided against prosecution, ostensibly on the basis that the evidence was insufficient. However, in his subsequent legal write-up, he opined that those materials were "permissible" because "battle cries and invectives are a commonplace feature of the rhetoric surrounding the [Middle East] conflict." As Lambertz would later confirm, this material, in his estimation, was lawful because it was being used in the context of the Israeli-Palestinian conflict.[258] So long as terror is being promoted against Israelis, and it can be justified in the context of war, to the most senior representative of justice in Sweden, the law allows for such incitement.

And yet, as if this affair could get any more outrageous, in 2006, the state ordered the closure of the website of the Swedish Democrats, a far-right party, for posting the infamous Danish cartoons of the Prophet Mohammed. As Elman points out, "The government's closure of the far right's website distinguished Sweden as the first Western state to block the re-publication of the caricatures of Mohammed," adding that "the government dressed its capitulation to Jihadist threats beneath a cloak of tolerance and pluralistic sensitivity."[259] Somehow, a cartoon depicting a religious prophet warranted state intervention and was regarded as a greater evil than texts that advocate the slaughter of Jews. This pronouncement ran contrary to the various agreements Sweden had signed up to, for instance, the Organization for Security & Cooperation in Europe (OSCE's) 2004 Berlin Declaration. This, however, did not seem to bother Swedish officials. In their commitment to multicultural Scandinavia, they remained, true to form, jejune and negligent.

---

[258] Elman, *The European Union, Antisemitism, and the Politics of Denial*. p.91.
[259] ibid, pp. 94-95.

What we see here, and certainly not only in the examples, is that the violence is never really the fault of those who go out and commit acts of violence. In the case of antisemitism, the perceived Jewish hegemon, in the form of the Jewish State, is given as an excuse by some politicians for not only violent Jew-hate, but extremism itself. For instance, in 2015, following the November Islamist terrorist attacks in Paris, in which 130 were killed and nearly 400 were injured, the Swedish foreign minister, Margot Wallstrom, somehow, without invitation, managed to bring Israel into the conversation. Talking about radicalism amongst Europe's Muslims, she held the Jewish state, at least partly responsible, by stating, "Here, once again, we are brought back to situations like the one in the Middle East, where not least, the Palestinians see that there isn't a future. We must either accept a desperate situation or resort to violence."[260] Although Jews were not specifically targeted this time around, this senior politician in the Social Democrats, the governing party, sought to absolve those criminals of any and all responsibility. It seems the Jews are at fault - even when we are not the targets!

Those elected have, at best, failed, and, at worst, betrayed their Jews. In the case of Sweden, and elsewhere, this is driven by a lack of incentive to implement policies which will protect this small community, i.e. an inappreciable size of the electorate, and increasingly, an awareness of what such policies might do to the electoral appeal of the parties seeking the support of Muslim voters. Back in 2006, the former leader of the Swedish Liberal Party, Lars Leijonborg, encapsulated the policy of mainstream parties in the country, which continues to this day, "For once, the Swedish parties are very much in agreement. We want the best possible relationship with the Muslim world."[261] He uttered these words after the cartoon affair, giving his support to the government action in this matter. And while this sentiment of Mr Leijonborg may have been motivated by laudable communitarianism, this pursuit of "the best possible relationship" has

---

[260] "Swedish Foreign Minister Criticized for Accusations Against Israel." *International Middle East Media Center,* November 27, 2015. https://imemc.org/article/74123/

[261] Cited in Elman, *The European Union, Antisemitism, and the Politics of Denial.* p.95.

meant, as correctly noted by Tossavainen, that antisemitism is ignored, hushed-up, or worse, blamed on its Jewish victims.

It is for this reason, in Sweden and elsewhere, that politicians who identify as progressive and/or liberal, have retreated from their liberal cause, and have got into bed with those who are patently illiberal and totalitarian. In addition to some of the examples considered, one that is particularly telling is when Sweden's first Social Democratic woman leader, Mona Sahlin, who would become deputy Prime Minister, marched alongside Hamas flags at what was, at least in name, a pro-immigrant demonstration. This female politician, a proud feminist, stood by the flags of an organization that rejects any notion of female dignity and autonomy. With Hamas flags being waved and Israeli flags being burned (also raising raises the question: what does this have to do with Swedish immigration policy?), Elman argues "she assumed the resulting photos would prove a greater asset than liability."[262] This incident, though not a regular occurrence, says a lot about what Jews in the country face. While they may say the correct words about the need to stand up for Jews, many Swedish politicians, with their interest in pursuing good relations with the country's Muslim population, not least for their votes, are prepared to ignore antisemitism and even to lend credence to antisemitic notions. For the very simple fact, these votes really do matter. For instance, one report in 2009 found that between 70 to 75 per cent of Swedish Muslims backed the Social Democrats, which was in government for several years, and an additional 10-15 per cent gave their support to one of the two parties in the red-green alliance, a coalition of left-wing parties.[263] Given that the country is made up of over 10 million people, and the Muslim population is growing, these parties need Muslim voters.

Observations like this are often shrugged off as fearmongering. And while these votes on a national level may not seem significant, election results on a micro level, particularly in the larger areas (specifically three largest cities: Stockholm, Gothenburg, and Malmö), where there are

---

[262] ibid, p.86.
[263] Cited in Olsen, Henry. "How the Muslim Left Is Shaping the Future of the Western Left." *UnHerd,* April 10, 2018. https://unherd.com/2018/04/muslim-left-shaping-future-western-left/?fbclid=IwAR0PuRrRhdZL8gczMIfKrvuTH69Ro4QXOSOTDexAEkvnCdwGJbDEp84sB1A

higher concentrations of Muslim voters, have a potentially determinative effect on which party will take office. The success of these parties in areas where there are high numbers of Muslim voters can be the difference between being in government and being in opposition.

The national election of 2022, in which the Social Democrat-led coalition was ousted from government, attests to the electoral indispensability of the country's Muslim population. In the face of the mounting pressure from the anti-immigration Swedish Democrats, who wound up achieving an informal position in government, the Social Democrats adopted more conservative positions on immigration and integration. This did them no favors, especially for their popularity amongst Muslim voters who felt this bloc had abandoned them. For 28,000 voters, most of whom had voted for this bloc in prior elections, turned to the newly-formed, Islamist-linked, Nuance Party. And given that they succeeded in those larger cities, where the concentration of Muslim voters is higher, they were the largest party that did not make it into the Swedish parliament.[264] This party, whose founder, Mikail Yüksel, was expelled by the Center Party for his relations with the Turkish fascist terror group, Grey Wolves, put up only Muslim candidates and campaigned on issues facing Muslims in the country.

After the election, Yüksel declared, "We went down in history as the party that overthrew the Social Democrat government," adding, "The Muslim voters punished the Social Democrats."[265] It's a bewildering source of jubilation since his "success" helped to ensure that what is routinely dubbed an Islamophobic and racist party achieve a position of power. Nevertheless, despite his self-adulating words, the Social Democratic coalition, according to Abdullah Bozkurt, a Swedish-based investigative journalist, lost the election by approximately 26,000 votes. Although 28,000 votes went to Nuance, other larger and mainstream parties also witnessed losses to other smaller competitors. What is indubitable, however, is that this party for disgruntled Muslims, given the

---

[264] Bozkurt, Abdullah. "Sweden: Islamist Party Leader Claims Muslims Face Oppression." *Middle East Forum,* January 12, 2023. https://www.meforum.org/sweden-islamist-party-leader-claims-muslims
[265] ibid.

way votes are distributed in the country, put a dent, and quite a visible one, in the electoral aspirations of the social- democrat bloc. It's worth noting that the Netherlands also witnessed something similar in the 2017 election, in which the Denk Party, won 2 per cent of the overall vote (with over a third of voters of Turkish and Moroccan descent giving their support), wining over 5 per cent of the vote in four of the country's largest cities, and so earning three seats in the Dutch Parliament. Like in Sweden, this certainly came at the expense of the Dutch Labor Party.[266]

In both cases, it becomes evident that mainstream parties, particularly in those large urban, metropolitan cities, rely on the support of Muslim voters. To lose their support, runs the risk of losing elections, both local and national. Consequently, representatives, in Sweden and elsewhere, face a critical question: why should they formulate and/or implement policies which run the distinct risk of alienating a support base they cannot do without, especially for the sake of a small minority of Jews, just over 0.1 per cent of the population? So long as these parties opt for what is in their interest, as any party would do in a democracy, then this negligence is not simply motivated by ideological considerations; it is also inevitable. Put simply, politicians lack the incentive to address the crises faced by their small Jewish communities without the influence of substantial numbers. And while this situation may be most pronounced in Sweden, the nation of ABBA and IKEA is far from alone.

Across Western Europe, centrist and left-wing parties are increasingly recognizing the importance of these voters in their campaigns. One might find this bamboozling given that the parties in question, for the most part, boast their support for social-progressivism (increasingly, being antisemitic has become part of being progressive, of course), whereas Muslim voters, on the whole, tend to be more socially conservative, for instance, when it comes to homosexuality and gender affairs. Nevertheless, due to a range of factors, including economic and foreign policy stances, Muslims who participate in elections are, overwhelmingly, attracted to these parties, largely on the left. As noted by Rafaela M. Dancygier in her thought-provoking study, *Dilemmas of Inclusion: Muslims in European Politics*, these parties have been willing to overlook

---

[266] Olsen, Henry, "How the Muslim Left Is Shaping the Future of the Western Left."

their differences. For the straightforward reason, winning votes trumps all other concerns, even where the voters do not share the same social values as the party they are voting for.

What does this development mean for the future of those traditional mainstream and anti-racist parties? We shall see, but following Henry Olson, a columnist at the Washington Post, we should view the Muslim vote, specifically for left-wing parties, in a similar vein to the Evangelical Vote for the Republican Party in the US. While the former is not the pre-eminent political base for social-democratic and socialist parties in our region, the latter plays a fundamental role for US Republicans. It would be politically detrimental for those parties seeking power not to take this growing constituency of voters seriously.[267] Moreover, it has been rightly argued that the high concentration of Muslims in urban areas influences the way in which mainstream parties electioneer, or campaign for votes. This manifests in multiple ways, often making use of platforms given by religious and communal institutions to communicate their ideas and policies to prospective Muslim voters. And this vote becomes even more of a necessity for left-leaning parties when considering that not only is the Muslim population in these areas is growing, but there has also been a noted decline in what was once their traditional voter base, the white-working class (in some cases, white- native populations have become a minority). Predictably, in these places, parties have sought to win the support of this growing electorate, which is becoming ever more politically engaged.

None of this is to say that Muslims are a homogenous voting bloc, or for that matter, monolithic. Being Muslim does not dictate voting patterns. Just like any other group, there is diversity of thought, and this plays out in multiple areas, no less in the ballot box. Notwithstanding, given how Muslim communities are politically engaged, coupled with how parties campaign for votes in these places, there is, de facto, a distinct and growing 'Muslim vote.' And it matters.

In the case of both the UK and France, countries with the highest Muslim populations in all of Western Europe, mainstream politicians realize just how much of a game-changer these voters can be. In both

---

[267] Olsen, Henry, "How the Muslim Left Is Shaping the Future of the Western Left."

places, the success of mainstream parties, especially those that lean leftwards, is increasingly reliant upon the support given by those areas which are home to a high and growing concentration of Muslim voters.

In the UK, the Muslim Engagement and Development organization (MEND), which is dedicated to engaging British-Muslims in the political, civic, and social spheres, found that the results in a staggering 50 seats across the country could be swung or impacted by Muslim voters (with the Muslim Council of Britain suggesting that Muslim voters could swing 31, specifically in marginal seats, in which the incumbent has no comfortable majority).[268] The MEND report added that Muslim voters make up approximately 10 per cent or more of the electorate in 83 seats, and that 25 constituencies have Muslim electorates of over 20 per cent or more (with Braford West and Hodge Hill, Birmingham having Muslim electorates of over 50 per cent). It also found back in the 2017 election, 25 constituencies with the largest estimated proportion of Muslim voters, Labour candidates were re-elected with larger majorities than in 2015, and that Muslim voters were crucial in overturning Conservative Party majorities in the constituencies of Bedford, Keighley and Peterborough.[269]

This 'Muslim vote' can indeed be decisive. As Zara Mohamed, the former Assistant Secretary General at the Muslim Council of Britain in, astutely pointed out in 2019, "It's important that we all – young and old – realize our potential to make change through political participation. Our votes matter. Be it the mosque, community organization, student society or women's group, each of us can make a difference. This is as true in Ealing as in Edinburgh – we all have a responsibility to encourage as many

---

[268] Sherwood, Harriet. "Muslim Voters Could Swing Marginal Seats, Research Shows." *The Guardian,* November 18, 2019. https://www.theguardian.com/politics/2019/nov/18/muslim-voters-swing-marginal-seats-research

[269] See the following: MEND (Muslim Engagement & Development). Muslim Manifesto 2019. London: MEND, 2019. https://www.mend.org.uk/wp-content/uploads/2019/11/MEND-Muslim-Manifesto-2019_15.11.19.pdf. Ismail Gulam Sufyan, "Why British Muslims Hold the Balance of Power in Britain's General Election," *Byline Times,* November 25, 2019, https://bylinetimes.com/2019/11/25/why-british-muslims-hold-the-balance-of-power-in-britains-general-election/
"What Matters to Muslims in an Election?" *MEND (Muslim Engagement & Development),* November 21, 2019. https://www.mend.org.uk/what-matters-to-muslims-in-an-election/

people register to vote."[270] One study found that in the election of that year, 86 per cent of British Muslims backed Jeremy Corbyn's Labor Party.[271] Although the party was defeated, the seats they retained in that general election, and have since retained and earned in various by-elections, in many instances, were made possible by this Muslim-vote. And losing the support of these voters, certainly in the case of the British Labor Party, runs the risk of jeopardizing their ambitions for office.

The situation in France, the country with the highest Muslim population in the entire region, is even more transparent. The significance of the Muslim vote in France became evident back in the 2012 election between the center-right incumbent, Nicolas Sarkozy and the leader of the Socialist Party, Francois Hollande. According to French sociologist, Ali Saad, French Muslims voted overwhelmingly for Hollande, in the second-round, after the commitments he made to fighting racism and Islamophobia, in which, allegedly, Sarkozy was indulging. Saad cites the French Institute of Public Opinion (IOFP), which found that 86 per cent of Muslims, who represented 5 cent of the population, gave their vote to Hollande. In fact, according to Saad's calculations, Hollande won the elections with around 51 per cent of the national vote, meaning the support he earned with Muslim voters "tilted the balance in favour of the socialist candidate."[272] While some may challenge the idea that these votes were decisive, it is a just extrapolation that Hollande would not have won without his Muslim voters.

In subsequent elections, we have seen a similar trend. No less in 2022, when in the election's first round, 69 per cent of Muslim voters, according to IOFP, lent their support to Jean-Luc Mélenchon, France's populist-left

---

[270] Muslim Council of Britain. "MCB Finds Muslim Voters Could Swing 31 Marginal Seats." November 18, 2019. https://mcb.org.uk/mcb-finds-muslim-voters-could-swing-31-marginal-seats/

[271] Cited in Shabi, Rachel. "There Are Muslim Bricks in Labor's Crumbling Red Wall..." *Hyphen,* June 21, 2022. https://hyphenonline.com/2022/06/21/there-are-muslim-bricks-in-labours-crumbling-red-wall/

[272] Saad, Ali, "Can the Muslim Vote Sway the French Elections?" *Al Jazeera,* April 20, 2017. https://www.aljazeera.com/opinions/2017/4/20/can-the-muslim-vote-sway-the-french-elections

candidate.[273] Making a series of promises about fighting Islamophobia, as well as his stances on the economy and foreign policy issues, notably Palestine, he came within 1.2 per cent of Marine Le Pen, who came second, thus earning herself, for the second time, a place in the final round.[274] It seems the 92 per cent of Muslim voters who backed Macron in the previous second-round in 2017, felt let down by him. This abandonment of Macron, the incumbent centrist candidate, was due to many factors, but one was his legislation challenging "Islamist separatism," identifying it as "an ideology which claims its own laws should be superior to those of the Republic,"[275] which was roundly criticized by the French-left, not least by Mélenchon. As such, the final round between Macron and Le Pen was, for many French Muslims, described like choosing between 'the plague or cholera,' but fears of Le Pen becoming President, especially after her anti-immigration stances and calls to ban the headscarf in public, led the many Muslims that backed Mélenchon in the first-round, to back Macron in the second.[276] In the words of the Haitian-born mayor, Dieunor Excellent, who represents Villetaneuse, a banlieue located on the outskirts of Northern Paris, "This is not a vote of conviction, because I am not convinced by the ultra-liberal policies that Macron has been pursuing, it is about responsibility."[277] Excellent, who backed Mélenchon in the first round, as did 65 per cent of other voters in this town, many of whom are Muslim, added, "Marine Le Pen's program is racist, xenophobic and Islamophobic," therefore, with

---

[273] Cited in Bechiche, Hanna. "French Muslims Overwhelmingly Backed Mélenchon. Will the Left Take Note?" *Novara Media,* April 29, 2022. https://novaramedia.com/2022/04/29/french-muslims-overwhelmingly-backed-melenchon-will-the-left-take-note/

[274] ibid.

[275] "Macron Launches Crackdown on Islamist Separatism in Muslim Communities." *Reuters,* October 2, 2020. https://www.reuters.com/article/world/macron-launches-crackdown-on-islamist-separatism-in-muslim-communities-idUSKBN26N212/

[276] Cited in Bechiche, Hanna. "French Muslims Overwhelmingly Backed Mélenchon. Will the Left Take Note?"

[277] "Banlieues Hold Fate of Macron in Their Hands." *The Times,* April, 2022. https://www.thetimes.com/article/banlieues-hold-fate-of-macron-in-their-hands-8rt69bsdz

reluctance, he said, "I have no hesitation in putting a vote for Macron in the ballot box."[278]

This is a sentiment which spoke, and speaks, to many. This becomes particularly evident when looking at the data which compares the results of both rounds in areas with a disproportionately high concentration of Muslim voters. In such areas, many of which gave Mélenchon a majority in the first round, saw the prospect of Le Pen as far more unpalatable than a further 5 years with Macron. For instance, in Excellent's town, in the second round 77 per cent of voters backed Macron. In Marseille, France's second-largest city, with a population of around 862,000, of which, an estimated 250,000 are Muslim, Mélenchon won the first round by 31.12 per cent, beating Macron by almost eleven percentage points, but giving the latter victory in the second round with nearly 60 per cent of the vote.[279] Although never explicitly telling his voters to back Macron, he made it clear to those that supported him, to keep Le Pen out, at all costs, which many interpreted as a call to vote, though reluctantly, for Macron. It is worth noting, however, in the legislative election which were held a few weeks later, Mélenchon's left-wing coalition, NUPES, retained and took many of those areas, once held by Macron's Renaissance Party, as did Le Pen elsewhere, and this led to Macron losing his majority in Parliament.

Nevertheless, what is of importance here is that the Muslim vote, as in elections elsewhere in the region, was fundamental to Macron's retention of power. According to Abdennour Toumi, an expert in North African affairs, given the Muslim population make up around 10 per cent of the electorate, Macron would have needed 60 per of the non-Muslim vote to have succeeded.[280] Since he did not achieve this, it is plausible that Muslim voters played the role of "king-maker," or, at least, they ensured he achieved the majority needed to stay in office.

Overall, given that in the UK and France, Jews make for such a small percentage of both countries' populations, 0.4 and 0.6 per cent

---

[278] ibid;France 2022 - Presidential election - Second-round results - France 24
[279] See results by region here: France 2022 - Presidential election - Second-round results - France 24
[280] Toumi, Abdennour. "Does Muslim Vote Really Weigh-In in French Elections?" *Daily Sabah,* Oct, 2021. https://www.dailysabah.com/opinion/op-ed/does-muslim-vote-really-weigh-in-in-french-elections

respectively, and that Muslim voters are an electoral-game-changer, it is no wonder that mainstream parties have been negligent. There is no incentive to, politically speaking, cut off your nose to spite your face. And why should they? It would be like asking the British Conservative Party to abandon and alienate pensioners, on whom they depend. It's not going to happen. And similarly, the left and other parties have no real appetite to deal with this crisis because it would be, in places, electoral suicide.

However, not only do those parties demonstrate a lack of political will to take on the issues addressed. As we saw in Sweden, and we see this across the region, large sections of the left have succumbed to the political opportunism which at best turns a blind eye to, and at worst is complicit in, Jew-bashing. There is a recognition that opposition to Israel which, in practise, is exceedingly difficult to divorce from antisemitism, wins votes. An important ideologue who recognized the political utility of anti-Israelism was Pascal Boniface, a member of the French Socialist Party, and Director of the Institute for International and Strategic Affairs.

In the April of 2001, Boniface issued a memorandum to leading members of the party, including the then Francois Hollande, who was the party's First Secretary and Mayor of Tulle, urging the party adopt policies which would help them to win the "Muslim vote," particularly with regards to foreign policy. In this letter, which would later appear in an article for Le Monde, Boniface stated that since there are ten-times more Muslims than Jews in the country (6 million, and 600,000, respectively), the party adopt a decidedly pro-Palestinian stance, and not be home to pro Israel positions. The failure to do so, he argued, would not sit well with an estimated five to six million Muslim voters, on whose votes they could not do without.[281] Come the election, the party would come third , behind the runner-up, Jean-Marie Le Pen, leader of the far-right National Front, by less than 200,000 votes. While it would be inaccurate to suggest that they lost the election because of their policy in the Middle East, perhaps had they adopted Boniface's suggestion, this gap would have been closed

---

[281] Cited in Suzan, Bénédicte, and Jean-Marc Dreyfus. "Muslims and Jews in France: Communal Conflict in a Secular State." *Washington, D.C.*: The Brookings Institution, March 2004. https://www.brookings.edu/wp-content/uploads/2016/06/suzan20040229.pdf

further, even resulting in them clinching second place. In any case, today, large swathes of the left in Western Europe have heeded Boniface's call. For the very practical truism that such views win votes in places where national elections are won and lost.

This point, however, is often overlooked in the analysis of contemporary leftist anti-Israel tendencies. Few commentators have been willing to identify this factor in their study of contemporary leftist-antisemitism. But any understanding of both Corbyn and Mélenchon must take into account this factor. Although coming from different places, both geographically and politically, they not only shared a philosophical identification with the New Left, from which their breed of leftism owes its origins, but a recognition of the electoral benefits of their anti-Israel positions, which are well-documented.

In both cases, despite losing the elections, they relied upon the support of young-progressive-white-middle class voters, as well as those of a religiously and culturally conservative Muslim background. And amongst such groups, who ostensibly have little to nothing in common, this hostility towards the Jewish-State, far from deterring voters, was pivotal in winning their support. After all, they both did well, even best, in areas where the concentration of these demographics (but particularly Muslim voters) is higher. Although not the sole interest of these voters, electioneering of this kind has now become an indispensable tool for the mainstream left. So long as the demography of these areas remains the same, or, as predicted, continues to grow, there is no sign of change. The bitter invective against, and calumnies told of the Jewish State, is a vote winner. They avoid this, it seems, at their own electoral expense.

Although there are several examples of this, one case in point that sticks out in my mind is the Batley and Spen by-election of 2021. The Labor candidate, the sister of Jo Cox MP, murdered by a far-right terrorist, Kim Leadbeater, had set out her stance on Palestine, on at least one of her campaign leaflets.[282] Not much was said, just the vacuous, but à la mode words, condemning Israel and its defensive actions against Islamist terror. During the campaign trail, she also posted, on her Twitter page, a picture

---

[282] Cited in Maguire, Patrick (@patrickkmaguire). *Twitter,* June 14 2021. https://x.com/patrickkmaguire/status/1404342131410587650

of herself along with several activists wearing t-shirts which showed the map of Israel today covered in a Palestine flag, which, at best, is a call to peacefully dismantle the state, or at worse, destroy it.[283]

Why, need I ask, would the Labor Party, in a Yorkshire town, thousands of miles away from the Middle East, need to put the issue of Palestine in their campaign? In one sense, they were motivated to do so because of the threat posed by Leadbeater's opponent, and fellow left-winger, George Galloway, a veteran politician and lifelong anti-Zionist, who also included his ardent support for the Palestinian cause on an election leaflet. With his previous successes in Bradford West, as well as Bethnal Green and Bow, constituencies with a high concentration of Muslims, he realized the importance of using the Palestinian cause to galvanize the Muslim vote. As such, Leadbeater wanted to show that she, not Galloway, would be the one to champion the Palestinian cause. However, like Galloway, she also did it because there was realization that this issue is fundamental to scores of these voters, even if most have no direct connection to the region. In a similar way to how scores of Jews view Israel as a central issue in their engagement in the political arena, many Muslims, regardless of cultural and ethnic differences, have similar feelings towards the Palestinian cause. And given the fact there are many constituencies in the UK, and beyond, which can be determined by these voters, there is no reason why those running for election should dismiss this cause as a parochial issue.

In the end, she just about won the election, with Galloway coming third. Had she not made use of the Palestinian cause,, it is more than conceivable that she would have lost those voters, and therefore, possibly, the election itself. This was by no means the only case of a Labor politician utilizing the politics of the Middle East to win votes. Across Western Europe, mainstream, left-wing parties are increasingly aware that to win elections, they must avoid alienating Muslim voters. If anything, their incentive is not to challenge antisemitism in our Muslim communities, but

---

[283] Shared on Ofer, Tal. "Why is a @UKLabour PPC is posing with people whose t-shirts calls for destruction of Israel?." *Twitter,* May 27, 2021. https://x.com/TalOfer/status/1398009250836799492

put one of its most common expressions, in the guise of opposition to Israel and Zionism, to good use, as a means of winning support and votes.

It is dismaying to be faced with mainstream politicians who have been negligent, with a growing number complicit, in the proliferation of Jew-hate. Many say the right words, and yet stay well away from any meaningful action on this issue. But this shouldn't lead you to spill your tea in shock horror. What decides the behavior of those seeking power in any democratic society is determined according to what is desired amongst the demos, the people. And that is what democracy is all about. For our purposes, since Jews hold too little electoral weight for mainstream politicians to act, and since this hate is worsening in communities which do hold electoral weight, this negligence, along with the support given to anti-Jewish ideas, has been a political inevitability.

This situation has left many Jews to think: can we really lend our support to mainstream parties if they are failing on this issue? Recent elections have seen a number of Jews turn from traditional left-leaning centrist parties towards populist-right parties. The rise of Eric Zemmour in France, a conservative commentator of Jewish origin, and man who is set on becoming the next French President (he ran in the last elections, but came fourth), has succeeded in speaking to the sensibilities of many Jews in France. Many French Jews, and Jews across Western Europe, are deeply frustrated by the failure (willful in some cases) of mainstream politicians to have dealt with what presents a genuine risk to their safety and future.

As Jews down the ages have asked, "are they good for the Jews?" There are indeed opportunities with populist forces. If a Zemmour, a Le Pen or a Wilders were to take power, we could see much needed reforms in several areas, including in the realms of immigration, integration, law-enforcement, and an end to state reluctance to deal with vehicles of anti-Jewish and anti-democratic extremism in our Muslim communities. The success of populism could well prompt mainstream parties to change their tune. The victory of these parties may be what is needed to influence a vital paradigm shift within centrist, mainstream politics. We already can see a glimpse of this. For instance, Macron's 'Separatism Law,' passed in the September of 2020, was motivated not by ideological consideration, but by the prospect of Le Pen ousting him from office come the next election. And the increased success of populism keeps mainstream politicians on their toes; and perhaps is the only means of getting such politicians to reclaim the issues populists have taken charge of.

It is, though, extraordinary that parties with historic connections to Holocaust-denial and/or fascism, such as the French National Rally (formally National Front) or the Swedish Democrats, offer policies, which are conducive to dealing with the crisis of Islamist Judenhass. Yet, while populism may be the catalyst for change within mainstream parties, in the long run, movements which some might dismiss as reactionary, are not conducive to a sustainable future, not for Jews, nor for anyone. Those who have read Animal Farm will know that short-term benefits do not, necessarily, lead to long-term prosperity. Napoleon may be well-intentioned and magnanimous in the beginning, but relying on forces which have illiberal tendencies, may well pave the way for the erasure of processes which keep us all safe and free. And yet, so long as those charged with the welfare of liberal democracy remain negligent, perhaps Jews will have to look for change elsewhere, including in populism.

For now, as this section has explored, negligence is motivated by a very simple reality: in the realpolitik, our elected politicians have little reason to tackle this crisis of antisemitism in our Muslim communities. And to deal with this issue is to potentially hamper their chances at the ballot box. So long as the status quo remains, however, Jews will have little confidence in those who represent us to deal with this worsening crisis. Perhaps Jews will be left with no choice but to abandon parties which were once their natural political home for those which were once, not long ago, their worst fears. Indeed, what a damnable and hideous state of affairs.

Whereas this chapter has thus far explored governmental failure through the prism of social and political considerations, it is important to understand negligence on a level which goes beyond mere on-the-ground realities. For this negligence runs much deeper. It is rooted in a crisis of identity, culture, and values within Western Europe.

Section Three: The Politics of Identity

Let's begin this section at my high school. My own boisterousness, chaos, and tomfoolery aside, my alma mater was, and is, a brilliant, but very peculiar place. Although a Modern Orthodox Jewish High School, which continues to celebrate all Jewish holidays (including Israel's Independence Day), most students are not Jewish. This school, which was once entirely Jewish, is now largely comprised of Christian and Muslim pupils, and is home to over 50 languages, as well as over 30 nationalities. This voluntary and state funded comprehensive school, located in one of the most diverse areas of the country, is truly a multicultural institution. And I think for the better.

It should be reiterated – even with these demographic changes – the school has not lost its Jewish character. To this day, all food remains Kosher, male pupils must cover their head with a skullcap, the school runs a biannual trip to Israel, an annual trip to Poland, Jewish studies is taught, as is Hebrew to early years. I distinctly recall how in our Hebrew class, it was the non-Jewish pupils who would speak better Hebrew than us Jewish kids. Funny old place, eh? Expectedly, whenever I tell someone about King Solomon, I am met with bemused grins. For how, people routinely ask, can a school without a Jewish majority continue to be Jewish? Indeed, how does such a school even work?

To their astonishment, and even to mine, the school remains both Jewish and cohesive. Of course, this isn't to say the school is a haven of kumbaya. The issue of Israel-Palestine, as one can expect, creates some degree of tension between Jewish and Muslim students. Having said that, this isn't an issue that causes irreconcilable divisions, at least, nothing remotely like what we see a few miles from the school grounds on the weekends. Despite being diverse, remarkably, this unique institution has maintained a unifying and shared identity, which has ensured an impressive degree of cohesion and sense of togetherness within this institution. In fact, it has also led to some unexpected developments. One moment that left its mark was on our trip to Poland. As a large and diverse group of students, we visited sites which were used, in living memory, for unspeakable evils. Regardless of where we were, be that in Auschwitz or in Treblinka, both factories of death, all of us, proudly representing a

Jewish-high school, stood as one. We cried as one. We comforted each another as one. In the end, we rejoiced as one. This occurred because our school imbued in us a recognition that while difference is enriching, there is virtue in an identity which we can all share and believe in. And it was my experience not only in Poland, but throughout my entire school career, which led me to reason that diversity, so long as it is well managed and that which unites remains central, can, and indeed does, bring out the best in all of us.

Some, however, remain unconvinced. There are those who will raise their eyebrows when they hear about KS, and they often suggest that given these demographic realities, the school should discontinue its distinct Jewish-character. Yet the school remains obstinate. And rightly so. In my estimation, the school's success in maintaining cohesion has been because not despite of the identity it refuses to lose, and most importantly, is unafraid to assert. As a former head teacher put it, "Multiculturalism has often been conflated with a purported lack of identity, but we do not suffer from this."[284]

I begin with my former school not only as I am hopelessly mawkish, but because this was an institution that recognized that shared identity is the glue that brings an eclectic range of people together. In the absence of that which unites - shared identity, symbols, and culture - you have individuals with all their various, and often egomaniacal, `isms`. Without wishing to ruffle the feathers of my libertarian and Thatcherite chums, I believe in society, and the responsibility each person has towards the other. In its absence, if people have nothing they share, beyond a physical geographical space, then they may exist side-by-side, but ultimately, not really, together. The specter of atomization then haunts us. My school avoided this. But, as I shall now argue, our societies have not.

To understand shared identity in the context of society and state, and why it matters, it is worth dwelling on the luminous words of the late Sir Roger Scruton. Arguably the greatest English philosopher of the past fifty years, Scruton wrote extensively on a range of topics, not least on the role of shared identity. He impressed upon the need to foster "an inclusive identity that will hold us together as a people," adding, "the substitutes of

---

[284] formerly on the KSHS website.

modern times--the ideologies and "isms" of the totalitarian states--have transparently failed to provide an alternative." He reasoned, "we need an identity that leads to citizenship, which is the relation between the state and the individual in which each is accountable to the other. That, for ordinary people, is what the nation provides."[285] The concept of nationhood, or belonging to a nation, is that which transcends our own personal cultures and identities. And it is this which gives us, on a societal basis, shared-identity.

For Scruton, the nation is "a people settled in a certain territory, who share institutions, customs and a sense of history and who regard themselves as equally committed both to their place of residence and to the legal and political process that governs it."[286] While it is the case that a sense of nationhood is not an exclusive social tie, he rightly said that it is the "only form of membership that has so far shown itself able to sustain a democratic process and a liberal rule of law."[287] The power of such an attachment is that it marginalizes "loyalties of family, tribe and faith, and places before the citizens' eyes, as the focus of their patriotic feeling, not a person or a religion but a place." And "this place," he says, "is defined by the history, culture and law through which we, the people, have claimed it as our own."[288] A sense of nationhood, therefore, is the means of achieving unity without having uniformity. As he argued, "you cannot immigrate into a tribe, a family or a faith, but you can immigrate into a country, provided you are prepared to obey the rules that make that country into a home."[289]

Also speaking of this idea of 'home' was the late Chief Rabbi Sacks, a student of Scruton's, for whom multiculturalism led Britain to look less like a 'home,' and more like a 'hotel.' By this, he explained, "you pay for services rendered and in return you get a room, you get room services - beyond that, you are free to do whatever you like so long as you don't

---

[285] Scruton, Roger. "The Case for Nations." *Ethics and Public Policy Center,* June 3, 2017. https://eppc.org/publication/the-case-for-nations/
[286] Scruton, Roger. *England and the Need for Nations.* London: Civitas: Institute for the Study of Civil Society, 2006. p.12.
[287] ibid p.10.
[288] Scruton, Roger. "The Case for Nations."
[289] ibid.

disturb the other guests." As he averred, however, "that is great, except a hotel in principle generates no loyalty." Indeed, he explained, "a hotel is somewhere where you don't belong. It isn't a home. It's a convenience. And therefore, when society becomes a hotel, as it has become in the past 50 years, you get no sense of national identity, of belonging, of common history, of common good, of moral consensus, of social solidarity - and that is where we are now."[290] Like Scruton, the late and great Chief Rabbi saw the absence of a 'home' as not only leading to a fragmented and broken society, but one in which there is a lack of fraternity and social solidarity between citizens. This can only be a recipe for disaster.

As such, it is here where we locate the last, but perhaps the most important source of governmental failure and negligence. Whereas previous sections have concentrated on how factors of fear and political expediency have left successive governments reluctant to act, here I argue that negligence is not only the consequence of political considerations. It is also product of a societal and cultural reluctance to define and cultivate, much less celebrate, a shared-nationhood, or shared-national-identity, which goes beyond merely owning a passport, or civic national-identity. Over the past eighty-odd years, Western Europe, in the face of globalism and inestimable social and intellectual change, is struggling to establish what the role is, if any, for nationhood in an era which underscores the importance of 'thinking beyond the nation state.' For many Western Europeans, and indeed many Westerners, the nation is obsolete, as it is regressive and dangerous.

However, without establishing a shared nationhood, from which we are able to establish our own collective values, we cannot adequately draw up what Karl Popper described as the 'boundaries of tolerance.' For what, after all, does it mean to stand up for 'our values' if our societies have not yet established what those values are, and the boundaries of their inclusion? Some retort with the vague and recycled platitudes of our societies being 'open' and 'tolerant,' and insist this is what defines who we are, but does it? The biblical call to 'love thy neighbor as thyself,' the

---

[290] Sacks, Jonathan. "Society is Not a House or a Hotel, It Should Be a Home." *The Independent,* November 17, 2006. https://www.independent.co.uk/voices/ commentators /jonathan-sacks-society-is-not-a-house-or-a-hotel-it-should-be-a-home -223850.html

maxim of our age, and the one which underpins the philosophy of contemporary multiculturalism, may be laudable on paper, but what is this 'thyself,' and what are the limits of its 'love'? Since this has not been defined, our societies have ended up tolerating that which is not really deserving of our tolerance and loving that which is not deserving of our love. This section shall, therefore, argue that governmental negligence is the symptom of a society that has not had a reckoning with its own identity, and consequently, the benevolence of its tolerance has become self-negating and self-destructive.

I have been cognizant of this crisis of identity for several years. But my trip to France in 2021 was an eye-opener. I was in the city of Rouen, the largest in the Normandy region. With the most spectacular architecture, ravishing landscapes, and chic cafes, it really is a special place. One day, aimlessly strolling through the city, I arrived at a very large bridge, which is over the 777-kilometre-long Seine River. At this point, it was pointed out to me that the city is, in fact, divided according to the 'left bank' and 'east bank,' and up till then, I had only seen the latter. With my somewhat insatiable thrill for adventure, I decided to cross, and suddenly got the impression that the city no longer looked like the bourgeois paradise I had spent the past few days enjoying. This 'left-bank' was immigrant heavy, poor, crowded, and, on the face of things, disconnected, both socially and economically, from the city I had quickly come to love. Walking through this modern Anatevka, it struck me that the city is home to sociétés parallèles, or parallel societies, in which diversity is not matched with the commensurate shared identity and shared-culture that holds these people together in one city. The large bridge is not only a geographical divide; it is one between cultures, peoples, and a way of life. And this boundary, both physical and metaphorical, is one replicated throughout the region.

The Dutch, for instance, are well experienced in this regard. Discussing diversity in the Netherlands was Paul Scheffer in his stirring 2003 essay, '*Het multiculturele drama*,' or 'The Multicultural Fiasco.' Scheffer, an academic and prominent member of the Dutch Labor Party, was the first on the Dutch left to talk about what his fellow social democrats had got wrong about diversity. He argued that the failure to cultivate a shared identity not only perpetuates the social, political and economic disparities which the non-native population are burdened with, but is the source of society disharmony, or lack of cohesion.

Describing this as a policy of "pacification," Scheffer stated that the indifference on the part of Dutch authorities to bring those from non-Dutch backgrounds, especially from the Middle East and North Africa, into a collective Dutch culture and identity constitutes a "lazy multiculturalism." Stating "we do not adequately express what holds our society together," he quipped, "We talk too little about our own limits, we cherish no relation to our own past and we treat our language with nonchalance." As such, "A society that disavows itself has nothing to offer newcomers." And this, as he rightly pointed out, with many are making the same points twenty years later, "we coexist without interacting: we each have our own bar, our own school, our own idols, our own music, our own faith, our own butcher and soon our own street or neighborhood." Concluding, "If we are honest we must admit that all these old and new inhabitants know little or nothing about each other."[291]

Over twenty years later, his words still ring true, and many continue to identify with Scheffer's words. But not only in the Netherlands. Throughout the region, there is not only a disturbing absence of social cohesion, but large numbers of the non-native population live on the peripheries. And without a shared identity and culture, without this collective sense of nationhood, healing divides, so as to build a 'shared home' is a mighty, perhaps even, an insuperable task.

It is the case, however, that most West-Europeans have not lost their sense of civic-national-identity. The majority of those in the region, despite variations according to age (especially this factor, younger people are less likely to identify with their nation), class and political views, still identify with the territory in which they reside. Various studies, including the 2021 European Commission Special Barometer report, Values and Identities of EU citizens, found that "Across the EU, an average of 73%

---

[291] See Scheffer, Paul. "The Multicultural Fiasco." *NRC Handelsblad,* January 29, 2000.

respondents said they identified with their nationality."[292] Much like with the FRA studies addressed in Chapter One, we see a difference between Western Europe and Eastern European states, with national identity in the latter being greater, but not, it should be added, substantially greater.

What, though, is notably different between the two places is the way in which national identity is viewed. In most liberal-democratic Western European states, with some differences, nationhood has gone from being inextricably rooted in shared culture to being what can be described as *passport-nationalism*, in which it is stressed that multiple people, of all different backgrounds, can exist as citizens, so long as they subscribe to the values and institutions of the society around them. This is what nationhood means today: something very legalistic, deprived of any cultural, indeed visceral, significance for the demos. Conversely, in Eastern Europe, nationhood has remained something much more embedded within the fabric of the culture, and one in which people are expected not to merely exist, but find belonging in the national and collective culture of their societies.

However, both Eastern European and Western European models of national belonging are problematic. In Eastern Europe, as evidenced in countries such as Poland and Hungary, national belonging is becoming increasingly predicated on ethnic grounds. This has rendered such attachments to be exclusionary, and no less xenophobic, and on occasion, racist. And such a trajectory is certainly undermining the liberal-democratic values of these and other Eastern European states. Whereas in Western Europe, although far more open and inclusive, nationhood, in the face of a profound cultural and intellectual shift, has lost much of its meaning, to the extent that it no longer commands the reverence and respect it once did. Like in Eastern Europe, what is happening in our region is also undermining our sacrosanct liberal-democratic foundations. But more on this further down. For now, to our liberal elites, nationhood in Western Europe embodies all that is parochial and dangerous about European society.

---

[292] European Commission. Special Eurobarometer 508: Values and Identities of EU Citizens. Conducted by Kantar Public, October-November 2020. https://publications.jrc.ec.europa.eu/repository/handle/JRC126943. p.71.

In the minds of those elites, who have sought to promulgate this 'think beyond the nation state' ideology, nationhood is dismissed as the very antithesis of progress. It is its enemy. This social attachment is treated as the great threat to the 'New Europe', which rests on eschewing nation-centric views. And yet, despite the efforts of liberal elites to move us away from thinking in terms of borders, be that through the rise of globalism or the intellectual assault upon the nation's legitimacy, this has not lured a great many Western Europeans away from wanting to reclaim and reaffirm their sense of nationhood. It is clear, as Scheffer propounds, that it is insufficient to reduce national identity to something merely civic. The success of conservative populism vindicates the appetite to move away from a vague and wishy-washy national identity, and cultivate one which is concrete and grounded in that which is more than owning a passport.

But those elites seem hesitant to change. In their mind, nationhood is obsolete as it is dangerous. In a Western Europe which is at the epicenter of globalization, as well as increased integration into supranational organizations, the question arises: do we really need nationhood? Perpetuating a national-centric view, after all, is a folly. For why put-up stumbling block to Western Europe reaping the fruits of globalism and internationalism? Why think in terms of national-borders when we are living in a Europe which is becoming progressively borderless? Why think of a national culture when there are global cultures? Why think of our relationship to our fellow countryman when we should be thinking in terms of our European and global citizenship? Why celebrate a nation when we should concern ourselves with the rights of oppressed peoples within that nation, and beyond? These questions are indicative of why nationhood no longer commands the cultural traction it once did. Those who should be the ones to make the nation relevant in our own age have abandoned it, as well as persecute its proponents, for the sake of achieving a world which is focused chiefly on the pursuit of material wealth and benefit.

However, although we are ever more interconnected and without borders, our age is one of hyper-individualism, in which people are thought of in their atomized individual state, rather than their place within, and their responsibility to, the wider whole, or, put simply, society. As such, the flags of those perceived to be oppressed carry much more social gravitas and acceptability than our national flag. I was reminded of this back in the June of 2023, Pride Month. In Regents Street, London, local council workers were taking down hundreds of Union Flags (Union Jacks), and were replacing them with the updated 'Progress Pride' flags for the forthcoming 'Pride Month.' Witnessing this, a passerby exclaimed, "You're taking the wrong f*****g flag down, mate." To which, the man taking down the flag replied, "You think I don't know that?"[293] In the same month, a similar incident occurred in Lyon, France. A group of LGBT+ activists were marching on the streets, with their rainbow flags, and allegedly, a local resident who objected to the parade put up a French flag on their balcony. In response, a protester climbed up, tore it off, threw it to the floor, and the crowd, typical of what the French describe as Bobos, or bohemian bourgeois, greeted such a move with cheers and applause.[294]

Although these incidents may seem to be isolated, they reveal why many feel disillusioned with contemporary liberalism. In a Western Europe plagued with identity-politics, to such elites, nationhood is no longer the identity which should unite peoples. Rather, in their mind, the flags of groups perceived to be oppressed and marginalized, especially the one of 'Progress Pride' (which, in actuality, has little to do with the commendable work of earlier incarnations of Pride), have far more virtue and value. And worse, national flags and national attachments, unless they belong to a country which is not white, Christian, or most importantly, Jewish, are that which restrain # human-progress.

Mostly seen at universities, the crucible of self-abasing anti-westernism, this propensity amongst Western Europe's intelligentsia and leading cultural figures to lambast all things tradition, not least the nation, is becoming increasingly mainstream. This was described by Rodger Scruton as 'oikophobia,' or hatred of home. As he pointed out though, it is much more than a hatred: it is the attempt to dismantle the very fabric

---

[293] Taken from Grimes, Darren. ""You're taking the wrong ****ing flag down, mate." "You don't think we know that?!" I'm with these guys.." *X* (formerly Twitter), June, 2023. https://twitter.com/darrengrimes/status/1646158597120729088

[294] "French Pride Parade Participants Triggered by National Flag, Tear It Down." *Rumble*, June 13, 2023. https://rumble.com/v2wh3k6-french-pride-parade-participants-triggered-by-national-flag-tear-it-down.html

of who we are. Owing its origins to the increased secularization of Western society, the oikophobe, Scruton averred, "sees that which is his 'own,' his inheritance, as an alien; he has fallen out of communication with it and feels tainted by its claims on him." Adding, "He wants to be free of that claim—free from the pressure to belong, to be with 'us,' to love something, believe in something, accept something what is his." Consequently, "he portrays his home as something Other, by means of a stereotype that seems to free him from all obligation towards it."[295]

Various intellectual developments over the past few decades, be that the emergence of the Frankfurt School or the spread of Critical Studies (or Critical Race Theory) on university campuses, have precipitated this intellectual war on what was once foundational. To the archetypal bastions of progress, both nationhood and nationalism, with no distinctions made, are viewed as the sources through which the worst of our civilization's past are reinforced and disseminated. Accordingly, any attempt to resuscitate, or even defend the nation, is seen as an assertion of wishing to perpetuate inequalities, racism, and oppression, all of which provided the backbone to Western Europe's historic participation in genocide, colonialism, and exclusion. No wonder there is a predilection amongst those elites to move Western Europe, and the world, away from its own borders. The nation can only be a purveyor of terror and destruction.

Reminiscent of the 'self-hating Jew,' for many who participate in oikophobia, they do so as a means of achieving acceptability amongst peers and wider society. And I don't blame them. The prospect, and it's a real one, of social ostracization naturally disincentivizes any kind of dissent from a new orthodoxy, which has become dominant on many university campuses; an orthodoxy which holds any patriot or any individual who still relishes in his or her national identity as a threat to human progress. Why risk losing friends or risk being treated as a 'racist' or perpetuator of 'orientalist thinking' (I face both charges regularly) for challenging the ideas which a small, but seemingly noisy and influential intellectual bunch, have come to regard as sacred? It seems anyone who

---

[295] Cited in Scruton, Roger. "Oikophobia." Excerpt from England and the Need for Nations. *Matiane's Blog,* April 10, 2020. https://matiane.wordpress.com/2020/04/10/oikophobia-by-roger-scruton/

greets their ideas with incredulity is a heretic, and must not only be exposed as one, but be silenced. In the words of Pascal Bruckner, who wrote in objection to Western "perpetual penitence," he remarked, "Nothing is more Western than hatred of the West, that passion for cursing and lacerating ourselves."[296] He continued, "By issuing their anathemas, the high priests of defamation only signal their membership in the universe they reject."[297]

Bruckner is certainly on to something. To borrow from Lady Macbeth, "All the perfumes of Arabia will not sweeten this little hand." In the case of Western Europe, although we have progressed from a time when our societies were plagued with evil, no matter what we do, to oikophobes, we shall forever remain in sin. Nothing can redeem us. We are eternally damned. And Douglas Murray, one of the leading intellectuals of our age, highlights this in his bestselling, The Strange Death of Europe.

In his analysis of Turkish cruelty towards the Armenians, as well as its brutal invasion and occupation of Cyprus in 1973, he opines, "One might concede that Turkey, as a historical force, has been no worse if certainly no better, than any other country in the world." Speaking of the country, he asks, "Who has not carried out an actual genocide against, run an empire for twice as long as the British and invaded a sovereign state in recent decades?" But states, "This is not what is striking." Rather, "what is striking is that so little of this is ever raised and Turkish people are ever rarely if ever made to feel guilty for Turkey's historic role in the world." In fact, the Turkish government have sought to regulate any condemnation of their nation, particularly through Article 301 of the country's penal code, which declares it is a 'crime to insult the Turkish nation.'[298]

In any event, Murray observes, "what is more surprising is that so few people would use these things against Turks as a people." As such, he rightly asks: "If the kind of history now taught and internalized in much of Europe is intended simply to prevent a replay of the worst aspects of that history, then we should ask who else should be treated this way?

---

[296] Bruckner, Pascal, *The Tyranny of Guilt,* p.33.
[297] ibid.
[298] See Murray, Douglas. *The strange death of Europe: Immigration, identity, Islam.* Bloomsbury Publishing, 2017. p.172.

Which other nations ought to be encouraged to feel shame for their past? And if none others do, relying not only on natural pride but also outlawing historical inquiry, does Europe not find itself in the strange situation of feeling unusually guilty for being only ordinarily so?"[299] These questions need answering. But not much has changed since these were written. To those of us who share such concerns, things have got much worse. In large sections of universities and media, any notion of Western European nationhood is frequently dismissed, though not necessarily explicitly, as the 'enemy of progress.' This became clear during the 2016 EU Referendum in the UK. Those who expressed legitimate concerns about national identity, immigration, and culture were regularly dismissed as backwards and racist. Even before the referendum, David Cameron, our former prime minister, dismissed UK Independence Party (UKIP), the party which triggered the referendum in the first place, as a party of "fruit cakes and loonies and closet racists."[300] Not only was this a shameful calumny of his own voters, but it is a sentiment which illustrates the state of many political elites in Britain's major parties: it is easier to malign those who believe in, as it were, nationhoodism, than discuss its place in society. Is it really surprising, therefore, why many, including lifelong socialists, have found political refuge in conservative populism?

The proponents of the 'think beyond nation-state' ideology have elected to demonize, often in the most classist terms, rather than engage with those who question the wisdom of their supposedly progressive and kinder politics. But this approach hasn't worked. And so long as nationhood is deemed as not only irrelevant, but inherently a violation of postwar renewal, our societies will lack that social cohesion which is necessary for the welfare of liberal democracy, and no less, for building a shared home.

It would, of course, be intellectually dishonest to ignore and/or deny the elephant in the room: atrocities have been, and continue to be, committed in the name of 'the nation.' It is a matter of historical fact that murder, violence, discrimination, dehumanization, and a disregard for the

---

[299] ibid, p.173.
[300] Cited in "Cameron refuses to apologize to UKIP," *The Guardian,* April 4, 2006, https://www.theguardian.com/politics/2006/apr/04/conservatives.uk

sanctity of human life, are all central tenants of a poisonous societal and political relationship to the homeland, which was at its zenith at the time of the Third Reich. Yet while it would be wrong to ignore this abuse of the nation for barbaric ends, it is important we are able to distinguish between positive and negative interpretations of what it means to belong. And to do this, I turn, once again, to the timeless sagacity of Roger Scruton.

In his short pamphlet, *England and The Need for Nations*, Scruton drew a critical a distinction, and one I share, between 'national-loyalty' or 'patriotism' (but what I have described as 'nationhood'), which he saw as positive, and 'nationalism,' which he saw as inherently problematic. Scruton regarded the former, much like Sacks, as being like an extended family, which comprises a plurality of people who form a collective in their shared territory, in order to work for the betterment of their society, both local and national. This nationhood respects the rule of law, it is democratic, and is inclusive without losing its distinct cultural flavor and identity. And this is miles away from nationalism. Rather, as Scruton observed, "nationalism is a belligerent ideology, which uses national symbols in order to conscript the people to war."[301] He saw this totalitarian and absolutist devotion to the nation as fundamentally dangerous, since it has no regard for the rule of law and democratic processes, and much less for the welfare of the demos, particularly its minorities. He thus reasoned, "this kind of nationalism is not a national loyalty, but a religious loyalty dressed up in territorial clothes."[302]

In reality, however, these distinctions in liberal circles have not been made. For those who proclaim to champion progressivism, no form of thinking in national terms can be accepted. Of course, it is the case that such people are well-intentioned. They regard national loyalties to be the principal reason why Europe plunged into totalitarianism and anti-democratic extremism. They make a credible observation. Nationalism did indeed lead to tragedy. But their readiness to repudiate any form of national-attachments has endangered social-cohesion, as well as democracy, and the very ideals, which they claim would be endangered if nationhood became, once again, the motor of societal unity.

---

[301] Scruton, Roger, *England the Need for Nations*, p.17.
[302] ibid.

The policy of 'pacification,' as Paul Scheffer puts it, has meant successive governments have been indifferent to the divisions, disparities, and tensions which have arisen from our societies becoming multicultural. Probably because many of those in government reside in places which have not been exposed to the issues which have emerged in this embrace of diversity, they do not seem to be overly perturbed by what is occurring in the local cities and towns which they claim to represent. And yet, they should be: a lack of cohesion amongst the demos endangers democracy. This point was, in fact, articulated two centuries ago by John Stuart Mill, one of the most prodigious and eminent political philosophers of all time. Writing in the midst of the 'spring of nations,' in which exclusionary ideas of Blut und Boden (blood and soil) were becoming increasingly more popular, he spoke of the 'principle of cohesion among members of the same community or state.' Dismissing the racialized and antisemitic interpretation of nationalism, Mill put forward what is arguably the first liberal defense of nationhood:

> *We need scarcely say that we do not mean nationality, in the vulgar sense of the term; a senseless antipathy to foreigners; indifference to the general welfare of the human race, or an unjust preference for the supposed interests of our own country; a cherishing of bad peculiarities because they are national, or a refusal to adopt what has been found good by other countries. We mean a principle of sympathy, not of hostility; of union, not of separation. We mean a feeling of common interest among those who live under the same government, and are contained within the same natural or historical boundaries. We mean, that one part of the community do not consider themselves as foreigners with regard to another part; that they set a value on their connexion—feel that they are one people, that their lot is cast together, that evil to any of their fellow-countrymen is evil to themselves, and do not desire selfishly to free themselves from their share of any common inconvenience by severing the connexion.*[303]

This astute analysis by Mill, later repeated by Scheffer and Scruton, is critical. A lack of shared identity not only leaves our societies more

---

[303] Cited in Orazi, Françoise. (2022) "The Elusiveness of Nationalism." *Revue française de civilization britannique, XXVII.* DOI: 10.4000/rfcb.9353

divided, as various places in Western Europe attest, but also serves to undermine democracy itself. The idea of nationhood is much more than a mere attachment: it is also a sense of responsibility to your fellow citizens, to your community, and to the welfare of your core national institutions. Without this, people become hungry for alternatives. The widespread disillusionment with mainstream parties and the growth of populist parties, both left and right, is evidence of an anger which many feel with the status quo. Although not exclusively for this reason, many are moving away from these parties because they no longer feel the current system is fit for purpose; it is not taking their grievances, their concerns, and their frustrations seriously. A healthy democracy is one in which citizens not only share a territory and responsibilities to one another, but also one in which people feel they are heard. Many in Western Europe feel unheard, and therefore, are at odds with what governs them. The rise of populism is, to no small extent, the symptom of a liberal politics in crisis. The onus is on such-minded individuals and parties to change their tune.

I am not the first, much less the first Jew, to address the consequences of this erasure of the nationhood. Contrary to the utterances of many liberal-philosophers of our day, Hannah Arendt, the great German-Jewish philosopher, in her Origins of Totalitarianism, argued that totalitarianism in the twentieth century emerged as the liberal-nation-state system began to decline. That is, totalitarianism is not the success of the nation-state, it flourishes when the system erodes. And antisemitism, she identified, is no exception to this. In the first section of her book, which is an analysis of modern Jew-hate, Arendt argues that it "grew in proportion as traditional nationalism declined, and reached its climax at the exact moment when the European system of nation-states and its precarious balance of powers crashed."[304] This is because the liberal-nation-state, which is different from nationalism, is the guarantor of the rights and liberties of all. Its erosion, it follows, imperils these protections, particularly concerning the rights of Jews.

However, Arendt's point could be taken further. It is not only the loss of the liberal-nation-state which presents a danger to a liberal-democratic

---

[304] Arendt, Hannah. *Antisemitism: Part one of the origins of totalitarianism.* Vol. 1. Houghton Mifflin Harcourt, 2012.

society. It is also the loss of nationhood which presents a grave risk to such a society. In some sense, this point was argued in Chapter Ten of her magnum opus, arguing that totalitarian politics requires an "atomized" society, in which citizens are deprived of that which binds them to one another. But the implications of this loss of nationhood need to be understood. In its absence, a vacuum emerges. And this is to the delight of anti-democratic forces. For in principle, nationhood is that which gives citizens a means of connecting with one another, and no less, a sense of belonging in a shared-territory. Where people no longer have a nation to identify with, they have sought belonging elsewhere. To illustrate why we all need place in which to belong, Yael Tamir, a leading scholar of nationalism, states that when her late-supervisor, Isaiah Berlin was asked which animal he identified with, he answered "A penguin." Explaining why, Berlin said, "Because penguins live in colonies, they cannot survive on their own." As Tamir explicates, "This was his way of saying something profound about himself and about humanity." Adding, "Humans may be able to survive on their own, yet even the loneliest of literary figures, Robinson Crusoe, had to find Friday to converse with and share the knowledge he had acquired back home— without the ability to converse he would have lost a significant part of his humanity." In sum, "It may be assumed that personal autonomy is dependent on our ability to free ourselves from the shackles of belonging, yet freedom is hollow outside of a meaning- providing system."[305]

For many in our region, Tamir's words ring true. In the decline of nationhood, people have sought alternative arenas in which to find belonging. For we all crave that which generates purpose and meaning. We live for those pursuits. This explosion of 'isms' in our society, this surge of 'ism-hood,' points to a Western Europe which is materialistically richer, perhaps we've never had it better, but ultimately, its people are crying out for that which goes beyond the rapacity for the accumulation of 'things.' We are indeed a spiritually malnourished culture. And, therefore, it is no shocker that people have attached themselves to various 'isms' which speak to their political, ideological, ethnic, or cultural affiliations, or desires. While many of these are perfectly innocuous, some have been

---

[305] See Tamir, Yael. *Why Nationalism.* Princeton: Princeton University Press, 2019.

more problematic, and do present a palpable threat to cohesion, to democracy, and, as ever, to the Jews.

There is no doubt that extremist groups of all incarnations, but particularly Islamist ones, have flourished unabated in a society of atomized, even broken, parts. Particularly for a growing number of young and aggrieved Muslim men, Islamist entities have sought to provide that which these individuals have not found in progressive society: belonging, purpose, identity, and thus, grounded-values, as well as a scapegoat for their grievances. No doubt this Islamist exploitation has been exacerbated by economic disparities, societal discrimination, and a state which has treated many of those who live in these deprived areas with contempt and bigotry. But these factors, though important, are a shallow interpretation of why a growing number find good company in the poison of fanaticism. In societies which share little and are bereft of a concrete identity, for pliant minds, the intoxication of hate becomes an almost irresistible force.

So how, then, did Western Europe end up experiencing this crisis of culture and identity? Of course, this did not emerge overnight. It has been brewing over the past eighty years. In this time, the region has undergone a major cultural, political, and social transformation. By exploring, in brief, this radical reshaping of our societies, we are able to understand the socio-cultural milieu in which multiculturalism, and by extension, governmental negligence, emerged. Throughout this book, I have worked on the supposition that the decades following 1945 have been characterized by a form of spiritual, cultural and social renewal. Although it is the case that the world has always been changing and evolving, what has developed since the end of the Second World War, but particularly from the 1960s onwards, has been unprecedented.

It is the case that, collectively speaking, much of this has been radically life-changing. Our societies are wealthier, and the opportunities for social mobility are greater. With healthcare being as universally accessible, our societies are indeed healthier. The countless legal protections for individuals and minorities as we presently have is historically unsurpassed. We have never had as much access to life-changing technology. The innumerable educational opportunities, regardless of socio-economic status, is not something my parents' generation had access to. As a result of globalism, consumerist goods are no longer restricted to those with inordinate sums of money, and poverty has been considerably reduced. And let's not forget the ground-breaking advances with social media, which have left us, more than ever before, interconnected with people from all walks of life. It is astonishing the extent to which our societies and lives have been revolutionized by the fruits of these advancements.

However, let's not kid ourselves: Western Europe is not yet a haven of equity and justice. And it probably never will be. Those ideals seem at odds with the current state of the prevailing neoliberal system. But compared to the poverty and war-ridden Western Europe my grandparents grew up in, we live in much more peaceful, prosperous, democratic, and economically fairer societies. Nevertheless, because of this extraordinary progress, Western Europe has witnessed what can be described as the 'decline of tradition,' or the erasure of that which was once central in our societies. We see this, for instance, in the dwindling numbers of those who identify as Christian and partake in religious services, in the unprecedented rates of divorce and decline in marriage itself, in the diminishing nuclear family, in the death of local communities, especially the high-streets, in the spread of multinational corporations at the expense of small businesses, in the radical reshaping of attitudes towards gender and sexuality, and of course, above all, the move to think in global, not national or local terms. We are a desperately lonely people. The anguish of this isolation seems to have no political antidote. And so, it is here, in the midst of this gargantuan civilizational reset, where we identify what underpins the delusion of multiculturalism, and why negligence is the inevitable symptom of this delusion.

For in this socio-cultural revolution, our societies no longer privilege, nor place any real virtue upon that which we share. Our societies have opted to become places of multi-culture, in which no culture is privileged over another, not even the one which allowed for this diversity in the first place. This has, in turn, led to a view, which many in our leading institutions hold to, that all cultures and their values are equal, and we should not impose our ideas and values on others. Such audacity, they argue, would constitute a form of cultural neocolonialism.

Often described as 'cultural-relativism' in scholarly circles, while some may view this as a means to further understanding between peoples, it is indeed the hallmark of a delusion to think one can achieve any degree of cohesion amongst the demos without having a framework which all are prepared to honor, and live under. For we cannot possibly be willing to assert shared values if we do not first define who we are, and what it is we stand for, and worse, if we consider every cultural value, some of which is outright sexist and racist, to be on an equal footing to our own. Of course, this is not to suggest well-managed diversity is objectionable. Societies which flourish are those which do make space for the 'other,' and those which value this 'dignity of difference.' And diversity most certainly does not preclude cohesion. There are, in fact, multicultural societies which have, in many ways, succeeded in reconciling diversity with a unifying nationhood. One such example of this is, perhaps to the surprise of many of you, the State of Israel. Although incredibly diverse, this state has managed, though not without challenge, to integrate vast numbers from various periods of large migration to its shores.

In fact, Douglas Murray cited a phone call between Angela Merkel and Benjamin Netanyahu, the Israeli Prime Minister, with Merkel allegedly wishing to find out how the Jewish state has managed to achieve such success in the realm of integration. Various possible reasons were given, such as mandatory national service and absorption programs, such as Ulpan. However, with his characteristic incisiveness, Murray points out, "what diplomatic discretion may have prevented Prime Minister Netanyahu from pointing out, but which might have been apt, was that Israel had an advantage in that nearly all of the arrivals into the country for decades had a common link in their Jewish heritage – whereas in the months and years to come Angela Merkel and her nation would have to recognize that few of the people they let in during 2015 were German Lutherans."[306] In other words, for the most part, those who migrate to Israel are Jewish – and, therefore, with some variations, the people moving to the country share a similar value and cultural system. This means Jews from Ethiopia and Jews from Russia, though from vastly different places,

---

[306] See Murray, Douglas. *The strange death of Europe: Immigration, identity, Islam.* p.124.

can dwell together in the same state. Their shared Jewish identities and shared sense of belonging, or nationhood, are the common denominators, which make this all possible. The State of Israel has discovered the benefits of being multicultural, but without having a policy of multiculturalism, which rejects a nationhood which all citizens can share. It is an example of a state which has retained its sense of nationhood and is unafraid to defend and assert it. This is not what we see many states throughout Western Europe look like. And we now see the consequences of our own delusions.

The very notion of establishing 'unity in diversity,' as the EU motto goes, without a defined sense of nationhood, and therefore, defined values and boundaries, is as unworkable in the same measure it is delusional. So long as Western Europe privileges a plurality of multi-culture above an overriding one, and so long as our societies move away from the virtue of nationhood, and the ability to assert that which unites, not only will our societies be more fractured, but this negligence will continue uninterrupted.

If our nations embrace a boundless tolerance, if our societies place little or no value, indeed no virtue, on a concrete shared nationhood, then the issues described in this work will get worse. Even if, somehow, society and government overcame their fears of confronting Islamism in Western Europe, and left-leaning parties put the welfare and future of liberal democracy before votes, so long as our societies have no understanding of its own identity, values and boundaries, then we shall see no end to that which divides, ferments hate, and ultimately, endangers all that we cherish in free liberal-democratic societies. The negligence of government, therefore, is the natural corollary of a society which has undermined and moved away from, its own soul.

These questions need to be reckoned with. If our societies persist in this reluctance to wrestle with such questions, not only will this negligence continue, but our societies will lack that which millions in Western Europe are crying out for: a home in which to find belonging, and crucially, believe in. And as my years at KS taught me, not only can this co-exist with a diverse population, but such well-managed diversity positively unleashes the best in all of us.

Concluding Thoughts

Throughout this chapter, various sources of governmental negligence have been explored. What is clear, from everything that has been said, is that inaction from successive governments, as well as that of traditional voices for anti-racism, cannot be reduced to or blamed on a single factor. This chapter has analyzed three main reasons why our governments have failed to tackle not only a threat to the rights of Jews, but a threat to the essence and future of our liberal-democratic societies. Yet it would be mistaken to think that these reasons should be used to excuse those who are responsible. This chapter explores what has disincentivized those in power from plucking the courage to address what needs to be addressed, not to justify their reticence. Before we turn to the next chapter, however, I would be remiss not to say a few words on another source of negligence: that of my fellow Jews, specifically, Jewish leaders. Although this is coming from a Jew living in Britain, I am sure Jews in Western Europe, and beyond, can identify with some of the following sentiments.

For the avoidance of doubt, I shall be clear from the outset: in no way is this to apportion blame on Jews for antisemitism. Such victim-blaming, although increasingly trendy these days, is sickeningly wrong. Nevertheless, this should not distract from the fact that Jewish leaders, particularly here in the UK, have simply taken a backseat on the issue of Islamist antisemitism. And on the rare occasion they do speak out, they will speak in terms of this issue involving a 'few-extremists.' I have encountered more courage in the Association of British Muslims, the organization I used to work for, since they, unlike senior Jewish bodies, are prepared to discuss the extent to which anti-Jewish thinking has become a part of our Muslim communities. They feel it is their duty, as practising and committed Muslims to speak frankly. The leaders of my community are patently falling short in this regard.

To illustrate this failure of leadership, I begin with an event which occurred some years ago, at the University of Essex. Here, I attended a conference about antisemitism. It was held on this campus because in the months preceding this event, a large number of students voted against the ratification of the Jewish-Society, on the basis that such society professed a desire to hold Zionist and Israel based events, which, of course, are close to the hearts of many Jewish students, of which there were not many. Much to the disappointment of those students who objected to the Jewish society, because of the fortitude displayed by the society's leaders, especially its inspiring president, it was eventually ratified. And subsequently, antisemitism became a hot topic on campus.

As such, university leaders sought to foster a better understanding of antisemitism, so as to avoid the university, once again, finding itself in hot water. The conference was one among several events put on to discuss this hatred. There were several speakers, each of whom offered insights and knowledge about the realities of the current situation, except, I must say, one. This one fifteen-minute presentation, about antisemitism on British university campuses, left me feeling deeply troubled. When it came to an end, I thought it was either, at best, a bad joke, or at worst, a volitional ignorance of reality. Unfortunately, this presenter was not joking. Well-acquainted with the issues facing Jewish students, this speaker gave most of their time, perhaps all of it, to the subject of the far-right on British campuses. Now, this speaker was not talking about your UKIP or Brexit activists; they were talking about neo-Nazis, fascists, skinheads.

Back then, when I was nineteen, I was travelling the country, speaking to Jewish students at various campuses about antisemitism, amongst other issues. If I was tasked with writing a list of the top twenty grievances Jewish students had on campus, the far-right threat would not make it. It would not even come close. This isn't to say we should shrug off the threat they might pose in the years to come, but at present, they are out of the picture. And yet this senior representative of a leading Jewish advocacy body ignored the actual problem. Presenting to an open-minded audience, eager to learn more about contemporary antisemitism, they had wasted an invaluable opportunity by inventing a problem to avoid discussing what really threatens Jewish life. But to us younglings in the room, we saw right through it. We knew what the threat was, and is. But the speaker would not dare say it.

Those who lead my community too often privilege well-intentioned interfaith work above calling out the unholy alliance and its threat to Jewish life on campus. They seem far more interested in encouraging Jews and Muslims to sit down with one another, where they eat sumptuous fruits, and talk, in the vaguest terms imaginable, about their commitment to make the world a better place. Make no mistake: this is lovely; it has its place, and no doubt makes those participants feel good about themselves. Spiffing! But there is no use in gliding over the issues that are the reason such interfaith forums exist in the first place. These much-needed conversations are, in my experience, routinely hushed up, as is any notion of leading figures in my community speaking publicly about the crisis of antisemitism in our Muslim communities. The current approach does not deal with the very real and worsening rifts between our communities. If anything, they are exacerbated by making such conversations taboo.

Be under no misapprehension, if they wanted to, they could speak out. These organizations are not insignificant. The Board of Deputies (BoD), for instance, is the second-oldest institution in Anglo-Jewry, and has established itself as an important British institution. It commands a great presence and much respect in journalistic and political circles. When it speaks out, its voice is not ignored. But even this reality has not prompted credible action on their part to speak out. In fact, they seem more enraged by those who discuss such issues than the issues themselves.

One episode that encapsulates this failure of leadership is the Samuel Hayek affair. A wealthy British-Israeli businessman and chairman of the UK branch of the Jewish National Fund, Hayek, in an interview for the Jerusalem Post, spoke about the future of Muslim migration into the UK. Making reference to the awful situation in France, Hayek declared, "maybe in 10 years, maybe less, who knows, Jews will not be able to live in the UK. I don't think anybody can stop it," but made it clear, that he is "not against any minority or against the Muslims in the UK or Europe, but against anyone who spreads hatred that harms Jews."[307] In a follow-up interview by the Jewish News, the most widely read Jewish newspaper in the UK, he said, "the demographic of British society is changing [due to] the number of immigrants coming to England." Asked if he was describing

---

[307] Harpin, Lee. "Charity Commission Is Investigating JNF UK After Comments by Chair." *Jewish News,* January, 2022. https://www.jewishnews.co.uk/charity-commission-is-investigating-jnf-uk-after-comments-by-chair/
Jaffe-Hoffman, Maayan. "Jews Do Not Have a Future in England." *The Jerusalem Post,* November 21, 2021. https://www.jpost.com/diaspora/antisemitism/jews-do-not-have-a-future-in-england-687711

Muslims, he replied, "You are not wrong. Our problem in the West is that we do not understand Islam. In Islam there is not a term for 'peace.'"[308]

While one is free to robustly disagree with Hayek, and challenge his views, this would have been an opportune moment for Jewish leaders to express the concerns of countless Jews in the UK and beyond. Hayek articulated a concern that many Jews identify with. But no. Leading British Jewish bodies, including the Board of Deputies, the Jewish Leadership Council, the Community Security Trust (CST), and even the Chief Rabbi, all came out to condemn Hayek's words. In a letter signed by over 46 members of the BoD, they called for Hayek to resign as chairman, and stated if this did not happen, they would encourage their synagogues and organizations not to have anything to do with the oldest Zionist charity in the UK.[309] A few days later, 105 Jewish school and student leaders have called for all JNF-related programs to stop because of the "Islamophobia and bigotry" of Mr Hayek.[310] And later, at a vote taken by the Board of Deputies, members voted, overwhelmingly, to censure the JNF for these remarks.[311] In the letter sent to the trustees of JNF-UK, which was made public, the President of the Board, Marie Van der Zyl, made their position crystal clear, "We note that the Chair of JNF has still not retracted his comments and nor has he apologized for them. It is also regrettable that you as Trustees have not been explicit in your condemnation of his comments. When you are unable to reject explicitly, anti-Muslim bigotry,

---

[308] Cited in Rocker, Simon, "Calls for JNF UK Chair Samuel Hayek to Quit Over Islamophobic Comments." *The Jewish Chronicle,* https://www.thejc.com/news/community/calls-for-jnf-uk-chair-samuel-hayek-to-quit-over-islamophobic-comments-enu15vl7
Cited in Harpin, Lee, "Charity Commission investigating JNF UK after chair's comments to Jewish News."
[309] Harpin, Lee, "Letter Signed by 46 Deputies Demands JNF UK Chair Resigns Over Islamophobic Comments." *Jewish News,* January, 2022 https://www.jewishnews.co.uk/letter-signed-by-46-deputies-demands-jnf-uk-chair-resigns-over-islamophobic-comments/
[310] "More than 100 student leaders back suspension of JNF UK schemes over chair's 'Islamophobia and bigotry'" *Jewish News,* January 2022, https://www.jewishnews.co.uk/jnf-ujs-letter-samuel-hayek-1/
[311] "Board Passes Motion Censuring JNF UK Over Chair's Bigoted Remarks." *The Jewish Chronicle,* January 23, 2022. https://www.thejc.com/news/community/board-passes-motion-censuring-jnf-uk-over-chairs-bigoted-remarks-j7z1t0u8?reloadTime=1650499200011

it undermines attempts to draw attention to, and combat, antisemitism from extremists in the Muslim community." And she concluded with, "The Board of Deputies look forward to the day when you address seriously the matters raised above."[312]

Many Jews look forward to the day when Jewish leaders take seriously the crisis of antisemitism within our Muslim communities, and the very legitimate concerns raised about the pace of future migration from Muslim lands to Britian and Western Europe. The fact that Jewish leaders failed to even engage with the contents of his statements, not to mention the President's dismissal of antisemitism in our Muslim communities to be the fault of 'extremists,' as if there is no larger problem in these communities, serves to highlight why those who claim to represent Jews in Britain are not reading the room. It would have been wholly legitimate had they come out and criticized the way in which Hayek voiced his concerns. They could have done this without dismissing his sentiments as expressions of hate. They weren't. On their part, this was an abrogation of responsibility, and this incident, as well as several others, has left Jews in Britian, and indeed across Western Europe, to think: do we really have the representatives we deserve?

This kind of response from Jewish leaders, of course, is nothing new. It speaks to a trend we have seen amongst diaspora Jews for millennia. It reminds me of the Jewish joke about two Jews in Tsarist Russia. For sure an old one, but nonetheless a profound truism is captured within its characteristic self-renouncing humor:

> Three Jews are about to be executed by firing squad. The sergeant in charge asks each one whether he wants a blindfold. "Yes," says the first Jew, in a resigned tone. "OK," says the second Jew, in a quiet voice. "And what about you?" he enquires of the third Jew. "No," says the third Jew, "I don't want your lousy blindfold," followed by a few choice curses. The second Jew immediately leans over to him and whispers: "Listen, Moishe, take a blindfold. Don't make trouble."

---

[312] van der Zyl, Marie (President, Board of Deputies of British Jews). Letter to the Trustees of JNF (UK), January 26, 2022. https://bod.org.uk/wp-content/uploads/2022/01/JNF-Letter-January-2022.pdf

This avoidance of rocking the boat is long-standing. And after centuries of persecution, this response to Jew hate really isn't surprising. It is to be expected. But this survival mechanism is misguided. If anything, it has left us even more vulnerable. In any case, it is no surprise that, in all the work I have done to shine a light on Islamist antisemitism, my nosiest critics have been liberal-minded Jews. Often, I should say, these leaders are plucked from affluent areas, with no direct experience with the issues addressed. Their social circles are kind of a bourgeois shtetl, in which they can avoid some of the unpalatable realities of the multiculturalism they seem intent on safeguarding. Part of the reason I joined the Association of British Muslims was not only to fight anti Muslim hate and reclaim the center ground from populism, but to be a part of an organization which has exhibited a willingness, and a courageous one at that, to address, unapologetically and assiduously, the worsening problem of Islamist-thinking in our Muslim communities. As I have said to the Sheikh, and Managing Director of this organization, 'You're the bravest Jewish non-Jewish leader we have in Anglo-Jewry.' It is indeed a scandal that we lack Jewish leaders like this Sheikh. It is indeed a scandal that we lack leaders generally who have the courage of this Sheikh. If we did, perhaps this book, at least this section, would not need to be written.

So far we have explored a crisis which is raging in Western Europe, threatening Jews and the entirety of our civilization. This chapter addressed one critical question: why has this been allowed to happen? In everything that has been said, negligence, be that of government or of societal institutions, has not emerged from a place of malice. Rather, as my father frequently reminds me, "the road to hell is paved with good intentions." In the name of good, this dire situation is spiraling out of control. And without profound change, the future, for us all, could well be bleak.

With that, we must now turn to the final chapter of this work: what, if anything, can be done to turn the tide?

Chapter Four:
How do we get out of this?

"We're finished. We're fucked. We're doomed."

With much foreboding, these gloomy words are being uttered by a growing number of Jews in Western Europe. Many have arrived at the unsettling conviction that this crisis is insoluble. Naturally, and unsurprisingly, this has given rise to a feeling of apprehension over what the future holds for generations to come. Such concerns cannot be easily brushed aside. This continent, the soil of which is soaked with centuries worth of Jewish blood, may have leaders who impress in their commitment to combat Jew-hate, but, on the ground, things are not getting better. It is by no means stupefying, therefore, why pessimism has taken root amongst a people who are all too aware of the dangers of complacency.

There are those who consider this view to be hyperbolic and the delusions of paranoia, but there is a historic virtue in pessimism. In fact, pessimism, regrettably, is often a duty. The illusions of comfort and safety have too often served to blind a great many Jews to reality, with all its stark and comfortless truths. I am not one for moroseness, but our ancestors have lived through times which were seemingly congenial and tolerant, and then, sometimes imperceptibly, things took a terrible, even bloody turn. And when prosperity turned to persecution, shattering those illusions of comfort and safety, Jews have too often responded with the disquieting words, "we did not see this coming." Perhaps this obliviousness and confutation is best exemplified in the experience Jews had in Weimar Germany, the new post First World War republic enshrined with liberal-democratic values and protections.

Scores of Jews, in the years preceding 1933, flourished in Germany. Even though there were active antisemitic movements throughout this

Goldenes Zeitalter, or 'Golden Age' of Weimar democracy, such as the Young German Order, with its 200,000 members, this wasn't mainstream. In fact, as pointed out by John Efron, a leading historian of Jews, "Under Weimar the last vestiges of exclusion were lifted and the nation's 564,000 Jews enjoyed unprecedented access to coveted positions in the state and society."[313] Across Western Europe, not least in Germany, Jews were disproportionately represented in the fields of medicine, law, and business. And these Jews felt bound and attached to the German land and culture, often prizing their national-identity over any other allegiance. It was only a few years after 100,000 Jewish men, or 18 per cent of the Jewish population served for Germany in the First World War; with 12,000 killed and 35,000 of these faithful Germans decorated. Speaking for many of German Jews in the 1920s, Gabriel Riesser, a leading German-Jewish lawyer and politician, declared, "If someone disputes my claim on my German fatherland, he disputes my right to my thoughts, my feelings, to the language that I speak and to the air that I breathe..."[314]

Most German Jews, therefore, greeted the prospect of the Nazi menace taking power with outright disbelief. They could not believe, after all they had contributed, and adopted German identity, that such an evil force could take hold anywhere, much less in Germany. This point was conveyed in Lion Feuchtwanger's novel, *The Oppermanns*. Published in 1933, the year in which the Nazis took power, it explored the rise of National Socialism through the prism of the Oppermann family, an assimilated Berlin-Jewish family. In a city which was the cradle of cultural and intellectual enlightenment, members of this family, with alacrity, scoffed at the Nazi threat. In one instance, Feuchtwanger describes how Rector Francois and Gustav Oppermann were reading passages from Mein Kampf, while simultaneously laughing. Although Rector confessed to his discomfort hearing such passages, both just saw the Nazis as a marginal, indeed, irrelevant force. And they had good reason to think this. Even in

---

[313] See Efron, John, Steven Weitzman, and Matthias Lehmann. *The Jews: A History*. Routledge, 2018.

[314] Riesser, Gabriel. Gesammelte Schriften. Translated by Gelber and Paul Mendes-Flohr. In "The Paulus-Riesser Debate, 1831." In *The Jew in the Modern World: A Documentary History,* 2nd ed., edited by Paul Mendes-Flohr and Jehuda Reinharz, 145. Oxford: Oxford University Press, 1995.

the 1928 national-election, the Nazis only achieved a measly 2.6 per cent of the vote. It was not until after the Wall Street Crash, and the subsequent economic despair which gripped Germany that the Nazis made huge electoral strides.

Even then, when Hitler and his Nazi Party came to power, most Jews did not have any idea how things would play out. In fact, in the June 1933, the Liberal Central Union of German Jews, the largest Jewish organization at the time, declared, "The great majority of German Jews remains firmly rooted in the soil of its homeland, despite everything. There may be some who have been shaken in their feeling for the German Fatherland by the weight of recent events. They will overcome the shock, and if they do not overcome it then the roots which bound them to the German mother earth were never sufficiently strong."[315] Such a sentiment, also captured by Feuchtwanger, points to a hopeless optimism by which many Jews in Germany were seduced. Indeed, as Efron points out that when the Nazis came to power in 1933, out of the 525,000 Jews in Germany, "only 37,000 left that year, in large part, because none of those who remained could predict the catastrophe to come."[316] There were certain prophets amongst European Jewry who were urging Jews of the imminent dangers, including Alfred Weiner and Ze'ev Jabotinsky. But such people were in a minority, and often, much like today, were lambasted as mongers of fear and alarmism.

Despite being a minority, those who could see catastrophe on the horizon, were right. Speaking to this, the great twentieth century Hollywood film director, Billy Wildier, born in the Austro-Hungarian Empire, is attributed to having said in the years after the Shoah, "The pessimists are in Hollywood and the optimists are in Auschwitz."[317]

---

[315] Cited in Wiener, Alfred. "The Position of the German Jews, as Seen by Alfred Wiener, of the Leadership of the Centralverein: Between Heaven and Earth." In *Documents on the Holocaust, Selected Sources on the Destruction of the Jews of Germany and Austria, Poland, and the Soviet Union,* edited by Y. Arad, Y. Gutman, and A. Margaliot, 50-51. Jerusalem: Yad Vashem, 1981. https://www.yadvashem.org/odot_pdf/Microsoft%20Word%20-%205403.pdf

[316] In Efron, John, The Jews: A History .

[317] Mort Laitner, "When It Comes to the Jews, the Glass Is Always Half Full," *Mort Laitner's Blog,* https://mortlaitner.com/when-it-comes-to-the-jews-the-glass-is-always-half-full/

Though not literally true, and perhaps melodramatic, there is a penetrating wisdom couched within this unpropitious aphorism. In Wilder's own life, astutely recognizing the trajectory of Nazi tyranny, he fled Berlin in 1934, where he had been living for several years, and found refuge in Paris, before ending up in the US, where he would achieve global fame. His family did not leave, and tragically, he lost several loved ones to the Nazis. Stories of this kind are not unfamiliar. Those who were fraught with deep worry, and left when they could, generally, survived. Those who remained optimistic, hoping '*Gam Zeh Yavor,*' this too shall pass, and stayed put, generally, did not. It is a salutary reminder of the unsettling and cruel irony that the values of hope and optimism, upon which Jewish religious tradition is centered, has often imperiled the people who live by such sanguinity.

This is not to say Jewish history can be reduced to a paradigm of pessimists who survive, and optimists who die. Plenty of pessimists were not so fortunate. Nevertheless, in the context of the Shoah and other events in Jewish history, those who could see where things were going, and took action to escape, overall, did not suffer the same fate which befell their counterparts who remained. Though not a particularly glamorous position, perhaps even an ignoble one, pessimism has ensured the survival of many. And today, it would be imprudent to rubbish those who paint a dispiriting picture of the years to come.

Despite the protestations of the optimists amongst us that Jews are living in a time of unparalleled safety and security, as the historical record demonstrates, this is no credible guarantor for long-term safety. In fact, it could be argued, when things are relatively prosperous, this gives us Jews even more of a reason to be suspicious; even more of a reason to question, and be skeptical. Yet even when things are beginning to change, many Jews suffer from a kind of 'Voldemort-Effect,' a term popularized by Maajid Nawaz.[318] Much like in Harry Potter, where those magical elites refused to admit Voldemort had returned, much less name him, our optimists, terrified by this explosion of *Judenhass*, exhibit similar qualities. Not only are they reluctant to give the hatred a name, but much like the Ministry of Magic, they deny it has returned, and indeed denigrate

---

[318] Cited in Collier, D. C. My Origin, My Destiny: Christianity's Basic "Value Proposition." WestBow Press, 2016.

those who dare to raise the issue. This may assuage some fears, but its responses of this kind which makes this situation all the more troubling. As the great contemporary German author, Cornelia Funke, warns, "Nothing is more frightening than a fear you cannot name."[319]

This tension between pessimism and optimism, amongst Jews, has existed for a long time. Although the circumstances are different, such debates continue to rage. The eternal question, however, which underpins this contestation is clear: will we and our children have a safe future in the lands which we call home? My response is that things could well be hopeless, but we must act as if they are not. It could well be the case that our pessimists are right, and yet, we are obligated to do all we can to ensure their grim predictions do not come to pass.

In recent years, owing to the resurgence of populism, mainstream politicians have been compelled to speak more about multiculturalism and what some have argued to be its 'failings.' Back in 2011, former British Prime Minister, David Cameron, in a speech he gave to an audience in Munch, argued, "Under the doctrine of state multiculturalism, we have encouraged different cultures to live separate lives, apart from each other and the mainstream." He added, "We have failed to provide a vision of society to which they feel they want to belong. We have even tolerated these segregated communities behaving in ways that run counter to our values." He, therefore, averred, "Frankly, we need a lot less of the passive tolerance of recent years and much more active, muscular liberalism."[320] Notwithstanding the fact that liberalism, by definition, is a rejection of muscular politics, similar sentiments have been expressed by several other mainstream politicians in the region, including Angela Merkel, and most recently, Suella Braverman, the (former) British Home Secretary. While it is encouraging to see those on the center discuss some of the shortcomings of diversity management (or lack thereof) in Western Europe, the policies have not matched those important words. As usual, in the realpolitik, mainstream politicians, at least on a policy front, keep their distance.

---

[319] See Funke, Cornelia. *Inkheart*. Translated by Anthea Bell. London: The Chicken House, 2003.
[320] Cameron, David. "PM's Speech at Munich Security Conference." GOV.UK, February 5, 2011. https://www.gov.uk/government/speeches/pms-speech-at-munich-security-conference

This worsening situation, however, is not yet immutable. It is indeed late, but not too late, to do what is necessary. This chapter, therefore, is a plea to my fellow centrists: act before we reach this dreaded point of no return. This is not only a crisis of Jew-hate. This is a crisis for us all. It is about the very future of the dignity and dearness of otherness. For societies to remain free, democratic, and prosperous, those entrusted with responsibility must change their tune. It could well be the case that my hope in liberal-democratic politicians and intellectuals getting their act together, is misplaced. And yet, if nothing is done, then there is a grave and distinct possibility that those prophets of gloom and doom will become prophets of truth. This must be avoided. To that end, not only must we see a change within the realm of policy, but as the likes of Adorno opined, to tackle antisemitism and prevent another tragedy against Jews, society must undergo a major cultural and civilizational shift.

A radical shake-up of this kind could well be implausible and downright delusional. Nevertheless, the gravity of what we are facing demands, at the very least, we attempt to shift the tectonic plates of civilization. As such, I present five antidotes to this deteriorating situation, namely, 1. To Confront Reality and Reclaim, 2. Prevent & Enforce the Law, 3. Non Jewish ally- building, 4. Amplification, not Reformation, and 5. Restructuring Society: A New Vision for Western Europe. Although aspirational, and unlikely to be achieved in the next few years, in the long run, these provide the propitious conditions for lasting change. Perhaps, if implemented, those who sound the alarm will have reason to challenge their somber prognosis.

However, as I sit in a café, in Central Paris, and write these words, I think to myself, the words in this chapter could well prove to be nugatory. Perhaps the future, as those pessimists predict, is already set in stone. Yet beyond this proverbial warning, if things are to get better- and I believe they can- the status quo must change. Something profound must be done to disrupt the current course. If so, maybe, just maybe, there might be a light at the end of this tunnel. And no, it will not be a train heading towards us!

On that cheery note, let us turn to the first of these proposed antidotes.

Section One: To Confront Reality and Reclaim

When ignorance is bliss, and when a problem cannot even be named, it is easy to pretend it doesn't exist. Such a pathology is common in delusional thinking, often leading those afflicted to construct alternate realities. Regrettably, this phenomenon is evident amongst Western Europe's liberal-elite. Not only have they harbored unrealistic visions of what our societies should look like, but when confronted with uncomfortable truths, they've also resorted to denying and obfuscating the facts, even inventing their own. If there is to be any chance of the situation improving, and before any policies are put forward, disrupting this pathology of falsehoods is a must.

When reality is intentionally unaddressed and/or is purposefully twisted, malevolent forces thrive uncurbed. Our liberal elites, in their timorousness to have a reckoning with the harsh truths of contemporary multiculturalism, have allowed for this crisis to go unchecked. This has not only endangered Jews and other targets of Islamists, but has contributed to the erasure of centrist politics, upon which our liberal-democracies, and all our rights for that matter, depend. The ferocity of this situation demands not only breaking the silence on discussions deemed 'taboo,' but also for those in power recognize this issue for what it is: a threat to Jews, democracy, and societal cohesion, which emerged as a consequence of the liberal elite's sacralization of their own delusional and wishful thinking. Only by acknowledging reality, and speaking candidly, will governments spark change, without which, there can be no security.

Few within mainstream politics have the spunk to do this. It's a red line, and most, understandably, keep well clear of it. There are brave individuals here and there, but at present, there is no mainstream movement within normative politics which is willing to take these issues head on. And life is not easy for those who dissent from the ranks, and boldly challenge the elite bien pensants of our time.

In Paris, I met up with a few journalists, two of whom work for Charlie Hebdo, the left-wing and secular satirical magazine. In a media landscape where few dare to tread, Charlie Hebdo stands alone. This magazine excels in upsetting everyone. Even me at times. If you will, it discriminates indiscriminately. No one is safe. But Charlie, it seems, is not in a great place. Not only do its journalists face threats against their lives, with some even requiring 24-7 police protection. The magazine also finds itself isolated from those who stand against its principles as well as from former allies within the left-wing circles and mainstream media. These are the same voices that once celebrated their audacity. The magazine's sin? Tackling subjects deemed too controversial for comfort and venturing into areas others desperately avoid. And to many connected to Charlie, this provocative and disruptive publication is on its own.

Yet, the tumultuous experiences of Charlie have repercussions which go beyond the walls of its new, ultra-secure, secret office. These wretched experiences not only unearth the dangers of leaving intellectual disruption to a few intrepid journalists but also highlight the impact upon the fabric of mainstream politics. As detailed in the preceding chapter, fear exerts a stifling influence, suppressing the voices of the most vocal spokespersons for liberal politics. The chilling prospect of what going against the tide might mean for personal safety, and the potential for social and political backlash, disincentivizes any kind of discourse on these issues which begins to be open, honest, and necessary.

Put simply, these discussions are not encouraged in polite society. Whilst Charlie's approach may be distasteful, and whilst we shouldn't look to cause unnecessary offense, we require its chutzpah in smashing this pathology of denialism which has gripped our elite. Confronting the fallacies which they have labored under can no longer be sacrificed at the altar of politeness. Those who are on the mainstream need to reclaim these conversations, and speak in a way that is responsible and considerate, but importantly, firm. By dispersing and spreading this burden, a broader range of mainstream voices will be emboldened to speak up, which in turn, with any hope, will thrust these critical issues into the spotlight and onto the agenda of policy makers.

Some mainstream politicians are beginning to recognize this. I serendipitously stumbled across the words of Ann-Sofie Hermansson, the former Social Democrat mayor of Gothenburg, who spoke in the July of 2023. In an impassioned article discussing Islamism in her city, she began with a brave admission: "If there is one thing I regret during my active years in the political world, it is that I did not pursue the issue of Islamist extremism more vigorously."[321] In fact, when she became mayor in the January of 2016, she explained, "I had not fully realized how bad things were in Gothenburg until I became chairman of the City Council [mayor]." Interestingly, she notes that she was "alerted by several courageous individuals to the degree of Islamist radicalization," but they "were met with silence or were suspected of doing the bidding of racist organizations." Citing the Rosengård Report, which looked into radicalizing in the city of Malmö, she takes from it a chilling sentence, "We lost the opportunity for an incredibly important discussion about radicalization when there was still time to take action to curb a harmful development." And added, as we have seen in other similar contexts, "Instead, a lot of journalists, decision-makers and opinion leaders devoted their time and energy to denying the problems." On that, she rightly concludes, "It was, and still is, the anxiety to speak clearly about extremism that is our worst enemy."[322]

That said, this former mayor, is one individual. It is precisely courageous reckonings of this kind, undertaken by her ideological counterparts in mainstream parties, which will be the impetus for change. This will only occur, however, if those in elected office realize, as Ann-Sofie Hermansson did, that dealing with this crisis is about the very future of Western society, and the values upon which it is grounded.

The alternatives are clear: either this crisis goes unaddressed, and the forecasts predicted by our pessimists will come to pass, or we entrust our futures to the hands of populists. If the issues continue to be ignored by the mainstream, because they are regarded as politically inexpedient, or a breach of their progressive worldview, more people will feel incentivized to revolt against the center-ground. And they would be right to. A reason for normalizing conversations of this kind is because, as this work has repeatedly asserted, the only ones prepared to discuss these realities are, it seems, populists. If we accept that the debate can only take place on the fringes of the body politic, then we serve only to reinforce parties and

---

[321] Hermansson, Ann-Sofie. "In the Fight Against Islamism, Sweden Lost a Valuable Time." Translated by Fondation pour l'innovation politique. *Fondapol*, July 12, 2023. https://www.fondapol.org/en/decryption/in-the-fight-against-islamism-sweden-lost-a-valuable-time-2/
[322] ibid.

individuals with illiberal tendencies. As such, if there is to be change, which goes beyond nice words, the center must be willing to embrace the likes of Ann-Sofie Hermansson, and take heed of their honest and gutsy evaluations. For if dissidents are ignored, hushed up, or condemned and marginalized, the acrid and abominable isolation of Charlie Hebdo will become the norm in Western Europe. And not only for writers and artists. A society that closes itself off to its disruptors is one which is on a perilous path to its own demise.

Whether or not others follow Ann-Sofie Hermansson's example remains to be seen. If more do, this must be coupled with better recording, data, and research on the extent to which antisemitism and concomitant extremist thinking exists within our Muslim communities. At present, while we have data that attests to the seriousness of this problem, the evidence is not as far-reaching as it ought to be. Although it may give us a flavor of the sources of antisemitism, as well as other extremist ideas in our Muslim communities, the data needs to be better. And this cannot be left to sparse, infrequent academic studies. Government agencies must fund and take the lead in funding this research.

On several occasions in this book, the limitations on the data available has been noted. In turn, this not only leads to a state of 'antisemitism distortion,' so that the realities on the ground are twisted and denied, but also, in part, has led policy makers and law enforcement, both of which are of course responsible for ensuring the safety of those targeted by this poison, to fail to recognize the urgency of this strain of antisemitism. And this has had concerning repercussions. If we return to the FRA studies, which looked into Jewish attitudes towards contemporary antisemitism, it found that the bulk of Jews, who are the victims of an antisemitic incident, do not report it to the police or other relevant organizations. The 2018 survey, which was the largest of its kind, found that 79 per cent of the respondents who experienced antisemitic harassment in the five years before the survey did not report it to the police.[323] Almost half of them said they did not report it because they feel nothing would change. When it came to young Jews, who are much more likely to experience antisemitism than their elder peers, the 2019 survey found that 80 per cent of those who

---

[323] FRA, 2018, p.12.

experienced antisemitic harassment, and 51 per cent of those who experienced an incident of antisemitic violence in the year before the survey did not report it to a relevant authority.[324] Clearly, for Jews of all ages, the situation is much worse than what the already alarming data suggests. It's just that most victims of antisemitism do not report it.

For sure, it is certainly possible that if those in positions of power grasped the enormity of this problem, and were to deal with it, more Jews might be inclined to report these incidents. As it stands, however, those in positions of power are keeping their distance from this crisis, all the while the situation is becoming increasingly more intolerable for Jews, and for liberal democracy. Is it a shock that despondency is increasingly in vogue?

For this to change, while it still can, honesty is the first step. Those who are well-intentioned and good must break away from the pathology of delusion, acknowledge this crisis, call a spade a spade, ensure the necessary recording measures are in place, and reclaim these conversations from the realms of taboo. Without this step, which admittedly is more of a leap, the following sections in this chapter are meaningless and unachievable. But time is running out. Before we reach for the dreaded words "too late," surely the most arresting phrase in the English language, a confrontation with the unvarnished truth is an imperative.

On the hope my fellow centrists recognize what is at stake, we can address the second of these five antidotes: Prevention and Law Enforcement.

Section Two: Prevent & Enforce the Law

A confrontation with reality, and candid words, are never easy. And this situation is no exception. Anyone willing to stick their head above the parapet, and challenge the current trend of indifference and negligence, is certainly brave. Especially in this climate of intimidation and fear. But those in power cannot be all words and no trousers. What has been laid out is not a theoretical, intellectual, nor a philosophical dilemma. This is an issue anchored in reality; one which has tangible consequences, and one

---

[324] FRA, 2019, p.21.

which will determine who we are, and what we shall become, as a collective, as a people, as a civilization. The magnitude of what has been discussed, therefore, deserves more than frank speeches and sentiments. This crisis demands action.

Before we turn to what this may look like, it must be recognized that as with many other psychoses, antisemitism is an irremediable disease of the masses. The fabric of our culture is, at least to some extent, rooted in the exclusion and vilification of Judaism, Jews, and Jewishness. While the Holocaust led to profound changes in the way Jews are perceived, this psychosis did not die after Auschwitz and Treblinka. And so, while eradicating this poison is fanciful, containing its spread, influence, and potency is, I believe, possible. This is what this section explores: a new approach on how best to manage this social disease.

If action is to be effective, it must be pragmatic. The utterances of various leaders, both Jewish and non-Jewish, about the need to rid our societies of rampant antisemitism are reassuring, but of course, impractical. More must be done in the realm of educating wider society about Jews, yet if there is to be change on the ground, the efforts of those in power must be focused on what is feasible, and therefore, prioritize the most pressing threats we face. As such, though a problem for all sections of society, a new approach to this crisis must concentrate on the anti-Jewish thinking that emerges from our Muslim communities, where this problem is particularly acute.

Following more comprehensive research, the state must be prepared to enforce the law and prevent this venom from spreading. The various sources of violent and murderous Jew-hate in our Muslim communities need to be investigated, and if it is found that those sources are inciting criminal behavior, those responsible must face prosecution. It is critical, however, that this itself does not become an anti-democratic measure itself. As such, two points need to be made. The first, social conservatism, should not be conflated with extremism. It is now conventional to spurn the views of conservative religious people as extreme, especially with regard to their views on homosexuality, abortion, gender, and all other hot and contentious topics. But this is a mistake. People are entitled to believe and share certain ideas, even those which are disagreeable, so long as these ideas do not explicitly incite violence or retribution against any individual or group. The state must ensure it is dealing with illicit activity, not disagreeable views. Following on from this, at all costs, free speech must be protected and preserved. Even for those we regard as repugnant. It cannot be the case that people who express views, especially those that offend, face criminal charges. The alternative may be good in its intention, but could well pave the way for the erasure of all our liberties and protections. Besides, as will be discussed further down, while free speech may allow for egregious ideas to be voiced, that is the necessary price we pay for allowing the voices of those who are working for change, often themselves in a minority, to be heard.

While preserving liberty is essential, as it is the most effective tool at our disposal to push back against the allure of totalitarianism, there is always a line. The late Supreme Court Justice, Oliver Wendell Homes Jr, in 1919, articulated an important distinction, "The right to extend my hand stops where your nose begins." The harm principle matters, and it is apposite for our purposes. No institution, Muslim or otherwise, can encourage violence with impunity. However, there is, as we established in Chapter Two, a particular issue of this within our Muslim communities. The state must be willing to take action to ensure the influence of such places is contained. In practice, policies can only really make a dent, as the evolving role of social media, coupled with the major influences of the home and family, renders any action necessarily limited. There are areas into which the state cannot easily trespass, let alone police. But this is not true of all places or spaces. Where possible, the state has a responsibility to act. And, at least in one country, France, the state is beginning to take action. Back in the February of 2021, Emmanuel Macron had his 'Anti-Separatism Law' passed by the French legislature, and by the July of that year, the government had put this policy to good use. It deported extremist preachers, and the Ministry of Interior stated that it suspected 99 of the 2,623 mosques in the country of being radical, and consequently closed 24 of these.[325] Since then, more venues of extremism and hate have been

---

[325] Cited in U.S. Department of State. "2022 Report on International Religious Freedom: France." U.S. Department of State, https://www.state.gov/reports/2022-report-on-international-religious-freedom/france/

closed. This may prove to be more dangerous, since it leaves preachers of hate to take their views underground, or worse, online, leaving them with even larger audiences. Despite this risk, and not one to be ignored, this action from one government demonstrates the power, both real and symbolic, that the state can exercise over institutions that preach ideas dangerous for the people who live in close proximity to these breeding grounds of radicalization.

While encouraging, on its own, closing the hate-hubs down will not suffice. Such measures must be blended with policies addressing the other, underlying issues at play. Amongst these, the most significant include blocking funds from and/or to those involved or connected to Islamist sources, as well as regaining a grip on immigration, in terms of both its quantity and quality. Together, these measures allow the government to mitigate the risks of poisonous influences, and the capacity each has for violent and murderous activity. With that, let us consider each of these potential areas of action.

On the first, any organization found to be in receipt of funds from, or having any connections to, Islamist movements or states, must be condemned and discredited by Western European leaders. Although not representative of all Muslims, these organizations with dubious connections are, to varying degrees, influential. And so long as these extreme associations remain unsevered, such organizations, which span Western Europe, cannot be treated with respectability, or worse, invited to any discussions around policymaking. These entities not only groom the minds of the biddable and young, but as made clear in the last chapter, have funneled money into several universities, institutions which are duty-bound to be unbeholden to any external influence, and ensure intellectual investigation remains unrestricted. Although an assault on our benevolence through the front door, this again does not seem to startle those in power. It is as if what is happening is perfectly permissible, and any attempt to call this out is itself more problematic than the propagation of anti-democratic, anti-civilizational, antisemitic, ideals.

Meanwhile, these same politicians, since the illegal invasion of Ukraine, have been eager and emphatic in condemning Russia, striving to, as it were, purge the region of Russian state influence. So why is there a dulling of their liberal appetites when it comes to tackling Islamist sources? We established reasons for this in the previous chapter. Nonetheless, if they are serious about democracy, then fine, let them prove it. Otherwise, as we have become all too well accustomed, their words are meaningless as they are sublimely dull. The ball is in their court.

Lastly, and to our second factor, while the problem of endemic Islamist thinking is already here, we must be mindful of the future. Even without further migration, as noted in the PEW Survey at the end of Chapter Two, our Muslim communities will grow. And yet, given that the numbers arriving from the Muslim community have not sharply declined and could become even higher in the next few years, along with the lack of credible integration policies in place, this situation, as it stands, is set to get worse. The pace of this kind of ill-considered migration to our shores has led to a strain on public services, as well as high rates of inequality and a profound sense of disillusionment with liberal-democratic politics. If the situation is permitted to carry on, and the government has no plan of action for adequately managing the flow of people to Western Europe, we will reach a point where it will be too late for government, of any ideology, to restore order to this chaos.

This is not to say, of course, that our borders should be run by overzealous and xenophobic tyrants. A country can have effective borders, as well as credible quotas on rates of immigration, and be tolerant and open, as well as mindful of its legal and moral responsibility to protect those fleeing from persecution. Society does not need to turn its back on a commitment to making space for the stranger in order to rectify the failures of successive governments. And yet, conversely, those who play down the need for tougher borders and a more active state in the integration process are also pushing for the impossible. A healthy society needs a middle ground. We need a goldilocks migration policy. But seldom do we hear of this centrist approach.

Our first task is to regain control of our borders, the numbers who enter, the quality of those arriving, and the way in which they are integrated. While this is no panacea to this crisis, which is already here, by having control, a grip, over these areas, it will certainly serve to prevent this crisis from becoming worse, at an exponential and irrepressible rate.

In her most recent, and many would say chilling, book, published in early 2021, *Prey: Immigration, Islam, and the Erosion of Women's Rights*, Ayaan Hirsi Ali spoke in some detail about what can be done to ensure our borders are fair and welcoming, all the while rigorous and well-managed. In her last chapter, of her six suggestions, three addressed how the region can regain control. It is worth dwelling on these points, for they speak to the urgency of this alternative, much-needed, middle-ground approach.

The first of which was dedicated to repealing the current asylum framework, which has been exploited by scores of people to claim status as refugees. On the day of writing this, Suella Braverman, the controversial British Home Secretary, in an address to the American Enterprise Institute, a center-right think-tank based in Washington DC, asks whether the United Nations Refugee Convention 1951, which came into effect a few years after the Holocaust, is "fit for our modern age?" Speaking to Rishi Sunak's policy of 'Stopping the Boats,' one of his Five Promises to the electorate, Braverman explains, "the convention was created to help resettle people fleeing persecution, following the horrors of World War Two and the Holocaust, and was - initially at least - centered around Europe." This, she says, was "an incredible achievement of its age," but continues, "more than 70 years on, we now live in a completely different time." Observing, "When the Refugee Convention was signed, conferred protection on some two million people in Europe," but citing analysis by Nick Timothy and Karl Williams for the Center for Policy Studies, "it now confers the notional right to move to another country upon at least 780 million people." As a result, she submits, "It is therefore incumbent upon politicians and thought leaders to ask whether the Refugee Convention, and the way it has come to be interpreted through our courts, is fit for our modern age? Or whether it is in need of reform?"[326] She argues, of course, for the latter.

This argument was pre-empted by Hirsi Ali. Stating that "I do not make such a statement lightly," she argued, "the global asylum and refugee

---

[326] Braverman, Suella. "It Is Incumbent Upon Politicians to Ask Whether the Refugee Convention Is Fit for Our Modern Age: Braverman's Speech in America – Full Text." *ConservativeHome*, September 26, 2023. https://conservativehome.mystaging website.com/2023/09/26/it-is-incumbent-upon-politicians-to-ask-whether-the-refugee-convention-is-fit-for-our-modern-age-bravermans-speech-in-america-full-text/

system is no longer fit for its stated purpose." Explaining, like Braverman did two years later, the Geneva Convention, specifically the section 'Relating to the Status of Refugees,' was ratified shortly after the Holocaust, and was aimed at offering a relatively small numbers of persecuted individuals a safe-haven. As she points out, "it was intended as a temporary solution to a postwar problem, not as a long-term system." In fact, she noted that from 1967, this "convention was extended universally so that anyone living in a dangerous place, not just those personally persecuted by the state, had grounds for asylum." And this, it seems, is where we are today, with a world population which has trebled since 1951. The distinction, as she observes, "between migrant and asylum seeker has become blurred to such an extent it is no longer useful."[327]

Therefore, for Hirsi Ali, once an asylum seeker herself, and now it seems for the (then) British Home Secretary, the system needs to be repealed, for one which, while willing to support genuine refugees, privileges not motivations for leaving these countries, but "the main criterion for granting residence should be how far they are likely to abide by the laws and adopt the values of their host society." As she explains, "...These would be individuals with the highest probability of entering the labor market, rather than the welfare state, and those who genuinely wish to become Dutch, French, or British and living among, as opposed to just near, their fellow citizens."[328] For those who live in a major Western European city, with a high concentration of migrants from the Middle East or North Africa, the picture Hirsi Ali paints is recognizable. She believes necessary for this change is for "armies of officials" who review asylum applications to not focus on petty questions, but rather, "what skills they have and have a frank conversation about what life will be like for them in Germany and France [amongst other places]." And concludes with a rather displeasing assertion, but one which should, I believe be considered, "Those migrants who are unwilling to embrace the laws and values of the host society should be given a reasonable time frame to demonstrate their

---

[327] Cited in Hirsi Ali, Ayaan, *Prey: Immigration, Islam, and the Erosion of Women's Rights.* Harper, an imprint of Harper Collins Publishers, 2021. Pp. 258 -260.
[328] ibid.

adaption to the West, say a year or two, and if this is unsuccessful, they should be ordered to leave or be deported."

However, to ensure we are able to regain control of our borders, as she puts forward in her second section, Western European leaders must also 'Address the Push Factors.' That is, she explains, "It is impossible to reform the asylum system or solve failed integration policies without first addressing the causes of mass migration." She, therefore, urges governments to invest more in resources which address the security and economic issues in countries concerned from which people are arriving. Observing that the EU and individual countries have relationships with various 'refugee-producing nations,' she says "trade agreements, development aid, and diplomatic pressure should be tied to progress on the migration issue such as forcing countries to accept the return of their repatriated migrants." In fact, Hirsi Ali urges for European nations to take the lead on stabilizing those countries, which includes effective military interventions, especially countries with an epidemic of militias and people smugglers. She opines, "Europe must stop pretending that the stabilization of the Muslim world is somebody else's problem," and adds that Europe must support the rebuilding of institutions and the rule of law in effected countries.[329] If not, it is only inevitable that hundreds of thousands will look for a better life elsewhere. And where better than across the Mediterranean?

Of course, though, this must be coupled with far more investment in border enforcement, whom, she notes, are severely underfunded. The very idea of 'borders,' however, as explained throughout this book, is anathema to those who subscribe to this 'think beyond-nation-state' ideology. Indeed, quoting Margaret Thatcher in 1985, who refused (thankfully) to sign the UK up to the Schengen Agreement, "It is a matter of plain common sense that we cannot totally abolish the frontier controls if we are also to protect our citizens from crime and stop the movement of illegal immigrants." The images coming from Poland of using its border force, and other security forces, to prevent migrants from entering on the Polish-Belarusian border, may have made for 'bad optics' by appearing needlessly extreme, but not entirely impolitic. While, again, I do not

---

[329] ibid, pp. 260-264.

believe our borders should be guarded by an iron wall, given the seriousness and gravity of what is on the line, European leaders should not be so dismissive, critical, and reluctant to employ its security forces to deter the vast numbers arriving, as well as the defeating the people smuggling gangs cruelly exploiting migrants.[330]

There is a reason why many do wish to come to Europe: the life here is good. And then some. In her third section, Hirsi Ali says to ensure our borders and migration is controlled, we must also address the 'Pull Factors.' She argues the attractiveness of Western Europe, particularly for its welfare-state, has left many wanting to move to Europe and establish home here. As Hirsi Ali argues, however, "The original welfare start was predicated on a notion of reciprocity, but to its newcomers it looks more like a universal basic income." For her, therefore, regional leaders must adopt a 'carrot-and-stick' approach. Citing Austria as an example, since 2018, this country has ensured migrants sign an 'Integration Declaration,' which commits them to meet certain obligations in order to continue to receive government assistance, as well as maintain their residential status in the country. She points out that those who do not comply with integration requirements, which includes German-language proficiency, values training, and more, face sanctions. Indeed, those who are still averse to comply after two years, can be sent home. As Hirsi Ali opines, "This threat of penalties – the form of cuts to welfare -works." Speaking anecdotally, she states when her team visited the Austrian Integration Fund (ÖIF), in Vienna, several months after the Integration Declaration came into effect, large numbers of newly-arrived migrants were queuing up for courses and language training. In one such class, thirty people, comprised of both men and women, of different ages and nationalities, engaged in a conversation about gender relations in the country. Some of the younger males, she says, found it amusing that girls could be allowed out at night just like the boys. However, by the end of the conversation, one of the female participants lowered her head scarf. Now while wearing a head-scarf in no way precludes integration and being a good citizen, as Hirsi Ali explains, "her subtle action symbolized exactly what an integration course

---

[330] Ibid.

should do: provide exposure to the values of one's new society and give them the confidence to adopt them for themselves."[331]

Austria is not alone in instituting policies of this kind. The Danes have also begun to ensure welfare provisions are given according to efforts to integrate and be a part of the host society. In any event, if more countries in the region were to implement this 'carrot-and-stick' method, not only will those who have no intention of being a part of the society not be permitted to remain, but the caliber of migrant will improve, which is in the interest of both the labor market and society-at-large.

What Hirsi Ali proposes may seem like a radical deviation from the current status quo, but it is called for. Her suggestions, if adopted by leaders throughout Western Europe, will certainly place Western European leaders in a better place to exert control over number of people entering, the kind of people who do enter, and how such people are integrated. This alternative, middle-ground approach of taking people in based on manageable numbers, as well as an expectation of integration and financial independence, will serve to bring the numbers of those arriving down, by a considerable amount, and will prevent this ongoing influx of culturally disillusioned individuals who cannot be integrated.

This section has laid out how Western European governments can ensure that this crisis is better managed. It has detailed how to prevent this from reaching the point where any notion of control becomes impossible and inefficacious. I am, after all, a realist. It is not my expectation that we shall be rid of the tidal wave of Islamist thinking anytime soon. It is far too late for that. But it is not too late to contain how this menace is spreading, and the violent and lethal consequences that go with it.

As ever, though, this is not exclusively a threat to Jews. This is a threat to us all. And so, I turn to the third of our five antidotes.

Section Three: Non-Jewish ally-building

"In every generation," it is written in the Passover Haggadah, "they rise up against us to annihilate us." Emerging around the Middle Ages, the story of the Israelites' flight from bondage to liberation in Ancient Egypt,

---

[331] ibid, pp. 262-263.

was well ahead of its time. Its authors recognized, even then, that Jews, so long as they exist, will be treated as the great and eternal other, subject to exclusion, rejection, and persecution. The question, however, which has not yet been raised in this work, nor in many other texts which wrestle with antisemitism, is that of why? That is, why, regardless of civilization or time, Jews face trouble. We regularly hear, and I have even said it in this work, "what starts with the Jews never ends with the Jews," but few ask, why does it not end with Jews? By understanding what underpins antisemitism, we can understand why it has clear implications for humanity at large.

In some sense, however, it is strange to even ask questions of this kind. After all, would one ask the same of anti-black or anti-Roma hatred? Surely the answer in those cases, as in the case of antisemitism, is obvious: it is plain, unadulterated racist hate; and that's the end of the matter. But antisemitism is ontologically distinct as it is peculiar. While it can be expressed in racist terms, it is a categorical error to place antisemitism in the same league as racism. Christopher Hitchens, in fact, saw antisemitism as the 'godfather' of all other prejudices. This is a plague which needs to be understood on a level that goes beyond material factors. It cannot be denied that certain negative beliefs about Jews have added, and continue to add, fuel to the fire, but they are not, contrary to popular opinion, the spark. If they were, the antidote would be apparent, and it would not have found social and political refuge across societies, both advanced and regressive. There is a reason why the doctrine of hating the Jews has been the force of all forces which unite those who seem to share little else or nothing in common. And this reason is located far beyond factors of money, resentment, or bigotry.

There is a consensus amongst most that it derives from the emergence of its theological opposition, Christianity, and in particular, the accusation of deicide, or the killing of Christ. The spark for this hatred was in the belief that Jews killed Jesus Christ, a manifestation of God, and will forever be in guilt for this crime (this would later be rescinded in the Second Vatican Council). In some sense, this charge of deicide has a kernel of truth. But not for the reasons given by Christian authorities through the ages. As David Patterson explains, this hatred emerged "not only because the Jews are the millennial witnesses to the uncompromising commandments of the God of Abraham, but also because, in a sense, the Jews are indeed the original deicides – the deicides who slay the false gods of those who would be as God."[332] Citing Jewish texts, Patterson notes, "According to Jewish tradition, Abraham, the first to be called a Hebrew, was the original slayer of false gods. The Midrash relates a story about the young Abram, who was left alone one day to attend to his father Terach's idol shop. While his father was gone, Abram took a stick and smashed all the idols but one, the biggest one. When his father returned to the shop he was outraged and demanded to know what happened. Abram explained that the big idol smashed the other idols with the large stick. "Do you take me for a fool?" Terach demanded. "It is nothing but clay!" To which Abram answered, "Precisely" (Bereshit Rabbah 38:13)."[333]

Although one could make the case that this Christian accusation sprung Jew-hate into momentum, its etiology cannot be understood by merely considering its historical foundations. For if the hatred owes itself to a fictious and unforgivable lie, this poison would have died long ago, and its proponents with it. As such, Jews have not been hated for killing God, but rather for inventing Him. The radical, revolutionary, eternal and universal declaration of there being one God, in whom all are equal, is a proposition which originates in Judaism. For this, it seems, Jews will never be forgiven. As Daniel Sibony, a French philosopher, put it, "The origin of the hatred is the hatred of the origin."[334] This is because the 'origin' is the ultimate antithesis of the core impulse of the 'authoritarian personality': to become a god. A mangod.

After all, not only does this original doctrine hold that all are equal before the divine, and that no man himself can be a god, but that in the Other, in the Stranger, we find beauty, the presence of the divine, and in doing so, our own humanity. The late Chief Rabbi, Jonnathan Sacks, opined, "We encounter God in the face of the stranger." He added, "That is, I believe, the Hebrew Bible's single greatest and most counterintuitive

---

[332] Patterson, David. *Judaism, Antisemitism, and Holocaust: Making the Connections.* Cambridge University Press, 2022. p.115.
[333] Patterson, David. *Anti-Semitism and Its Metaphysical Origins.* United Kingdom: Cambridge University Press, 2015. p.19.
[334] Cited in Joel Kotek lecture, Oxford Summer Institute, 2022.

contribution to ethics." Concluding, "The human other is a trace of the Divine Other."[335] The most frequently repeated commandment in the Torah is to love the stranger and view the divine in the stranger. Explaining why this is counterintuitive, David Patterson averred, "I do not have to be reminded so often to love my neighbor, the one who is like me, who shares my outlook on the world." He went on, "He is a regular guest at my table. We watch the games together, and together we enjoy a beer now and then. But the stranger? The one who does not look like me or think like me, the one whom I regard as a nonbeliever and as politically backward, if not barbarous? I need to be repeatedly reminded to love him."[336] This call to love the one not like us is irreconcilable with the mindset which has no regard for the sanctity of life and for the diversity in the world around us.

This 'original message,' which Jews throughout the ages are called on to champion, stands in opposition to this totalitarian mindset. It is the negation of this socially Darwinian and despotic view of humanity. It follows, therefore, that Judenhass plays such a central role in most, if not all, totalitarian movements, past and present. As Professor Patterson puts it, "It doesn't end with the Jews because the Jews represent, by their very presence in the world, a testimony to the truth of the infinite responsibility that each of us has for the other, who is infinitely dear." For the visions of man-gods to come to pass, be that Hitler or Sinwar, it is inevitable that they wage a war on Jews, the people who embody that which serves to remind man of what is central in our humanity: the belief that all life, including that of the Other and of the Stranger, is holy. Intrinsic to the war on Jews is a war on otherness, on the very sanctity of life, and indeed, regardless of whether we believe or not, a war on the enduring presence of God. It is for this reason that antisemitism is not only a divine hatred but a hatred of the divine.

Consequently, those in power, responsible for the future of all our rights and dignities, must recognize that the assault upon Jews is an assault upon everything the Jews, by their presence, seem to represent. Our

---

[335] Sacks, Jonathan. *The dignity of difference: How to avoid the clash of civilizations.* Bloomsbury Publishing, 2002. Pp 59-60.
[336] Patterson, David, *Judaism, Antisemitism, and Holocaust: Making the Connections*, p.34.

civilization is confronting a threat to Jews, but more, to the right to be other, the hallmark of liberal and free democracy. A threat which disregards the right to be different, the right to be an individual, the right, indeed, to be human. And so, it is not enough to implement policies that serve only to prevent acts of criminality against Jews. To date, this has been the extent of government action. Several governments in the region have invested more in maintaining and updating the security apparatus within Jewish communities, and this is both encouraging and necessary. One will struggle to find a synagogue, or any other Jewish institution in most Western European states, which is not gated and secure, often including the protection of state police and/or military. On its own, however, these measures only touch the surface of this problem. To effectively combat antisemitism, it is necessary to understand the depths of this poison, and where it leads.

And, therefore, whereas the previous section considered how best to prevent the spread of Jew-hate, this section addresses how to prevent the spread of this lethal creed into wider society. The first step is that any effort to manage Judenhass must recognize how others, not only Jews, are at risk in the Islamist, totalitarian orbit. This section encourages the formation of alliances between targeted communities, and impresses upon the importance of ensuring that these communities do not go unnoticed by those in power. Secondly, critical to disrupting the trend of Islamist thinking, which leads to acts of harassment and violence against members of such communities, is to protect and amplify the voices of those within our Muslim communities working for change, who have been abandoned, shamefully, I hasten to add, by successive governments.

On the first, as with any kind of extremist politics, Jews may be the first who are targeted, but rarely, if ever, the last. As laid out in Chapter Two, the 'intersectionality of antisemitism' means that negative attitudes to Jews is often bound to negative, even extreme attitudes towards other communities, and its people. And Islamism is no exception to this trend. In the proliferation of Islamist thinking, disturbing attitudes towards other minorities, including women, LGBT people, and other religious communities, particularly Jews and Hindus, run rife. These attitudes go further than socially conservative and legitimate convictions. They actively challenge the dignity and rights of individuals concerned. They indeed provide an atmosphere in which violence and criminality can flourish.

There is, as such, a desperate need for the formation of closer ties between communities who are the subject of Islamist vituperation and dehumanization. In practice, this means spokespersons for these communities, as well as other human-rights activists, ensure governments are doing all they can to resist this danger. This isn't a concern to only one community; a range of people are at risk, and so it is necessary that a diverse group of voices, representing various communities, work together to give these shared fears a voice. And, indeed, as ever, the more this gets spoken about more likely it is policy policymakers will listen. We established in the previous chapter that, on their own, Jews command little political and electoral weight. But by other communities speaking out together, this will no longer be an issue mainstream politicians can ignore, or more accurately, afford to ignore.

Fundamental to ally building is also to engage those who are feeling concerned by what is occurring around them, often in their own cities and towns. Throughout Western Europe, there is a sense that there are places which no longer feel or look like a part of the nation; to many, it feels as if there are colonies within our shared homelands. For the majority who feel this way, such a feeling is not driven by racial prejudice. But a concern that we no longer live in a society, in which we share a collective identity, culture, and value system. Far too often, however, people expressing their concerns, largely (though not always) from white-working class backgrounds, are easily and wrongly dismissed as xenophobes and racists. But there are areas in Western Europe which have fundamentally, perhaps irrevocably, changed because of mass migration, especially from Muslim majority nations. Scores of people believe that this has occurred without democratic consent, and in doing so their communities have been wrecked, and have been treated as a dumping ground, even as a social laboratory, for mass migration by an out of touch liberal elite who are at best indifferent, at worse contemptuous, to those who are indignant at what this has done to their local communities. It is by no means surprising that this has left the door wide open for reactionary groups, often with violent and extreme elements, who have taken to the streets, sometimes in these local towns, to protest these changes. If local communities are expected to bear the brunt and strain of ill-managed migration, then, of course, there is going to be backlash. The question is, however, how long before the next group, this time much worse, comes to town?

An engagement with wider society is not only to avert a situation like this, but to rebuild trust in liberal-democratic institutions and processes. To make liberal democracy relevant. That can only happen when governments and wider society, take seriously these concerns about immigration, community life, and working-class grievances. It cannot be permitted that images of loutish groups are the pretext used by liberal-minded politicians and commentators to deflect from the very legitimate issues at play. The cornerstone of responsible governance ensures that those affected no longer feel unheard and left out, often by the parties that reiterate their commitment to working-class interests.

This section has tackled why working with a wider society for change is vital. However, while building connections outside of our Muslim communities will encourage politicians to engage with these issues, as I shall now outline, it is equally important to build similar partnerships within these communities.

Section Four: Amplification, not Reformation

For change that extends beyond putting this crisis on the policy agenda, it is necessary to empower and support those working for renewal within European Islam. Although there are a number of Muslim organizations with concerning ties to Islamism, as Jikeli points out, "as in Germany and France, the majority of British Muslims (51 percent) do not feel represented by any existing Islamic organization." Adding that while "the existence of a number of Islamist organizations and the influence of Islamism in major Muslim organizations in Europe, the observation of Muslim organizations should not be the only approach to evaluating attitudes among the diverse Muslim communities."[337] Just because there are such organizations, some of which are significant, this does not mean

---

[337] Jikeli, *European Muslim Antisemitism*, p.15.

they speak or represent all members of these communities. There are other bodies which are working to challenge the authority of these organizations, and thus for wider change in our Muslim communities. One such body is the one I have worked with, the Association of British Muslims.

From its inception in 1889, this organization has sought to promote the reconciliation between a strong Muslim identity along with a proud British identity. To this very day, this organization, co-run by Sheikh Paul Armstrong, views no contradiction between a committed and devout Islamic lifestyle along with a belief in the virtues of secular-liberal democracy. Speaking to me, Sheikh Armstrong told me that AoBM "isn't just an advocate for Muslims, but for every citizen valuing a unified Britain. In the face of rising division, we champion mutual respect and understanding." He added, "Our mission transcends religion, appealing to all who hold dear the principles of democracy and liberalism." He went on to say, "Our collective identity as British citizens is paramount." And proudly declared, "we work tirelessly to ensure that our shared values triumph over division. In an age where fragmentation looms large, supporting AoBM means endorsing a vision of Britain that celebrates

unity through diversity."

If there is to be change, it is essential that Sheikh Paul, and others like him are supported and indeed, amplified. Unfortunately, these voices, dedicated to improving Muslim communities, have been abandoned and left to fend for themselves by successive governments.. They receive very little, if anything, in the way of social, political, or financial support. Instead, Muslim organizations with concerning affiliations have risen to prominence. To gain insight from someone with firsthand experience, I spoke to Charlotte Littlewood, the former UK Government Coordinator for Prevent, and the former Counter Extremism Coordinator for East London Boroughs, where the issue of Islamist extremism and radicalization has worsened in recent years.

Reflecting on her time in local government, Littlewood shared, "Personally, I experienced a local authority that cowered at the task of supporting such liberal voices for fear of losing votes in a local election. This simply cannot be accepted." She emphasizes that "the British central government and all its local authorities need to be staunch and steadfast in their protection of freedom of speech and brave in challenging those who try to stifle it through ingenuine claims of islamophobia or threats to those deemed "blasphemous."" Explaining why the UK government has ended up here, she argues, "Strategically the British Government made a detrimental error in its approach to countering extremism in the UK, in a bid to curb violent extremism it supported extremist elements to tackle violent elements. Muslim brotherhood affiliated groups were platformed and at times funded." As such, "illiberal spokespeople have found a way into positions of power and influence, whether that be through leading charities, lobbying via APPGs and entering politics." Although she observes that, "the government since changed its approach and set out to support liberal voices such as the Quiliam foundation and various community groups that value equality and tolerance and stand against extremism," it is the case that "the issue faced was any such community or group was then attacked by Islamists, branded non-Muslim and delegitimized." And, therefore, Littlewood concludes despondently, stating, "the risk liberals face to be heard has become such that for many it is simply not worth it. People are intimidated and most just want to go about their daily lives with their religion being something personal not something public and political. These voices will never come forward as the risk is simply too great for them."

This is not an acceptable situation. The governments of Western Europe are vital partners in supporting the work and activities of Muslims working to fend off these poisonous influences, or as my friend Haras Rafiq would put it, working to "reclaim the soul of Islam from extremism." This dire situation, though, is augmented by Western liberals who, as laid out in the previous chapter, have empowered Islamist forces by abandoning those who dare to challenge or offend Islamism's orthodoxy. Perhaps liberals in the West have it too easy. If they were to step in the shoes of their intrepid and indefatigable liberal comrades in Iran, fighting for female empowerment and to be freed from the shackles of Islamist rule, they would be compelled to appreciate what is at stake. As it stands, however, our progressive class in Europe has betrayed its partners overseas and has become the useful idiots of those who oppress and tyrannize. At the time of writing, and to its shame, the Danish Ministry of

Justice is proposing a bill which will criminalize "improper treatment of objects with significant religious value." If passed, (and I believe it was passed) it will be an expansion of Section 110 (e) of the Penal Code, which already restricts "publicly [insulting] a foreign nation, a foreign state, its flag or other recognized national mark or the flag of the United Nations or the European Council." If found guilty, fines can be imposed, as can a two-year custodial sentence. This legislation was introduced after a series of recent Quran burning incidents in Sweden. In a piece refuting the claims made by the Danish government, the organization committed to defending freedom of speech, Article 19, points out, "the bill emerged in a highly secular country where the political establishment consistently defended satire and mockery of religious figures and symbols and where the most recent conviction on charges of blasphemy took place in 1946."[338] Yes, that's right: the Danes, in the face of fear of Islamist reprisals, are preparing to pass a de facto blasphemy law. This not only raises immediate questions about what 'objects' will be protected by this law (what, after all, constitutes an object of 'significant religious value?'), but what does this mean for those who do dare to offend? Time will tell, but certainly this speaks to a worrying pattern throughout Western Europe, namely, the abandonment of anti-Islamist Muslims, and as a consequence of liberal cowardice, the emboldening of Islamist Muslims.

It is now time to abandon extremists and defend and amplify those striving to reclaim the center ground. Any legislation, proposed or passed, which gives, even a scintilla of credence to Islamist actors, must be scrapped. The law must not only protect the right to dissent, but also the right to be free of retribution. And society must celebrate those Muslim voices working for renewal. Not only because a healthy society embraces diverse voices, and recognizes the virtue in the marketplace of ideas. But because once an idea becomes immune from being scrutinized and offended, that is when totalitarian impulses flourish to an unceasing degree. All the while the people who suffer are not only the various communities targeted by Islamists, but non-Islamist Muslims, of whom there are many, who justly believe that their identities and deep-rooted

---

[338] ARTICLE 19. "Denmark: Scrap the Blasphemy Law Proposal." September, 2023 https://www.article19.org/resources/denmark-scrap-the-blasphemy-law-proposal/

faith have been hijacked and perverted. And, therefore, as well as scrapping any laws provide fodder for Islamist actors, what is needed in the European Muslim landscape, and around the world, is not reformation, but critically, amplification.

As established in the introduction, Islamism is a credible interpretation of Islamic texts, but it is far from the only interpretation. It is time that Muslims who interpret their texts, their religion, and their identity, in a way which is commensurate with liberal-democratic values, discover the support of liberal politicians, activists, and commentators. This is precisely what Donald Trump called for when he was running for President back in the August of 2016. To an audience in Ohio, speaking of 'radical Islam,' he asserted:

> Nor can we let the hateful ideology of radical Islam—its oppression of women, gays, children, and nonbelievers— be allowed to reside or spread within our own countries . . . [W]e must use ideological warfare as well. Just as we won the Cold War, in part, by exposing the evils of communism and the virtues of free markets, so too must we take on the ideology of radical Islam. Our administration will be a friend to all moderate Muslim reformers in the Middle East, and will amplify their voices.[339]

In her short 2017 book, The Challenge of Dawa: Political Islam as Ideology and Movement and How to Counter It, Ayaan Hirsi Ali noted that this speech, "heralded a paradigm shift away from President Obama's doctrine of focusing solely on the violence committed by "extremists" to a more comprehensive approach that seeks to undermine, degrade, and ultimately defeat political Islam (or Islamism) as an ideology and a movement seeking to infiltrate and undermine our free society."[340] In other words, Trump recognized that the key to defeating Islamism, as with any other totalitarian ideology, is not necessarily through military intervention, but through empowering genuine moderates in the battleground of ideas.

---

[339] Cited in Hirsi Ali, Ayaan. "The Challenge of Dawa: Political Islam as Ideology and Movement and How to Counter It." Stanford, California: Hoover Institution Press, 2017. https://www.hoover.org/sites/default/files/research/docs/ali_challengeofdawa_final_web.pdf. p.1.
[340] ibid.

This was coming from someone on the right. And far too often, those who wish to embolden the voices of genuine moderates (meaning those who are actively engaged in working or change) are often those who are not so moderate themselves. It is, therefore, vital that liberals and centrists amongst us are willing to replicate this 'paradigm shift' here in Western Europe.

By encouraging and supporting those who work for renewal from within, we are able to see much more in the way of meaningful change in these communities. As Pascal Bruckner puts it, "It is time to create a great chain of help for all the rebels in the Islamic world, whether moderate, unbelieving, free-thinkers, atheists, or schismatics, just as we used to support the dissidents of Eastern Europe." Adding, "But the problem with the moderates is that they are precisely . . . moderate, and never rise to the level of radicals. Europe, if it wants to construct a secular Islam within its frontiers, should encourage these divergent voices, give them its financial, moral, and political support, sponsor them, invite them, and protect them."[341] And concludes, "Today there is no cause that is more sacred and serious or that more affects the concord of future generations."[342] Bruckner is correct. We needn't strengthen those who are indifferent to the normalization of Islamist thinking, but those working to root it out.

The state must be an active partner in the process of integration and reconciliation. These are both exceedingly difficult to achieve and are a two-way street. The state must help to provide the conditions necessary to push back against extremism, which includes, tackling poverty in these communities, which too often runs rife, as well as challenging discrimination against Muslims (as well as all other minorities), and ensuring that counter-extremism does not lead to the stigmatization or unnecessary essentialization of all Muslims, thus leading to even more alienation and extremism. While in Paris, meeting with journalists, I was saddened to hear from Robert McLiam Wilson that in France, immigrants, particularly those of a Muslim background, will refer to their fellow white, indigenous citizens as 'French people.' For many new arrivals in France, including first, second, and third generations, they see themselves

---

[341] Bruckner, Pascal, *The Tyranny of Guilt,* p.47.
[342] ibid.

disconnected and isolated from the society, the culture, and the very identity that surrounds them. In France, and elsewhere, the lack of state support in integration gives rise to a quandary which many wrestle with, either be Muslim, and separate yourself from the country you call home, or be a part of the national-community, and therefore, relinquish all that which is unique to your personal and cultural identity.

It does not need to be the case, however, that Muslims need to be any less Muslim to find a home in the countries in which they reside. As part of our emboldening of the 'shakers' in our Muslim communities, is to help those working to cultivate a new identity, one which embraces the hyphen. That is, just as I identify as a 'Jewish-Brit,' the same duality of identities ought to be encouraged amongst members of our Muslim communities throughout Western Europe. In the case of the Jewish experience, particularly here in Britain, our institutions have always been mindful of the importance of this hyphen. And they have embraced it. Even more, they have sought to disseminate its importance to young Jews. One such organization, existing for over 125 years, is the Jewish Lads and Girls Brigade, or JLGB. From its beginnings, first known as JLB, as the historian Sharman Kaddish, put it, JLB sought to make of young Jews, a 'Good Jew And A Good Englishman.' With its British military style uniform and discipline, it boasts a long-standing commitment to British society, both inside and outside the Jewish community. Never did it see any contradiction in these identities. For the very simple reason: there isn't. In the case of our Muslim communities, the same applies. It is precisely an organization of this kind that is needed for Western European Muslims. One that does not expect Muslims to abandon the principles upon which they are grounded, but one that encourages this way of life to co-exist alongside an active and proud national identity, which is committed to the values of liberal democracy.

If we are to unlock the potential benefits of a multicultural society, governments can no longer take a nonchalant approach to our minority communities. The government must fulfil its end of the social contract, and support the development of organizations like the Association of British Muslims. Because it does not need to be the case that people of faith need to be any less devout to be a part of a pluralistic liberal democracy. But it is time liberal democracies engage with faith communities in a way which emphasizes openness, but also underscores the boundaries of tolerance, and the responsibilities of living in a liberal democracy. The alternative will not only mean our diversity will suffer, but we will eventually see the complete marginalization of those voices working for change.

The past two sections have explored why building relations between communities is vital. This is a crisis that faces not one community, but several, as well as the very future and welfare of liberal democracies. It cannot be left to a few brave individuals here and there to put this on the policy agenda. As many activists subsequent to the Charlie Hebdo affair articulated, we must 'spread the risk,' and in doing so, not only do we mitigate the risks and fears which go with discussing and dealing with these topics, but we encourage this to be on the agenda of politicians, as one of the major issues of the day. Indeed, as part of this community building, we must support those actively engaged in efforts for renewal in our Muslim communities. On these organizations and people, we rely for lasting change. And on us, and the support of liberal politicians and commentators, their work depends. In sum, by working together, we not only are in a better place for politicians to come out of their state of negligence, but we are able to encourage fundamental change.

On this note of rebuilding, I turn to the last of our antidotes.

Section Five: Restructuring Society: A New Vision for Western Europe

This book is written during a time of intense, widespread concern over the future of our planet. Throughout the world, but particularly here in the West, scores of people, both young and old, are coming together, urging their respective governments deal with what they regard as a life-or-death ecological crisis. "Time is running out," they say, with the clever line, "There's no Planet B." While such activists regard government action as the imperative of humanity in the twenty-first century, they also stress the importance of 'individual responsibility.' Meaning while those in positions of power are responsible for driving our societies and economies towards greener policies, equally vital are the habits and behaviors of individuals. Everyone is responsible for ensuring their habits are sustainable and do as little harm as possible to the planet. As Nakul Jaidka, the Founder and CEO of Stella Moto, put it in an article for the Times of India, no less, "While we all agree that environmental changes for the better are needed, we leave it to others to bring about the change," adding, "but in actual fact to bring about significant changes it is the collective conscience of the people that is required to change, with alterations to one's personal behavior and lifestyle." He reasoned, "It is not enough to vent one's feelings or share pro-environment posts on social media, which at best only spreads some awareness along with affording one with some self-gratification. Each individual needs to bring environmental concern from the recesses of one's mind, right to the forefront while making choices."[343]

Many share the view of Mr Jaidka. They agree that merely addressing climate change at the level of government and rich corporations is not enough. Change starts with us. As Mahatma Gandhi put it, "If we could change ourselves, the tendencies in the world would also change. As a man changes his own nature, so does the attitude of the world change towards him. This is the divine mystery supreme. A wonderful thing it is and the source of our happiness. We need not wait to see what others do."[344] In the same way, the ecological crisis of our planet requires both political and social change, the same is also true for the future of the ecology of our societies.

The political arena, critical though it is, has its limitations. Where policymakers can work to manage and contain this crisis, society and its citizens can address the cultural factors that allowed for it to occur in the first place. Without grappling with the cultural undercurrents of this dangerous tide, which transcends governmental policy-making, the efforts of politicians will pale into vacuous unimportance. The roots of this crisis are not political; they are cultural, indeed philosophical. As such what is needed is not only credible policies, but a cultural reckoning and

---

[343] Jaidka, Nakul, "Individual Responsibility Towards The Environment." *Times Of India*, 2023. https://timesofindia.indiatimes.com/blogs/voices/individual-responsibility-towards-the-environment/

[344] Cited in Gandhi, M. "Chapter 153." In *The Collected Works of M.K. Gandhi,* vol. 13, 241. New Delhi, India: The Publications Division, 1960. p.241.

interrogation of the ideals which led us here. In short, as discussed in Chapter Three, our societies need to rediscover their own identity, culture, diversity, tolerance, and of course, boundaries. So how, exactly, do our we go about doing this?

The answer is desperately unsatisfactory, and for that I apologize, but not unrealistic: there is no defined path to cultural renewal. After all, at the heart of this, rests a question which reaches the very soul of our civilization, and human identity: who are we? And how, if at all, a society can tackle such an enormous question, is not clear. Maybe a question of this kind is without an answer. Some light, however, can be shed on what might ignite, at the very least, a discussion on this question of our age. To that end, it is worth returning to our climate activists.

As with any social and/or ideological movement, green activism was the progeny of what emerged within intellectual circles. What a relatively few number of climate scientists discovered, and continue to discover, has become the principal basis for large numbers to mobilize and urge governments and societies to go green. The common retort of such activists to their detractors, 'look at the science,' meaning, look at what those in positions of intellectual power are coming out with, is indicative of how significant the intelligentsia has been in planting the roots of this now worldwide movement. Whether one accepts their findings or not, it is clear the influence of a few experts has been extraordinary. And throughout history, the contributions of a minds, the churners of ideas and theories, has proven indispensable for inspiring of radical politics and social-change.

To no small extent, where Western Europe today finds itself, in this en masse confusion over its own soul, has been shaped by the intelligentsia. Some might even say the foundations of the region's transformation since 1945 owe its origins to those within these circles who conceived of post-war civilizational and cultural reset. It is certainly the case that the core attitudes of our liberal elites, especially towards race, nationhood, borders, immigration, and identity, emerged from intellectual thought. And so, in the same way intellectuals profoundly contributed to the cultural underpinnings of this crisis, it requires their thinking and influence to help take us out of it.

There is a chilling culture of disdain for, and silencing of, those who defy the positions of liberal elites. The number of those willing to challenge the status quo, given the fears of a backlash, is ever dwindling. The intoxication of conformity is overwhelming. Before our intellectual spaces, particularly our universities, become places in which dissent becomes virtually impossible, and they are purged of all who feel able to dissent, there must be a new intellectual movement, a new school of thought, one which consists of leading, centrist-thinkers, willing to lead and reclaim the debate on the contentious issues facing society. Indeed, in the same way we ought to amplify Muslim voices striving for change, we must also do the same for those within centrist, liberal-thinking, who wish to disrupt the bien pensants of our own elites.

Across the West, and particularly here in Western Europe, it has become apparent that the center ground is intellectually, spiritually, and philosophically undernourished. It lacks fresh and innovative ideas for how to address these concerns of culture, identity, and values. It has left such conversations to the populist right. The center ground is desperate for a renaissance of ideas and a shakeup of its orthodoxies. A diverse coalition of thinkers, concerned by the topics raised, must come together and forge an institute through which these questions facing the cultural fabric of Western Europe are answered.

Such questions this institution will explore includes, how to cultivate a sense of shared, inclusive nationhood? How to best maintain communities? How to ensure cultural factors are not dismissed in migration policies? How to ensure we remain tolerant of opposing ideas, but not to the extent that intolerance is allowed to flourish out of those ideas? Indeed, how to ensure we maintain a cohesive society? These are amongst some of the most important issues Western Europe faces, and to ensure the survival of the center-ground, they demand fresh thinking. At present, the choice facing Western Europeans is, it seems, a binary one. That is, either we maintain the delusions of our liberal elites, or we turn our backs on diversity and become exclusionary and hostile to outsiders. Neither option is at all sustainable, nor desirable. The alternative model, the reclaim of the middle-ground, as discussed in the previous sections, is not only a rethink of migration and integration, but the way in which society itself should look like.

There are those who may dismiss this middle ground option as unsexy or unremarkable. Yet it is anything but. For it is possible to embrace a multicultural Western Europe, without the delusions of multiculturalism. A coalition can press for the rights and protections of diverse groups, and can value difference, without having to celebrate that which divides us. It can call for welcoming borders, but demand defined limits and expectations from those who arrive. It can emphatically defend religious freedoms, but not make the unreasonable demand that the state must intervene in any kind of activity which threatens the rights of any other group, and, indeed, the welfare of liberal democracy. It can make the case for nationhood, which is inclusive, without having to indulge the exclusionary tendencies of populist nationalism. It can robustly challenge this tendency amongst our liberal elites to view any conversation about Islamism, our Muslim communities, and integration as racist, and at the same time, challenge the vile poison of anti-Muslim hate. In short, as I learned in my unique high school, it is possible to retain identity, clear values, and defined limits to tolerance, and at the same, remain inclusive, democratic, and fair. It is precisely this vision for society that this institute shall tenaciously defend.

This is not the first time this alternative has been presented. In fact, the leading Iranian psychologist, Fathali M. Moghaaddam, gave this vision a name: omniculturalism. By this he meant the recognition and celebration of that which we all share, our humanity. He argues that prior to learning about group differences, and even prior to valuing difference, our education system must begin on the recognition that we are all human. By first addressing that which we all of us are (the 'omni'), homo sapiens, it will better ensure we make the most of our diverse societies, and no less, ensure better cohesion and relations between diverse peoples.[345] While I would agree with Professor Moghaaddam, we need more than merely a recognition of our shared-humanity. We all need a sense of shared identity, which, in turn, provides belonging, meaning, and social responsibility. Regardless, the point is that others have certainly called for a greater social

---

[345] Moghaddam, Fathali M. 2012. "The Omnicultural Imperative." *Culture & Psychology* 18, no. 3: 304-30. https://doi.org/10.1177/1354067X12446230

and political emphasis on that which we all share. The role of this institute is to figure out how, if at all, such a vision can come to fruition. As ever, the emphasis must always be on action.

This section has described how this crisis, emerging from exponential cultural change, demands the efforts of not only politicians, but citizens perturbed about their shared futures in society. This serves not only to prevent a further deterioration of this crisis, but help to heal the wounds it has sown. This is contingent upon a discourse which is not toxic and reactive, rather, in profound socio-cultural interrogation of the factors which have paved the way to this crisis facing our Jews and our civilization. These critical conversations will only take place if the marketplace of ideas is rejuvenated by a newly formed coalition. By having one foot in the academic world, and another in the of media, these minds will work to take these conversations away from the realm of taboo and populism, as well as help to guide society in a way which ensures the preservation of our liberal-democratic foundations.

In thought, in ideas, in the disruption of orthodox thinking, there is an opportunity to better our societies; and to unleash the potential in what makes us all different and in that which we all share. The efforts of a few individuals, opening a new branch of intellectual and cultural thought, could make all the difference. For, as the record shows, what begins with a few people, can become a mass movement for social change. This is what the center-ground, what our societies, and, indeed, what our collective futures, are crying out for.

Final reflections

This chapter has offered a route out of this crisis. The road ahead is bumpy and arduous, and difficult things will need to be said, and, above all, done. While there is no silver bullet, these 'antidotes' put those in power, and our societies more broadly, in a better place to manage this crisis before it disintegrates into something unmanageable. To that extent, there is reason for some degree of optimism. This is not yet, I believe, a lost cause, and so long as there is a willingness to act, things can get better. But we are at breaking point. There is no time for intellectual dithering which has become all too commonplace. If our leaders are to get a grip, if this dire situation is to improve, the correct words must be met with action. The various issues raised in this book, though worsening by the day, have credible responses. Before we reach the point of no return, it is now up to those in power to make a difference.

We began this section on the return of pessimism amongst Jews. With all that has been said, an inauspicious view of the future would not be illogical, unwise, or futile. Difficult though this is to say, even if all these antidotes were implemented, it could just be too late for this small minority. Perhaps, for Jews, there is no future in Western-Europe. It could be the case, though I pray not, that the only antidote to this crisis is for Jews to get out. While we still can.

This is not an easy thing to say. And it is not said lightly. I am a proud British and European Jew; attached to this soil, connected to its culture, bound to its people, responsible for its continuity; in short, a patriot to my core. My future, I hope, remains in this country. But I end this chapter on an honest conviction: like many, I am afraid for the future. Notwithstanding my optimism that this situation can change, too many of our ancestors have fallen prey to the alluring and comforting 'Voldemort-effect,' and they did so at their own peril.

Writing this section, ringing in my ears, I have the words of Ze'ev Jabotinsky, a Zionist leader and leading-liberal, in a letter to Polish Jewry in 1938. On the lugubriousness of Tisha B'Av, the darkest day in the Jewish calendar, in which Jews commemorate the Roman destruction of the Second Temple, Jabotinsky wrote a stark and prophetic warning:

> ...it is already three years that I am calling upon you, Polish Jewry, who are the crown of world Jewry. I continue to warn you incessantly that a catastrophe is coming closer. I became grey and old in these years. My heart bleeds, that you, dear brothers and sisters, do not see the volcano which will soon begin to spit its all-consuming lava. I see that you are not seeing this because you are immersed and sunk in your daily worries. Today, however, I demand from you trust. You were convinced already that my prognoses have already proven to be right. If you think differently, then drive me out of your midst! However, if you do believe me, then listen to me in this 12th hour: In the name of God! Let anyone of you save himself

as long as there is still time. And time there is very little...[346]

Jews in Western Europe are not confronting what many of their ancestors did in Poland in 1938. But doubtless we are in dark times. And although in this `New Europe` of openness, tolerance and respect, this reality seems nigh on impossible, the volcano of Judenhass, in our day, is beginning to rumble. Parts of our region are becoming increasingly Judenfrei. The acute fear which we thought could not happen in this era has resurfaced. As such, we can only ask, how long before this volcano erupts? Who knows. But leaving things the way they are, perpetuating this trend of indifference, remaining acquiescent, will pave the way for an exodus.

This book was written some years after the signing of the Abraham Accords. It was an astonishing moment when Israel and Arab- Muslim-states, which once did not recognize the Jewish State, finally did so. Moreover, these accords laid out how states, former adversaries, could work together to make the Middle East, and the wider world, a more prosperous region. Today, although far from perfect, these states are building trade-partnerships, collaborating on cultural projects, and slowly (but surely), their citizens are beginning to interact and learn about one another. This was once impossible. But now it is reality. In that spirit, what seems impossible now, could well be reality in the not-too-distant future.

Admittedly, I have my doubts. And I would advise all, especially my fellow Jews, to keep a very close on eye on the current trajectory of our societies. We are, after all, at a precipice. But if we are to be buoyed, our hope rests in wider society recognizing what is at stake. It is much more than Jews. It is much more than civilization. It is indeed our very humanity. At present, with this frightening culture of indifference amongst the well-intentioned, I remain very sober about the future. With the way things are, we have little reason to be optimistic. But just like the Abraham Accords, with action, and with people of all faiths and none working together, there is hope. It is, indeed, upon the courage of good people, on

---

[346] Cited in Netanyahu, Benjamin. "Prime Minister Netanyahu Speech at Holocaust Remembrance Day—April 2012." *Jewish Virtual Library*. https://www.jewishvirtual library.org/prime-minister-netanyahu-speech-at-holocaust-remembrance-day-april-2012

their ability to reclaim the center ground, on their willingness to manage this crisis, on their efforts to build relations between communities, and on their willingness to grapple with major cultural questions, on which we all depend. The time for this is now.

Afterword: The Road to October 7th

In Israeli society, there is a before and after October 7th. This gut-wrenching onslaught was not just a flare-up in tensions, or an ordinary, but deadly, terror attack. To those living under siege, these are regular and expected occurrences. Yet, even for Israelis, a people well accustomed to the devastation of war and terror, the incomprehensible fiendishness exhibited on that Black Saturday, as well as the world's reaction to it, is unparalleled. Not since the Holocaust have Jews had to confront such unspeakable, indeed unimaginable, horror and gruesomeness. Many of us, including myself, thought nothing like this would ever happen again, at least, not on that scale. But given the magnitude of this event, we find ourselves in a new post-October 7th epoch, which can also apply to Western Europe, as it can to the wider world. The depredations of Hamas' barbarians, without doubt, changed the course of the world as we know it.

However, this afterword is not written to analyze the events of the 7th, nor the myriad episodes of hate and fanaticism since this atrocity. I would need a lot more space than a short afterword. And so, these few pages offer some reflections on this epoch, and unpack its implications for Jews, society, and civilization. Although readily dismissed by commentators as the inevitable corollary of conflict in the Middle East, the social issues that have become headline news in Western Europe run much deeper than a reaction to this bitter contestation. For what has become at the center of public attention since the 7th does not mark a rupture from, but an extension of, the various themes this book has outlined.

The past few months have been the worst for antisemitic and anti-democratic activity in a long time, and in several places, since records began. Much can be said about what has since occurred, but it is perhaps best to start on an area I know best: my family. Since our experiences are doubtless shared by many Jewish families across the world. As with many, we Markham's are as proud to be British in the same degree as we are proud to be Jewish. Both my grandfathers, as loyal and patriotic Brits, served in the armed services during the war, and to this day, we all take immense pride in the fact that prayers at our synagogue, on a weekly basis, are said for the welfare of our monarch, armed services, and wider country. This country, for all its flaws, inclement weather, and woeful absence of competent politicians, is our home, and we feel inextricably connected to the history, culture, and identity of this land. But for the first time, my family is beginning to question if we have a future here. My father, overcome with emotion, opened up to me and confided, "My whole life I have got on with my neighbors around me," and those neighbors came from all different backgrounds. Yet, he added, "For the first time, I feel this country no longer wants me." Far from his usual stoic self, he remarked despondently, "I can no longer take how lonely and vulnerable we all feel," and with a broken voice, concluded, "I believe our tenancy in this country is soon over." These words are not expressed by an impetuous and thoughtless individual. Far from it. They represent an unfeigned sense of distress and despondency that many British Jews, indeed Western European Jews, identify with. Along with others in a similar boat, it is a violation of every postwar principle that, once again, we are having to even contemplate, worse discuss, the prospect of our young family having to moving elsewhere. But because of what I have tackled in the previous chapters, the Europe in which we now inhabit, had its foundations laid in the decades before the autumn of 2023.

What is surprising, however, is that for many who lambasted the concerns of their fellow Jews prior to October 7th, by incredulously labelling such fears as paranoid and alarmist, they have come to realize the fragility of their skepticism in the convictions of their co-religionists. The following exchange reflects a prevailing and instructive mood within Jewish circles. Speaking to my British friends who live in Israel, I asked, "why not return home, where, at least, you're safe from rockets?" In response, all of them have said, "we'd rather have rockets flying over our heads than be in a country where we feel abandoned and alone." That says it all. There is a sense to which that to be in a country at war, with a government protecting us and standing up to threats, is safer than being in a country, though not at war, is home to a large number of people who are either out for Jewish-blood, or not much concerned if it spilt. While this isn't a Shoah, it seems, even for the most optimistic amongst us, these weeks have marked the beginning of the end of not only a sense of safety for the future, but our 'tenancy,' as Jews, in these lands we call home.

Within hours of this tragedy occurring, before even the full details of this monstrosity came to light, and when the bodies of those dismembered and brutalized were still warm, scores of Palestinian activists took to the streets in exultation. As if it were party season, those who have an apparent concern for the sanctity of life, rejoiced at this barbarism with flags, dancing, loud music, and, as is now customary in certain quarters when innocents are slaughtered, handed out sweets to passersby. As you do, of course, especially when the execrable evidence was beginning to flood social media. But do not labor under a misapprehension: this was well before Israel had begun a ground invasion or its bombardment of Hamas targets in Gaza. This was not a protest for a ceasefire or concern for the people in that small strip of land; these were gatherings of people, made up by predominantly Muslim men, celebrating the invasion, dehumanization, and mass slaughter of citizens. However, even after reading my previous chapters, knowing the degree to which our progressives have betrayed their ideological roots, you might be forgiven for thinking that they would distance themselves from this celebration of human evil. But no, au contraire.

Across the world, leftist circles joined this Islamist bandwagon, by describing the events of that day as 'legitimate armed resistance,' and demanding that barbarity be viewed 'in context of a 75 year armed struggle,' as if anything could justify what took place. This position would have us believe that the Israelis, not just because of their policies, but by dint of their very existence, are at fault. The Jews brought this upon themselves. Yet there are not only inversionists, but outright, unabashed, unashamed, uncompromising denialists. Whereas the deniers of only a few years ago were conspicuous by their swastika tattoos, today's Holocaust deniers, those who deny the events of October 7th, even when presented with the verified and incontrovertible facts, have metamorphosed into intellectuals on campus, activists in anti-racist circles, and those who society regard as politically mainstream, even progressive. Unlike those swivel-eyed fruitcakes of the past, denialism is no fringe phenomenon. It is commonplace, normalized, and for those who participate, exhilarating.

Equally trendy are the weekly, even daily, protests "for Palestine." I say that cautiously. It is hard to tell how many on those protests are for justice and peace in Gaza, which itself is a laudable proposition, and how many are Hamas apologists dressed up in rainbow flags. Because, of course, Hamas are widely known for their commitment to DEI, LGBT inclusivity, and the rights of individuals. Indeed, it is no less of a challenge to establish how many such activists have a sincere regard for all human life, since you would be hard pressed to find how many have attended protests for human-rights abuses in other parts of the world, many of which have resulted in a far greater loss of life than in Gaza. Notwithstanding, the number of people who have become full-time activists since Israel undertook defensive action is both revealing and crushing. Astoundingly, albeit we are well accustomed to this, most have no direct (or even indirect) connection to the region. They are largely white and young, who have joined the burgeoning fashion of western self-effacement. Without hesitation, and with alacrity, they have adorned keffiyehs around their necks, affixed hateful badges to their coats, and have taken to social media to post all sorts of recycled antisemitic blood-libels. This is not novel, but there is something particularly, even metaphysically, noteworthy about their language, specifically, in their demands for a ceasefire.

It is wholly unsurprising, but nonetheless shocking, how most of these self-declared voices for peace did not utter a word of condemnation of Hamas on October 7th, or in the days, weeks and months, which followed this tragedy. In what has become a usual practice in the face of dead Jews, our progressives maintained a deafening, but instructive silence. If they were vocal, it was to deny, justify, or distort what had happened. But the moment Israel reacted, as every country on earth would do, and defend herself from a deadly threat, these activists jumped at the chance to beseech European leaders to pressure Israel to withdraw, and implement an immediate ceasefire. Rather extraordinary given that there was a ceasefire until Hamas launched its vicious assault upon innocents. Conveniently escaping their notice, their insistence on a ceasefire is patently not a concern for the sanctity of human life. Were it otherwise, these demonstrations would be aimed at the murderous source responsible for this war, Hamas, and the way in which it has prosecuted its war against both Israel and civilization, and the way in which it has used its people, not to mention innocent hostages, as expendable pawns. It relishes in the suffering of the people it apparently champions. That is not to say valid criticisms of the Israeli war effort should be avoided. Where necessary, they should, and can, be made. But so long as Hamas remains in power, calls for a ceasefire are tantamount to accepting an endangered Israel as an acceptable price to pay. Some might respond by insisting that Hamas has been largely incapacitated, and that they would do no more harm. This commonplace observation glares over the various statements from Hamas officials that they would, if presented with another opportunity, repeat further October 7th-style attacks. And this begs the question: what would any country do, other than destroy a death-cult, which has not only declared its intention to repeat another bloodbath, itself a declaration of war, but has embedded its terrorist infrastructure amongst a civilian population and in a network of terror tunnels, the size of which is larger than the London Underground? There is a standard which is demanded of no other country; and to capitulate to such demands would be to further imperil the security of the already targeted Jewish-State, and to endanger the lives of those who live within it. But, of course, for an alarming number of people, this is not merely a preferable outcome. It is desirable.

For the roars of our ceasefireniks reached their explosive apotheosis not when Jews were being slaughtered, but a day later, when Jews launched a campaign of resistance to Islamist terror. On October 7th, most of our progressives greeted this savagery with indifference, and some, to their shame, were even elated that it had occurred. We Jews will forever remember how empty our inboxes were on that day; many of the people we regarded as friends, must have seen we were traumatized, but remained distant. Yet less than twenty-four hours later, the day on which the Israeli operation began, the perfervid and strident demands for a ceasefire became the most in demand product on the market of bourgeois activism. And many of our friends jumped at the chance to be modish. Their demands, though ostensibly well-intentioned, have connotations which reach well beyond geopolitical stability, and the concern for human life.

They speak to an age-old othering of Jews from not only society, but humanity, and its standards, at large. A rejection of the right of Jews to be held to the same standards as everyone else. In this case, the right and duty of Israel, as accorded to every other nation on earth, to defend herself from terror. If the Jewish State took heed of these apparently humane calls, not only would this lead to further massacres, but it would return Jews, not that this would disappoint antisemites, to a state in which they are disempowered, weak, and yes, even dead. The State of Israel is the negation of this othered, downtrodden, and defenseless Jew. Indeed, it is worth pointing out, had the same hand-wringing faux liberal cries about 'genocide' of innocent civilians been invoked 80 years earlier, when the allies fought an existential war against the Nazis, like Israel against Hamas, those liberals would not be here today. Contrary to the intellectual masturbation of the vanguards of human-rights, there is no moral equivalence between Hamas and Israel, in the same measure there was no moral equivalence between the Nazis and the allies. War is - and always has been - terrible for innocent life, and every loss must be mourned. But that does not mean we should be pacifists. War is sometimes necessary. It is sometimes, alas, a duty.

Recent events, though, accentuate the way in which some ancient ideas seem impervious to the test and progress of time. Well ahead of his time, five hundred years ago, this point was made by Shakespeare in a work often, but mistakenly, labelled as antisemitic. In his *Merchant of Venice*, we find perhaps the greatest refutation of the worldview of antisemites. The Jewish protagonist, Shylock, a money-lender, explains his desire for revenge, pointing to the fact that Jews are also bound by the same whims, desires, and feelings as anybody else:

> *He hath disgraced me, and hindered me half a million, laughed at my losses, mocked at my gains, scorned my nation, thwarted my bargains, cooled my friends, heated mine enemies, and what's the reason? I am a Jew. Hath not a Jew eyes? Hath not a Jew hands, organs, dimensions, senses, affections, passions? Fed with the same food, hurt with the same weapons, subject to the same diseases, healed by the same means, warmed and cooled by the same winter and summer, as a Christian is? If you prick us, do we not bleed? If you tickle us, do we not laugh? If you poison us, do we not die? And if you wrong us, shall we not revenge? If*

we are like you in the rest, we will resemble you in that. If a Jew wrong a Christian, what is his humility? Revenge. If a Christian wrong a Jew, what should his sufferance be by Christian example? Why, revenge.[347]

When Zionism achieved a Jewish-state, it put Shylock's words into action. From the May of 1948, Jews have had not only the power to defend themselves and be the masters of their own destiny, but also to be, as it were, normal. For that sin, Israel and its defensive campaigns will never be accepted by our ceasefireniks. Although they may conceal their views behind a facade of humanitarianism and kindness, in the pathology of this progressive creed, never can the 'Jew be like us;' never can the Jew be held to the same standards as everyone else; never, indeed, can the Jew be human. And to the disappointment and outrage of those philo-disempowered-semites, the State of Israel, by its very presence in the family of nations, issues an emphatic 'no' to the demand that Jews be once again without dignity, or without human equality.

While acceptable to be critical of how Israel has prosecuted its war on terror, though such people never seem to propose any other alternative other than "Israel has an iron dome," the Jewish-State can teach us in the West an important lesson in our own identity and values. While on a trip to the Holy Land, some months after the 7th, I was awestruck by the way Israeli patriotism is ubiquitous to the same degree it is unifying. Perhaps that is inevitable in war, but in Israel, this sense of national pride, regardless of political affiliation or ideological leanings, runs deep and is long standing. That isn't to say Israelis are a people of uniformity; far from it. But they are a people who know who they are, what they stand for, and what they must defend. For this reason, you will see streets awash with the country's flag, notice patriotic billboards on motorways, find strangers taking responsibility for one another, and even spot the words 'am israel chai,' the Jewish people will live, a patriotic slogan, on egg boxes! These small things may seem insignificant, or even ostentatious and jingoistic. Yet they are foundational in establishing something we so desperately need in the West: society.

---

[347] Shakespeare, William. *The Merchant of Venice.* Act 3, Scene 1.

For sure, we have a society in nominal terms, but we have abandoned that which brings all individuals, from every background, together. Israel has not lost this. For it is a society, though fragile, centered on families, mutual responsibility, a shared identity, a belief in a collective purpose, and above all, a people who have respect for the principles and traditions passed down to them. It is somewhat of an irony that the Jewish State, whose founders learned of statehood from their European counterparts in the 19th century, is now teaching the West a lesson of what it means to be a society, and by extension, a country. It is not only to ensure your citizens own a passport, or enjoy the national cuisine, not that we really have one here in Britain, anyway. Rather, as the Israeli example demonstrates, it is to embrace that sense of nationhood as a force of unity, pride, and identity, and to do so, not just when your country is at war, or involved in a sporting competition, but to make it a fundamental aspect of daily life. Perhaps it is easier for Israel, given it has ensured its waves of migration have, for the most part, shared the same identity and values. In any case, if we in the West are to resolve the cultural and philosophic issues which are at the heart of this crisis of civilization, we have much to learn from this small Middle Eastern nation. Indeed, Israel is willing to stand up for itself, and by implication, Western civilization. The question which we must ask is, are we?

That's for a separate book. In any case, my grandparents, joined by thousands of other Jewish servicemen, did not serve their country against fascism only for their descendants to fear a new generation of fascists. What is happening today is surreal, but with each passing day, our shared heartbreak even more excruciating. Informing a friend of how miserable we have all been, he said words to the effect of, "I understand your worries, but most people are not antisemitic," and "most Brits are against Jew-hate and extremism." He tried to comfort me, but it dawned on me that in the long history of atrocities against Jews, they never occurred against the backdrop of violent, hate-filled majorities. They happened because a minority of bloodthirsty, inhuman barbarians went unchallenged by silent and indifferent majorities. The silence of good people has enabled some of the worst episodes in human history. While it is true that most people are not supportive of this resurgence of Jew-hate and do not subscribe to the warped worldview of antisemites, the great many do not speak out. They leave a nasty and menacing few to carry on unchallenged and undisturbed. Despite the fact that we have been supported by some from other communities, our numbers are lamentable when set against the scale of the protests on the other side of this divide. That in turn creates an enormous sense of isolation and abandonment, which most of us identify as one of the most agonizing aspects in this new epoch.

What only serves to compound these feelings has been the response from various Western European states. Be that from government, high-ranking police officers, and many of our elected representatives, senior leaders of important public institutions, have been, to put it lightly, horrendously complacent, bordering on complicit, in what is decidedly the greatest threat to Jews and democracy in generations. In their idleness, they have allowed countless instances of Jew-hate and extremism, camouflaged as protest against the bombing of Gaza, to pass with little or no legal repercussions. All over the UK, on our campuses, some of the best in the world, pro-Palestine encampments have been established by students, in which they squat in public areas of their universities. In doing so, these squatters believe they will encourage their universities to implement the demands from BDS, and withdraw all their involvement in Israeli universities, business, and government. In working towards this aim, not only have they decided to disrupt the lives of other students and have flagrantly disregarded university regulations on what constitutes legitimate protest, but they have become hotbeds of hate speech, intimidation, and outright criminal activity. If this were a group of pro-Trump students calling for a halt to all immigration, the university would no doubt take swift action. But when faced with a coalition of incandescent Muslim students, supported by a significant number of non-Muslim leftist students and staff, universities are reluctant to act, or if they do, their tardiness is telling.

Nevertheless, whether this happens on campus, or barely concealed support for Hamas with calls for Jihad on the streets of London, we struggle to avoid the feeling that the authorities have been, by their fear of reprisals and backlash, more efficient in protecting antisemites from Jews than Jews from antisemites. Though it may be the case that those in power may repeat positive sentiments, after October 7th, in this new epoch, our states are no longer simply guilty of negligence as I laid out in Chapter Three. It has now become apparent that we have state-enabled antisemitism.

In some sense, this is not new. In May of 2021, with which I began this book, we caught a glimpse of some of the most upsetting, frightening, and disturbing facets, of Jewish life in contemporary Western Europe. But while writing this book, I thought it highly unlikely that we would see, in the near future, anything which could match, much less surpass, what we experienced over three years ago. While we are still in the midst of this raging storm, the events of this new epoch have made that May look like a breeze. One needn't be a historian to realize that it is never easy to be a Jew. Even at the best of times. Sometimes things are relatively convivial. But in the bedrock of liberal, progressive, and tolerant Western Europe, Shalom Aleichem's words are ever more prescient, shver tzu tzyan a yid, it is hard to be a Jew.

Even though it is hard, perhaps mightily so, civilization needs its Jews. In fact, civilization itself cannot do without its Jews, as well as its Judaic, foundations. They are bound together. This is why October 7th was such a pivotal moment. When those Hamas operatives struck on Simchat Torah, not only did their rapacious and megalomaniacal sadism unleash itself in an explosion of bloodshed, but they attacked the very people, the eternal witnesses, of that which is foundational in the West: The Torah, and its imperative that before God, all people, regardless of background, creed, or religion, are equal. This message, foundational in the West, was assaulted when Hamas began its sanguinary incursion. For this reason, what Israel is having to contend with is not just about ensuring a safe future for Israelis, and Jews worldwide, but the very sanctity of that which we could not live without.

This new epoch has brought the various themes I have outlined throughout this book to the forefront of public attention. The significance of these underlying issues has been exemplified in recent weeks and months, and no doubt they will become increasingly more influential in the months and years to come. Indeed, the consequent global insurgency against Jews exposes, in explicit terms, the consequences of the delusions of our liberal-elites, and how their policies and ideas are leading not only to a Western Europe, in which parts of it will turn Judenrein, but the erasure of everything which ensures our civilization remains peaceful, democratic and cohesive.

Yet, most do not see it this way. It is maddening, but most do not see how recent events are indicative and symptomatic of a broader assault upon that which they regard as the defining qualities of human rights. Yet it is precisely their silence that enables this kind of violence. It is, to their shame, the necessary precondition for this threat against our way of life. And they are mistaken, even delusional, to think that this will end at Jews. This is about us all. It is short-sighted of government, of any ideological leaning, to merely talk about stopping the spread of Jew-hate and extremist thinking. It cannot be done unless we are prepared to confront the underlying problems, as laid out in this book, which have led us to this wretched place. The current discourse on multiculturalism seems to involve either those who believe it has been a ripping success, or those who believe it has been a dismal failure. But, in my mind, it is neither. While countries experience different manifestations of multiculturalism, all have manifestly wound up experiencing societies in which we are deprived of that which ensures unity without uniformity. And the absence of this togetherness has created the fertile ground in which these divisions have spiraled out of control. The notion that a society can achieve social cohesion, in the absence of that which transcends individual identities, is delusional. Tragically, though, this delusion has gripped our region. And we are all paying the price.

This should have been avoided. We could have embraced diversity, and at the same time, rejected a policy and philosophy, multiculturalism, which places no significance or emphasis on what we can all share. But we were foolish. Nations suffering, for several decades, from a crisis of identity, culture and values, have no idea what brings us all together. The results are clear. The past months have been an example of what the future could well look like with no meaningful action. In response to such observations, many of multiculturalism's proponents will make it clear that this is somebody else's fault. They see the return of extremism, antisemitism, and right-wing populism, to be the products of economic disparities or social discrimination. This book does not dismiss these points, but in the saga of Europe's fixation with the civic-religion of multiculturalism, they are not causal. The crisis facing both Jews and society-at-large goes beyond a reaction to negative political, economic, and social circumstances. And nothing can change unless the deep-rooted factors are reckoned with.

Civilization is now on Lady Shalott's boat. If this situation persists, our candles will be extinguished, and I fear, so too, our humanity. But before they do, while there is time, there is an opportunity for the center ground to rebuild trust in liberal democracies, push back on the endemic state of Islamism, rethink diversity, and value the enriching qualities of difference, while being prepared to assert and celebrate that which we all share. It is now up to those in power to awaken from their slumber of indifference and seize this opportunity for change. If not for our sake, let it be for the sake of future generations that we do all we can to prevent this from becoming an immutable reality within Western Europe. For we know where this leads. It is my sincere hope, therefore, that what has been discussed is a valued contribution in advancing a rational, fair, and just approach to one of the most burning issues of our time.